Great Principles of Computing

Great Principles of Computing

Peter J. Denning and Craig H. Martell

The MIT Press
Cambridge, Massachusetts
London, England

MIT Press books may be purchased at special quantity discounts for business or sales promotional use. For information, please email special_sales@mitpress.mit.edu.

This book was set in Stone Sans Std and Stone Serif Std by Toppan Best-set Premedia Limited, Hong Kong. Printed and bound in the United States of America.

Library of Congress Cataloging-in-Publication Data

Denning, Peter J., 1942–
Great principles of computing / Peter J. Denning and Craig H. Martell.
pages cm
Includes bibliographical references and index.
ISBN 978-0-262-52712-5 (pbk. : alk. paper)
1. Computer science. I. Martell, Craig H., 1965– II. Title.
QA76.D3483 2015
004—dc23
2014022598

10 9 8 7 6 5 4 3 2

To Dorothy, Anne, and Diana
To Chaliya and Katie

Contents

Foreword

Peter Denning and Craig Martell have taken on a monumental topic: identifying and elucidating principles that shape and inform the process of coercing computers to do what we *want* them to do and struggling with the difference between what they *actually* do (that is, what we told them) and what we want them to do. Bugs (errors) are examples of the difference. Bugs are usually a result of inadvertently programming the machine to do something we did not intend. But errors are not the only source of bugs. A bug also arises when an unexpected behavior emerges from the execution of a program in a system. Networks of computers with their myriad variations in software and interactions are often the source of emergent behaviors. We sometimes speak of a *network effect* in which a trend becomes a predominant behavior that reinforces the emergence of some feature that might not have been envisioned or even intended. This can happen when an application is put to use in ways that were not anticipated. *Spam* and *phishing* are examples of emergent behaviors with email in large networks.

Such effects challenge our ability to understand, anticipate, and analyze complex behaviors arising in large-scale software systems in large-scale networks. Even if each component operates within its design parameters, the system as a whole can give indeterminate results because of unpredictable interactions among components.

Complex emergent behaviors also arise simply because computing machines are finite. Digitized information always contains small errors of representation. Tiny errors can accumulate into catastrophes over billions of computational steps. A very concrete example of unanticipated results arises from floating point arithmetic with finite precision. Round-off errors and other artifacts of handling very large or very small values can lead to catastrophic results, as William Kahan eloquently demonstrated in his paper on this topic in a symposium on numerical computation in 2005.[1]

These effects teach us that the business of getting computers to do things on our behalf is both a nontrivial and deeply intellectual exercise. This book aims to provide insight into some fundamental principles that can orient our approach to computing in its most general sense.

The authors organize their analysis into eleven chapters, each of which plays an important role in the panoply of activities we associate with computing. I think of these as foci for marshaling and organizing resources in aid of computational outcomes. By *computational* I mean to suggest achieving particular objectives through the use of computers and their software. This is intentionally unspecific. Making a computer game work is a computational objective as much as getting a complex, distributed, networked financial exchange system to work. Despite the disparity of computational objectives, designers are aided by definite principles for managing and marshaling resources—information representations, communications, computing elements, programs, memory, modeling, analysis, and so forth. I read that the book's overall intent is to codify the principles that facilitate achievement of these objectives. This effort is broad in its scope and depth.

One of the things that makes computing so interesting is the utter generality of binary representations. We can choose to make the bits mean anything we wish. We can manipulate these bits in myriad ways and choose to interpret the results in equally diverse fashion. Just as we convert algebraic word problems into equations that we manipulate according to straightforward mathematical rules to find answers compatible with the original equations, so also we write programs to manipulate bits following rules that lead to a chosen interpretation of the resulting bits. Large-scale simulations, big data, and complex visual renderings all share the property that they help us to understand and interpret the bits we manipulate.

One of the reasons I have been a strong proponent of teaching programming in middle school and high school (and perhaps even earlier) is the discipline it imposes on organizing thoughts to problem solving. One has to analyze the problem, break it into manageable parts, figure out what has to happen for the program to solve the problem (that is, produce the desired result), then work through the task of writing the program, utilizing preexisting libraries, if applicable, compiling and running the program, and verifying that it produces the desired result and nothing else. The last discipline, which we might call a combination of debugging and verification, is a skill that is applicable to more than programming. Although I am not an advocate of making everyone into a programmer, I think it is valuable for people to learn the skills that are applicable to successful programming because these skills are broadly applicable to many other problems.

Programming skills can be put to work dealing with complex system design and analysis. Here I think we reach a very important area that Denning and Martell emphasize in their chapter on design. Good design has many useful properties. I am reminded of the remark that "neatness is its own reward" because you can find things you put away when you need them. Good design is its own reward because it facilitates understanding of complexity and ability to evolve and revise the design to achieve new objectives. In design of the Internet we took a lesson from its predecessor, the ARPANET, which could not scale up in size. We envisioned the functionality of the system in *layers* and standardized the interfaces between the layers. The result was that while keeping these interfaces stable, we were able to allow for enormous flexibility in the implementation and reimplementation of the layers between the interfaces. The Internet Protocol is a good example. Designers of applications knew nothing about how Internet protocol packets were carried—the protocol did not specify. Nor did the protocol itself depend on what information packet payloads carried—the meanings of bits in the payload were opaque. One consequence of this design decision has been that the Internet Protocol has been layered on top of every new communication system designed since the early 1970s. Another consequence is that new applications have been placed in the Internet without changing the networks because the Internet Protocol carried their packets to software at the edges of the Internet. Only the transmitting and receiving hosts needed to know what the payload bits carried in packets meant. The routers that move Internet Protocol packets do not depend on the content of the packet payloads.

The role of design cannot be overemphasized in dealing with computing. Whether it is the hardware, the operating system, the application, the data, file and directory structures, the choice of language(s), it all comes down to thinking about design and how the ensemble, the system, will work. Sometimes one hears the term *system engineering* too infrequently. I am a systems person and take some pride in thinking along architectural lines. How do all the pieces go together? What should be a *piece?* How does the design facilitate adaptation to new requirements? Is the design maintainable? How hard is it to teach someone else how the design works?

An interesting test of a good design is to see whether someone who is confronted with the system de novo can figure out how to make it do something new without destroying its previously designed capabilities. In some ways this is a fairly powerful test of one's understanding of the program or system and its organization. You may not need to know everything about the system, but you have to know enough to be reasonably sure your change has no unintended consequences. This is the meaning of a clean design—it can be revised with a reasonable sense and likelihood of safety. I am glad that this book is so strong on design and emphasizes the role of architecture, and not just algorithms, in design.

There is a great deal more to be said about computing principles, but that is the point of the book that follows. Keeping these principles in mind should make the task of designing computing systems a lot more manageable. Read on!

Vint Cerf
Woodhurst, VA
April 2014

Note

1. W. M. Kahan, "How futile are mindless assessments of roundoff in floating-point computations: Why should we care? What should we do? (Extract)," in *Proceedings of the Householder Symposium XVI on Numerical Linear Algebra*, p. 17, 2005.

Preface

Just seven decades ago no one but a few specialists had ever heard of computers. Now computers, software, and networks are ubiquitous. They are generating bountiful benefits for our lives at an ever-accelerating pace in every part of the planet.

It is amazing that we have learned to design and build systems of such scale in such a short span of years. Computing technology is now automating knowledge work and amplifying productivity by supporting massive collaborations. The Second Machine Age is truly upon us.[1] How has this been accomplished? What big ideas have made this possible?

With the bounty come anxieties. Will automation by computers drive many workers out of jobs? Will computers erase our privacy by becoming the ultimate tool for surveillance? Will computers develop superhuman intelligence? Is there any limit to what computers can do?

We believe that an understanding of the principles and laws of computing would help people to appreciate how computing has accomplished so much and would ease their concerns. We wrote this book to help. Here we introduce some of the most important principles of computing, presented in a way that anyone with some familiarity with computing can follow.

Computer science is not just an engineering field that designs computing devices; it is a science of information processes. Computing is governed by scientific principles and laws that tell us what computers can and cannot do. The laws of information reveal new possibilities and constraints that are not apparent from the laws of physics. Many pundits have ascribed to computers powers that computing science tells us they cannot possibly have. They have also underestimated the powers computers do have.

Computer science interacts with many other fields. Many science and engineering fields have identified a "computational" part, such as computational physics, computational chemistry, bioinformatics, computational product designs, additive manufacturing, computational social networking, or computational cardiology.[2] Educators at all levels struggle to keep their crowded curricula up to date with computation. Many high schools, suffering from a teacher shortage in computer science, do not yet have a computer course. In business, buzz words such as "big data," "the cloud," and "cyber security" signal concerted attempts to use computing principles in data management, distributed computation, and information protection.

Computing has traditionally presented itself as a *technology field* that advances at the breakneck speed of Moore's law.[3] Our view is different. We believe computing is better described as a *science field* with fundamental principles that span all computing technologies and information processes both artificial and natural. We need a new language to describe computing. Like the telescope in astronomy or the microscope in biology, the computer is a tool but not the object of study.

The *great principles framework* of this book is a new language. It divides the principles of computing into six categories: communication, computation, coordination, recollection, evaluation, and design. By a computing principle, we mean a statement that guides or constrains how we manipulate matter and energy to perform computations. Computing principles are either (1) recurrences, including laws, processes, and methods that describe repeatable cause-effect relationships, or (2) guidelines for conduct. An example of a recurrence is the locality principle: every computation clusters its references to data into small subsets for extended intervals of time. An example of a conduct guideline is that network programmers should divide protocol software into layers. The purpose of all such principles is to enable good design by increasing understanding and reducing complexity.

Every computing technology draws on principles from these categories. The framework is broad and holistic, covering every part of computing including *algorithmics*, *systems*, and *design*.

Computing people have organized into dozens of computing domains—communities of practice such as artificial intelligence, cyber security, cloud computing, big data, graphics, and computational science. These domains are focal points for advancing the field and for interacting with other communities. They are all empowered and constrained by computing principles. A principles framework would be incomplete without the computing domains.

Because the six categories are so large, we decided to split our coverage into the eleven more manageable chunks you see in the table of contents. We have more to say about this in chapter 1.

From Machines to Universal Digitization

The computing *machine* was the center of attention in the early years of the computing field (the 1940s through the 1960s). Computation was seen as the action of machines performing complicated calculations, solving equations, cracking codes, analyzing data, and managing business processes. The leaders in those days defined computer science as the study of phenomena surrounding computers.

Over the years, however, this definition made less and less sense. The computational science movement of the 1980s maintained that computation was a new way of doing science, alongside traditional theory and experiment. They used the term "computational thinking" for a mental practice of inquiry and problem solving, not as a way to build computers. A decade later, scientists in several fields started finding natural information processes in their fields. These included biology (DNA translation), physics (quantum information[4]), cognitive science (brain processes), vision (image recognition), and economics (information flows). The emphasis of computing shifted from machines to information processes, both artificial and natural.

Today, with the digitization of nearly everything, computation has entered everyday life with new ways to solve problems, new forms of art, music, motion pictures, social networking, cloud computing, commerce, and new approaches to learning. Computational metaphors are part and parcel of everyday language with expressions like "My software reacts that way," and "My brain crashed and had to be rebooted."

In response to these changes universities have been designing new principles-based approaches to the teaching of computing. The University of Washington, one of the first at this, developed a course and book on fluency with information technology, now widely used in high schools and colleges to help students learn and apply basic computational principles.[5] The Educational Testing Foundation partnered with the National Science Foundation to develop a new Advanced Placement curriculum based on computing principles.[6] Many people now use the term "computational thinking" to refer to the use of computational principles in many fields and in everyday life, not just in computational science.[7]

As it has matured, the computing field has attracted many followers in other fields. We know of sixteen books that reached out to explain aspects of computing for interested nonspecialists.[8] Most of the books focus on individual parts such as information, programming, algorithms, automation, privacy, and the "guts" of the Internet. We wrote this book to examine the field as a whole and offer an account of how all the parts fit together. Readers will find a coherent set of principles behind all these parts.

In our own experience teaching graduate students who are transitioning into computer science, we have found that a principles framework is easier for beginners than a technology framework. Describing the field in terms of technology ideas was a good approach in the early days when the core technologies were few. In 1989 the Association for Computing Machinery listed nine core technologies. In 2005, however, ACM listed about fourteen, and in 2013 about eighteen. The six-category principles framework does not redefine the core knowledge of computing, but it does provide a new way of looking at the field and reducing its apparent complexity.

Origins and Aims

We are often asked about the origins of the six categories of principles. Author Peter Denning started this project in the 1990s at George Mason University. He collected a list of potential principle statements from many colleagues. He discovered seven natural clusters and named them communication, computation, recollection, coordination, evaluation, design, and automation.[9] When we put this book together, we realized that automation is not a category for manipulating matter and energy; it is instead the focus of the computing domain of artificial intelligence. In this book we deleted automation from the set of categories and included it among the computing domains.

The six categories do not divide the computing knowledge space into separate slices. They are like windows of a hexagonal kiosk. Each window sees the inside space in a distinctive way; but the same thing can be seen in more than one window. The Internet, for example, is sometimes seen as means for data communication, sometimes as means of coordination, and sometimes as a means for recollection.

This set of categories satisfied our goal to have a framework with a manageable number of categories. Although the list of computing technologies will continue to grow, and the set of computing domains will enlarge, the number of categories is likely to remain stable for a long time.

This book is a holistic view of computer science, focusing on the deepest, most pervasive, principles, "cosmic" principles.[10] It presents computing as a deeply scientific field whose principles affect every other field as well as business and industry.

We designed this book for all who use computing science to accomplish their objectives. Scientifically educated readers can learn about the principles of computing spanning the whole field from algorithms to systems. A person inside the computing field can find overviews of less familiar parts of this giant field, such as a programmer who wants to learn about parallel computing. The members of a "computer science for us" class in a college or university can find help to understand how computing technologies affect them, such as how networking and the Internet enable social networks. Budding scientists, engineers, and business entrepreneurs might find here a *Popular Science*–type approach to the whole of computer science.

Acknowledgments

Peter thanks the many people he met on his long journey with the principles of computing, which began when, at the age of eleven, his father gave him a remarkable book about the principles of machines, *How It Works*, published in 1911.[11] His high school math teacher and science club advisor, Ralph Money, encouraged him in 1960 to direct his energies toward computers, the machines of the future. When he became a student at MIT Project Mac in 1964, his mentors Jack Dennis, Robert Fano, Jerry Saltzer, Fernando Corbato, and Allan Scherr broadened his interests to include the fundamental principles behind all computing. His second published paper in 1967, on the working-set principle for storage management, came with the help of major inspirations from Les Belady, Walter Kosinski, Brian Randell, Peter Neumann, and Dick Karp. In 1969 he led a task force to design a core course on operating systems principles, where his teammates Jack Dennis, Butler Lampson, Nico Habermann, Dick Muntz, and Dennis Tsichritzis helped identify the principles of operating systems, with insights from Bruce Arden, Bernie Galler, Saul Rosen, and Sam Conte. In the following years Roger Needham and Maurice Wilkes provided numerous additional insights into the principles of operating systems. He joined with Ed Coffman to write a book on operating systems theory in 1973.

In 1975 Jeff Buzen drew him into his new field of operational analysis, an investigation of the fundamental principles for performance evaluation of computing systems. Erol Gelenbe, Ken Sevcik, Dick Muntz, Leonard Kleinrock, Yon Bard, Martin Reiser, and Mani Chandy all contributed to his understanding during that time.

In 1985 the ACM Education Board asked him to lead a project to identify the core principles of computing as a discipline, for use in designing the 1991 ACM/IEEE curriculum recommendations. He is grateful to the team for deepening his understanding of computing principles: Douglas Comer, David Gries, Michael Mulder, Allen Tucker, Joe Turner, and Paul Young.

In the mid-1990s he began to gather all computing principles under a single umbrella. Jim Gray enjoined him to look for "cosmic" principles—ones so deep and vast that they would be true in all parts of the universe at all times. He designed a capstone course called "The Core of Information Technology" and launched it in 1998 with help from his George Mason colleagues Daniel Menascé, Mark Pullen, Bob Hazen, and Jim Trefil.

In 2002 the Education Board of ACM asked him to set up a great principles task force to advise it on how a great principles framework might inform the design of future curricula. What a fabulous team came together to help: Robert Aiken, Gordon Bell, Fred Brooks, Fran Berman, Jeff Buzen, Boots Cassel, Vint Cerf, Fernando Corbato, Ed Feigenbaum, John Gorgone, Jim Gray, David Gries, David Harel, Juris Hartmanis, Lilian Israel, Anita Jones, Mitch Kapor, Alan Kay, Leonard Kleinrock, Richard LeBlanc, Peter Neumann, Paul Rosenbloom, Russ Schackelford, Mike Stonebraker, Andy Tanenbaum, Allen Tucker, and Moshe Vardi.

Rick Snodgrass, a kindred spirit with his pursuit of "ergalics," gave us much sage advice on what makes science in computing. Vint Cerf and Rob Beverly gave many helpful suggestions about the sections on networking.

Peter is most grateful to his wife Dorothy Denning for her constant insistence on clear logical flow and compelling grounding and for her unfailing encouragement for him to take the time needed for writing. He is grateful as well to his daughters, Anne Denning Schultz and Diana Denning LaVolpe, for their faith and support.

Craig Martell was attracted to co-authoring this book because he has the sometimes unfortunate characteristic of always wanting to parameterize the world. Computing as a field presents a particularly fascinating challenge in this regard in that it is equal parts science, mathematics, and engineering. He is constantly fascinated that these machines even work!

Craig would like to thank Mitch Marcus, with whom he co-taught "Information Technology and its Impact on Society" at the University of Pennsylvania. Working through the syllabus for that course began the process that led to his contribution here. He would also like to thank his co-author, Peter Denning; he made the writing process fun, as well as productive. Finally, he would like to thank Pranav Anand, Mark Gondree, Joel Young, Rob Beverly, and Mathias Kölsch, *sine qua taedium*.

Craig's contribution to this book would not have been possible without the patience and multifaceted support of his wife, Chaliya, and the adoring smile of his daughter, Katie. He is convinced that he is, in fact, the luckiest man in the world.

1 Computing

Computer science studies phenomena surrounding computers.
—Newell, Simon, and Perlis

Computer science is no more about computers than astronomy is about telescopes.
—Edsger W. Dijkstra

Computing is integral to science, not just as a tool for analyzing data but also as a method of thought and discovery.

It has not always been this way. Computing is a relatively young discipline. It started as an academic field of study in the 1930s with a cluster of remarkable papers by Kurt Gödel (1934), Alonzo Church (1936), Emil Post (1936), and Alan Turing (1936), who saw the importance of automatic computation. They laid the mathematical foundations to answer the question, "what is computation?" and discussed schemes for implementing computations. Their seemingly different schemes were quickly found to be equivalent, as a computation in any one could be realized in any other. It is all the more remarkable, then, that their models all led to the same conclusion that certain functions of practical interest, such as whether a computational algorithm terminates, cannot be answered computationally.

In the time that these men wrote, the terms "computation" and "computers" were already in common use. Computation was taken to be the mechanical steps followed to evaluate mathematical functions. Computers were people who did computations. In recognition of the social changes they were ushering in, the designers of the first digital computer projects all named their systems with acronyms ending in "-AC," meaning automatic computer or some close variant—names such as ENIAC, UNIVAC, EDVAC, and EDSAC.

At the start of World War II the militaries of the United States and the United Kingdom became interested in applying automatic computers to the calculation of ballistic and navigation tables and to the cracking of ciphers. They commissioned projects to design and build electronic digital computers. Only one of these projects was completed before the war was over. That was the top-secret project at Bletchley Park, UK, which cracked the German Enigma cipher using methods designed by Alan Turing.

Many people involved in those projects went on to start computer companies in the early 1950s. Universities began offering programs of study in the new field by the late 1950s. The field and the industry have grown steadily ever since, into a modern behemoth whose Internet connections and data centers are said to consume over 3 percent of the world's electricity.

Figure 1.1
(A) Charles Babbage (1791–1871) invented the Difference Engine, a mechanical calculator of tables of logarithms and other arithmetic functions. Later, he designed an Analytic Engine, which was to be a general-purpose calculator. (B) Ada Lovelace (1815–1852) helped him with the design. Lovelace saw possibilities beyond numerical tasks—music composition, graphic drawings, and even logical reasoning. In 1843 she laid out a program whereby the Analytic Engine could calculate Bernoulli numbers, for which she has been credited as the "first computer programmer." (Source: Wikipedia Creative Commons)

During its youth, computing was an enigma to the established fields of science and engineering. At first it looked like technology applications of math, electrical engineering, or science, depending on the observer. Over the years computing seemed to provide an unending stream of new insights and defied many early predictions that it would be reabsorbed back into the fields of its roots. By 1980 computing had matured in its understanding of algorithms, data structures, numerical methods, programming languages, operating systems, networks, databases, graphics, artificial intelligence, and software engineering. Its great technology achievements—the chip, the personal computer, and the Internet—brought computing into many lives and stimulated more new subfields, including network science, web science, mobile computing, enterprise computing, cooperative work, cyberspace protection, user-interface design, and information visualization. The resulting commercial applications have spawned new research challenges in social networks, endlessly evolving computation, music, video, digital photography, vision, massive multiplayer online games, user-generated content, and much more.

To keep up with the flux, the name of the field changed several times. In the 1940s it was called automatic computation, and in the 1950s, information processing. In the 1960s, as it moved into academia, it acquired the name computer science in the United States and informatics in Europe. By the 1980s the computing field comprised a complex of related fields including computer science, informatics, computational science, computer engineering, software engineering, information systems, and information technology. By 1990 the term "computing" had become the standard for referring to this core group.

Computer science became a recognized academic field in 1962 with the founding of computer science departments at Purdue and at Stanford. At the time, the leaders of the new field felt compelled not only to say what the field was about but to defend it from critics who thought there was no new content outside of electrical engineering or mathematics. In 1967 Allen Newell, Alan Perlis, and Herbert Simon argued that it was a science concerned with all aspects of "phenomena surrounding computers." However, many traditional scientists objected to the conclusion that the field was science; they held that true science deals with phenomena that occur in nature ("natural processes"), whereas computers are man-made artifacts. Simon, a Nobel Laureate in economics, so strongly disagreed with the "natural interpretation" of science that, two years later, he published a book *The Sciences of the Artificial*. There he argued that economics and computer science met all the traditional criteria for science, except for studying natural

Figure 1.2
Alan Turing (1912–1954) saw computation as the evaluation of mathematical functions. In 1936 he invented an abstract machine, known now as the Turing machine, to model function evaluation. His machine consisted of a finite state control unit traversing an infinitely long tape with symbols written in each square; on each move the machine reads a single symbol, possibly overwrites with another symbol, moves one square left or right, and enters a new control state. Turing showed how to build a Universal Machine that could imitate any other given its description. He argued that any function that might be called computational could be implemented by one of his machines. He also demonstrated that there are noncomputable functions, such a deciding whether a machine halts rather than going into an infinite loop. (Source: Wikipedia Creative Commons)

Figure 1.3
After Babbage's failure to build a working Analytical Engine, no one tried to design a general computing machine for the next 80 years. Then, in the late 1930s, the militaries of the United States and United Kingdom sought electronic machines to calculate ballistic firing tables and to crack ciphers. In 1944 the US Army commissioned the ENIAC at University of Pennsylvania under the leadership of John Mauchly and J. Presper Eckert. Its first programmers were Kay McNulty, Betty Jennings, Betty Snyder, Marlyn Wescoff, Fran Bilas, and Ruth Lichterman. The picture shows Jennings (left) and Bilas operating the ENIAC's main control panel. At the time, computers were people and computing was their profession; the electronic machines were called automatic or electronic computers. Programming consisted of wiring plugboards. (Source: University of Pennsylvania)

processes, and deserved to be called sciences even if qualified by the term "artificial."

Computing's Paradigm

For three decades after 1962 traditional scientists often questioned the name computer science. They could easily see an engineering paradigm (design and implementation of systems) and a mathematics paradigm (proofs of theorems), but they could not see much of a science paradigm (experimental verification of hypotheses). Moreover, Simon's protests to the contrary, they understood science as a way of dealing with the natural world, and computers looked suspiciously artificial.

Figure 1.4
Pioneers (A) John Backus (1924–2007) and (B) Grace Hopper (1902–1992) designed higher-level programming languages that could be automatically translated into machine code by a compiler. In 1957 Backus led a team that developed FORTRAN, a language well suited for numerical computations. In 1959 Hopper led a team that developed COBOL, a language well suited for business records and calculations. Both languages are still used today. With these inventions, the ENIAC picture of programmers plugging wires died, and computing became accessible to many people via easy-to-use languages. Many thousands of programming languages have since been invented. (Source: Wikipedia Creative Commons)

The founders of the field came from all three paradigms.[1] Some thought computing was a branch of applied mathematics, some a branch of electrical engineering, and some a branch of computational-oriented science. During the first four decades, the field focused primarily on engineering: the challenges of building reliable computers, networks, and complex software were daunting and occupied almost everyone's attention. By the 1980s these challenges had largely been met, and computing was spreading rapidly into all fields with the help of networks, supercomputers, and personal computers. During the 1980s computers had become powerful enough that science visionaries could see how to use them to tackle the hardest "grand

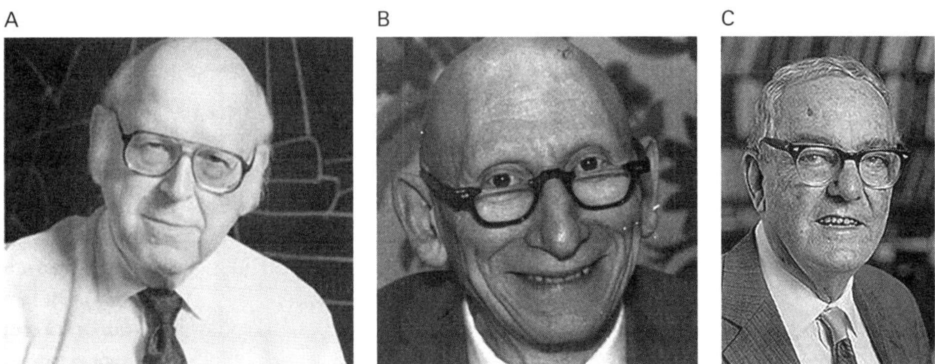

Figure 1.5
(A) Allen Newell (1927–1992), (B) Alan Perlis (1922–1990), and (C) Herb Simon (1916–2001) saw computing as a science of phenomena surrounding computers. In 1967 they argued that computer science was a necessary science that studied everything computational, from computing machines, software, intelligence, information, design of systems, graphics, algorithms for solving problems in other fields, and much more. Simon went further and argued that studies of phenomena surrounding man-made artifacts—sciences of the artificial—were just as much science as traditional sciences. (Source: Wikipedia Creative Commons)

challenge" problems in science and engineering. The resulting "computational science" movement involved scientists from many countries and culminated in the US Congress adopting the High-Performance Computing and Communications (HPCC) Act of 1991 to support research on a host of grand challenge problems.

Today, there seems to be an agreement that computing *exemplifies* science and engineering and that neither science nor engineering *characterizes* computing. What then does characterize computing? What is the paradigm of computing?

The leaders of the field struggled with the paradigm question ever since the beginning. Along the way, there were three waves of attempts to unify views. The first, led by Newell, Perlis, and Simon (1967), argued that computing was unique among all the sciences in its study of information processes. Simon called computing a science of the artificial (1969), implicitly agreeing with the common belief that computations are not natural processes. A catchphrase of this wave was that "computing is the study of phenomena surrounding computers."

The second wave focused on programming, the art of designing algorithms that produced useful information processes. In the early 1970s,

Figure 1.6
(A) Donald Knuth (b. 1938) and (B) Edsger Dijkstra (1930–2002) considered programming to be at the heart of computing. Around 1970 they argued that the processes of designing and analyzing algorithms are at the center of everything computer scientists do. To them, a master programmer was a master computer scientist. Unfortunately, this noble view was lost by the late 1990s; governments defined programmers as low-level coders. (Source: Wikipedia Creative Commons)

computing pioneers Edsger Dijkstra and Donald Knuth took strong stands favoring algorithms analysis as the unifying theme. A catchphrase of this wave was "computer science equals programming." In recent times this view has foundered because the field has expanded well beyond programming, and because public understanding of a programmer became so narrow (a coder).

The third wave came as a result of the Computer Science and Engineering Research Study (COSERS), led by Bruce Arden (1983) and funded by the National Science Foundation in the 1970s. It defined computation as the automation of information processes in engineering, science, and business. Its catchphrase was "computing is the automation of information processes." Although its final report successfully explained many esoteric aspects to the layperson, its central view did not catch on.

An important aspect of all three definitions was the positioning of the computer as the focus of attention. The computational science movement of the 1980s began to step away from that notion when it said that computing is not only a tool for science but also a *new method of thought and discovery in science*. The people in the computational sciences saw computing as an ally in understanding their information processes and what algorithms might govern them.

An important consequence of this new direction was that scientists began to acknowledge that natural information processes exist and can be studied with the same methods as the artificial information processes generated by computers. Biology was one of the first examples: Nobel Laureate David Baltimore (2001), echoing cognitive scientist Douglas Hofstadter (1985), said that biology had become an information science. David Bacon (2010) argued similarly for physics, saying that that quantum mechanics, which underpins quantum computing, is an information science. Erol

A

B

Figure 1.7

(A) Bruce Arden (b. 1927), a pioneer in computer systems, led a group (COSERS) that advocated a view of computing broader than programming. In the late 1970s his group defined computing as the study of "what can be automated." At the time, this view fit a public mood disposed toward robots, such as the two from *Star Wars* (B). This view did not stick because of the shift toward science that began a few years later. (Source: Wikipedia Creative Commons)

Gelenbe (2011) gave a long list of examples of scientific fields that actively study natural information processes. The conclusion that computer science methods also apply to natural information processes strengthens Herb Simon's (1969) argument that computer science is a genuine science.

More recently, Paul Rosenbloom (2012) has noted two other reasons that the "all computations are artificial" proposition is outdated. First, many scientists now accept humans as part of the world ecosystem and that human structures are as natural as beaver dams or ant hills. Second, our ability to modify natural processes at ever-finer levels of detail erases any boundary between natural and artificial, as in stem cell cloned organs, organically grown nanomachines, or genetically modified crops.

Great Principles of Computing

The maturing process of our interpretations of computing has given us a new view of the content of the field. Until the 1990s most computing

Figure 1.8
Tim Berners-Lee (b. 1955) offered a different view of computing than the prevailing view of a network of machines. In 1989 he invented the World Wide Web, a way of linking the information stored on machines and automatically following a link at the click of a mouse. He saw the web of connections established by people to each other's information as the host of many new kinds of computations that dealt with the meanings that people assign to information. (Source: Wikipedia Creative Commons)

A

B

Figure 1.9

Nobel Laureates (A) Ken Wilson (1936–2013), a physicist, and (B) David Baltimore (b. 1938), a biologist, were at the forefront of computational science, which held that computing was a new way of thinking and discovery in science. In the mid-1980s Wilson popularized the notion of "grand challenge" problems in science that could be solved by computational methods, and he advocated highly parallel supercomputers to do the job. In the 1990s Baltimore popularized the notion that biology had become the study of information processes embedded into cells and all life processes. Computer scientists were at first reluctant to be involved but have since embraced computational science and have started a science renaissance in computing. (Source: Wikipedia Creative Commons)

scientists would have described the field by naming its core technologies: algorithms, data structures, numerical methods, programming languages, operating systems, networks, databases, graphics, artificial intelligence, and software engineering. This is a deeply technological interpretation of the field. The principles interpretation used here emphasizes the fundamental laws that empower and constrain the technologies.

The principles of computing fall into six categories: communication, computation, coordination, recollection, evaluation, and design (Denning 2003, Denning and Martell 2004)[2] (see figure 1.10.). These categories are all concerned with manipulating matter and energy to produce intended computations. Table 1.1 defines and illustrates them, and notes which chapters of this book focus on them.

Table 1.1
Great Principles of Computing

Category	Focus	Examples	Focal Chapters
Communication	Reliably moving information between locations	Minimal-length codes, error-correcting codes, compression of files, cryptography.	3. Information 11. Networking
Computation	What can and cannot be computed	Classifying complexity of problems in terms of the number of computational steps to achieve a solution. Characterizing problems that have no algorithmic solution.	4. Machines 5. Programming 6. Computation
Recollection	Representing, storing, and retrieving information from media	All storage systems are hierarchical. No storage system can offer equal access time to all objects. The locality principle: all computations favor subsets of their data objects for extended intervals.	7. Memory 11. Networking
Coordination	Effectively using many autonomous computing agents	Protocols that lead the parties to have the same knowledge, eliminate conditions that cause indeterminate results, or synchronize. Choice uncertainty principle.	2. Domains 8. Parallelism 9. Queueing
Evaluation	Measuring whether systems produce intended computations	Predicting system throughput and response time with queueing network models, designing experiments to test algorithms and systems.	9. Queueing 10. Design
Design	Structuring software systems for reliability and dependability	Complex systems can be decomposed into interacting modules and virtual machines. Modules can be stratified corresponding to their time scales of events that manipulate objects.	10. Design

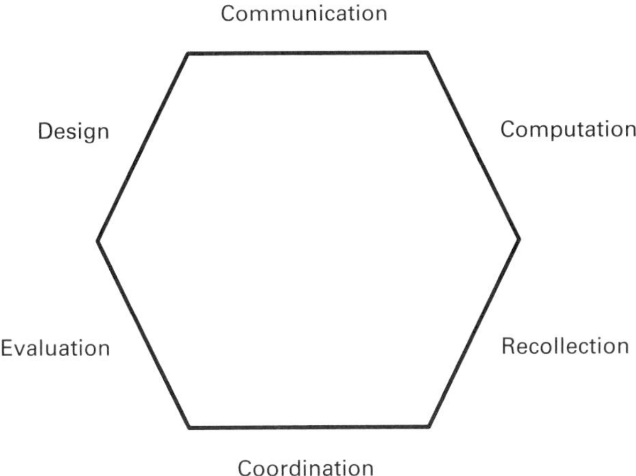

Figure 1.10
Each category of principles is a perspective on computing: a window into the computing knowledge space. (There is no significance to ordering of the category names around the sides of the hexagon.) The categories are not mutually exclusive. For example, the Internet can be viewed from the perspectives of a communication system, a coordination system, or a storage system. Most computing technologies use combinations of principles from all six categories; each category has its own weight in the mixture, but they are all there. These categories also represent mental perspectives people develop about computing. Some people see computing as computation, others as data, networked coordination, or automated systems. The framework can broaden people's perspectives about what computing really is.

There is more to computing than a set of principles and the core technologies that build on them. Computing professionals do the daily work as members of communities that specialize in many computing domains (see figure 1.11). In addition to their knowledge of computing principles, computing professionals are expected to be competent in four core practices: programming, systems thinking, modeling, and computational thinking. A practice is a skill set embodied through continuous practice and interactions with customers. A practitioner's skill can be rated as beginner, advanced beginner, competent, proficient, or expert. A beginning programmer, for example, would be focused on language syntax, getting programs to compile, and finding bugs; an expert programmer would be able to build large systems, solve complex systems problems, and mentor junior programmers. Principles and practices are in constant interaction. People put computing principles to work through skilled action; new principles are occasionally discovered from common practices people have developed.

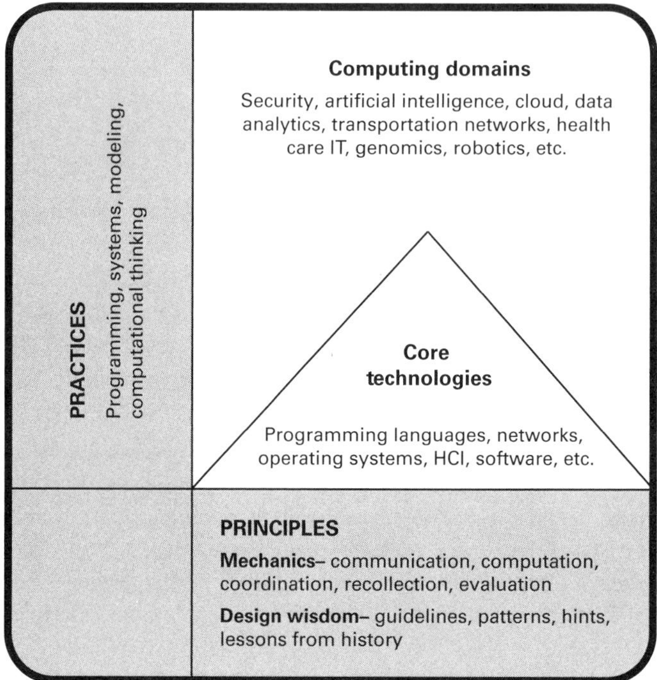

Figure 1.11
Computing as a whole depends on both principles and practices. The core technologies are pervasive tools used by practitioners to carry out their work in numerous computing domains. This book concentrates on the principles and their uses in several key domains, leaving core technologies and practices to other books. The principles are either *mechanics*—laws and recurrences—or *design wisdom*—accumulated knowledge about what works or does not work—to build computing systems that are dependable, reliable, usable, safe, and secure.

The communities in which computing people and their customers gather are called *computing domains*. There are dozens of domains. ACM (the Association for Computing Machinery) recognizes no less than 42 domains of professional interest to its members (Denning 2001, 2011), and there are many more under the heading of "computing applications." The next chapter examines four domains of high contemporary interest—security, artificial intelligence, cloud computing, and big data.

A great many of the computing domains interact with other fields outside of computing. In an analysis of how computing interacts with the three great domains of science—physical, life, and social sciences—Paul

Rosenbloom found two kinds of interactions: *implementation* and *influence* (Rosenbloom 2004, Denning and Rosenbloom 2009, Rosenbloom 2012). Implementation means that something from one domain is used to create or build something in the other. Influence means that something in one domain affects the behavior of something in the other. Implementation and influence can be single- or bidirectional. Rosenbloom built the chart of table 1.2 to demonstrate the rich set of interactions between computing and all of science in all these dimensions. He included a column for computing in his chart. He did this simply because computing is constantly implementing and influencing itself through the interactions among the many computing domains. There can be no question about the pervasive influence of computing throughout science.

Where Does Computing Fit in Science?

Because computing is so pervasive in its influence in science, and because no other scientific field is directly concerned with information, Rosenbloom came to the conclusion that computing qualifies as the fourth scientific domain.

What is so special about computing's approach to information? Information traditionally means facts that add to knowledge when communicated. It is an old concept, studied for centuries in philosophy, mathematics, business, the humanities, and the sciences. Science is concerned with discovering facts, fitting them together into models, using the models to make predictions, and turning validated predictive models into technologies. Scientists record all they have learned in the structure called the "scientific body of knowledge" for future use. Information has always played a strong role in the sciences.

Computing differs in two ways from the other sciences in its approach to information. First, computing emphasizes the *transformation* of information, not simply its discovery, classification, storage, and communication. Algorithms not only read information structures, they modify them. Moreover, humans constantly modify information structures—such as in the web—with transformations for which we yet have no computational models. Purely analytic methods cannot help us understand the dynamics of these information structures. The experimental methods of science are needed to make progress.

The second difference is that the structures of computing are not just descriptive, they are *generative*. An algorithm is not just a description of a method for solving a problem, it causes a machine to solve the problem.

Table 1.2

Examples of Computing Interacting with Other Domains

	Physical	Social	Life	Computing
Computing is implemented by:	Mechanical, optical, electronic, quantum, and chemical processes	Wizard of Oz, mechanical robots, human cognition, games with inputs and outputs	Genomic, neural, immunological, DNA translation, evolutionary computing	Compilers, operating systems, simulators, abstractions, procedures, architectures, languages
Computing implements:	Modeling, simulation, databases, data systems, quantum cryptography, 3D printing	Artificial intelligence, cognitive modeling, autonomic systems	Artificial life, biomimetics, systems biology	
Computing is influenced by:	Sensors, scanners, computer vision, optical character recognition, localization	Learning, programming, user modeling, authorization, speech understanding	Eye, gesture, expression, and movement tracking, biosensors	Networking, information protection, security, parallel computing, distributed systems, grids
Computing influences:	Locomotion, fabrication, manipulation, open-loop control	Screens, printers, graphics, speech generation, network science	Bioeffectors, haptics, sensory immersion	
Bidirectional influence	Robots, closed-loop control	Human computer interaction, games	Brain-computer interfaces	

The computing sciences are the only sciences with such a strong emphasis on information causing action.

No other field has taken up this view of information. Computing has, and the answers it has found have profoundly influenced every field of science. Computing does not fit as a subset of the physical, life, or social sciences. It seems to be a science domain in its own right.

What This Book Does

The computing sciences have grown so large that a complete survey cannot fit in a manageable book. Three books designed as "encyclopedias of computer science" present their summaries as a series of articles in 2030 pages (Ralston 2003), 770 pages (Abrams 2011), and 580 pages (Henderson 2008). Rather than attempt comprehensive coverage, we have selected a sampling of the greatest principles of computing.

Our sample is contained in nine chapters: information, machines, programming, computation, memory, parallelism, queueing, design, and networking (chapters 3–11). Each of the six categories is represented in at least one chapter (see table 1.1). Taken together, the set of chapters aims to convey a coherent view of the breadth, richness, and depth of the computing categories.

Chapter 1 is about the history and structure of the computing field and its interactions with other fields. Chapter 2 is about how computing domains draw knowledge from computing principles; security, artificial intelligence, cloud computing, and big data are featured examples.

Chapter 3 is about the nature of information, what machines can do with it, and how machines can deliver meaningful information to their users. Chapter 4 is about how computing machines are built, so that the programs we write can control the electronic circuits to perform the computations we intend. Chapter 5 is about programming, the art of designing computational solutions to problems, and how we can automatically translate programs into equivalent machine codes.

Chapter 6 is about computation itself: some problems are solvable by fast algorithms, others only by slow algorithms, and others not by any computing machine at all. Chapter 7 is about memory, how we store and retrieve information efficiently by naming it and positioning it in memory systems and networks.

Chapter 8 discusses parallelism, the quest for speed by mobilizing many cooperating parallel computers on the solution of one problem. Chapter 9 is about queueing, the methods we use to predict the throughput and response times of complicated networks of servers when many parallel jobs compete for their services.

Chapter 10 is concerned with design, how to plan and organize computing systems that are dependable, reliable, usable, safe, and secure. Chapter 11, a case study of the Internet, is about how we mobilize other principles to build a vast, reliable data communication network of links and hosts.

We have included a bibliography at the end of the book. The bibliography contains selected items that have inspired us; they are not meant to be historically complete summaries of literature. If you find someone's name in the text, you will also find at least one bibliographical item by that person.

Conclusions

Computing as a field has matured and exemplifies good science as well as engineering and mathematics. The science is essential to the advancement of the field because many systems are so complex that experimental methods are the principal means to make discoveries and understand limits. Computing is now seen as a broad field that studies information processes, natural and artificial.

The great principles framework reveals a rich set of principles on which all computation is based. These principles support many computing domains and a large number of domains within the physical, life, and social sciences.

Computing is not a subset of the physical, life, or social sciences. None of those domains is fundamentally concerned with the nature of information processes and their transformations. Yet this knowledge is now essential in all the other domains of science. The computing sciences may well be the fourth great domain of science.

Acknowledgment

This chapter is adapted from "Great Principles of Computing," by Peter J. Denning, *American Scientist 98* (Sep–Oct 2010), 369–372. Republished in *Best Writings on Mathematics 2010,* ed. Mircea Pitici, Princeton University Press (2011). Reused here with permission from *American Scientist* magazine.

2 Domains

Biology is an information science.
—David Baltimore

Computation is a third way of doing science, besides theory and experiment.
—Kenneth Wilson

Science and applications of science are bound together as the fruit of the tree which bears it.
—Louis Pasteur

The action of computing comes from people, not principles. Computing people have organized into numerous communities of practice, which we call *computing domains*. Each domain is centered on a technology or an application of technology. For example, the security domain is centered on security technologies and the privacy domain on applications of security technologies to safeguard personal information. The members of these domains share similar concerns, skill sets, methods, and interactions with other communities. They are empowered and constrained by computing principles. The great principles framework would be incomplete without the computing domains (Rosenbloom 2012) (see figure 2.1).

Numerical aerodynamic simulation is an example of a domain. Computer scientists have long collaborated with aeronautics engineers on the design of aircraft. Starting in the 1980s, aircraft companies turned to numerical simulation to design wings and fuselages for efficient, nonturbulent air flows. The traditional methods of wind tunnels and test flights were no longer practical for the size and complexity of aircraft. With new algorithms running on massively parallel supercomputers, engineers were able to design new aircraft that would fly safely on the first flight. The Boeing 777 was the first aircraft completely designed numerically. The teams of

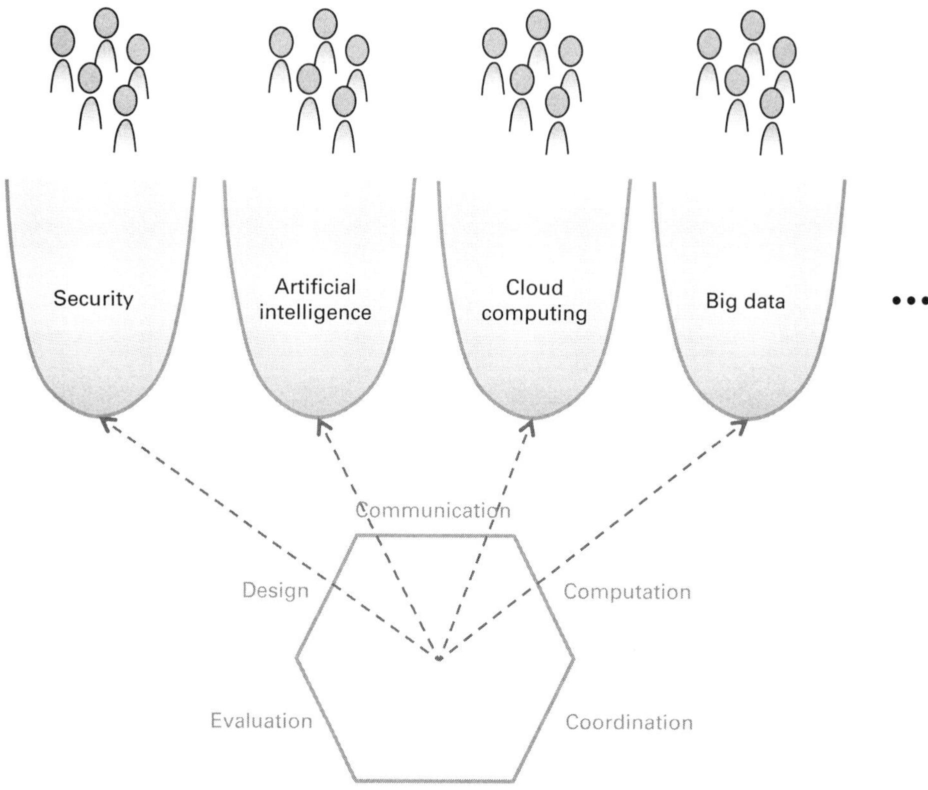

Figure 2.1
The six categories of the great principles framework (*bottom*) are all concerned with managing matter and energy to produce intended computations. In contrast, computing domains (*top*) are communities of practice; their people mobilize computing principles to support solutions to their problems, breakdowns, and interests (*dashed arrows*). The domains also feature strong interactions between computing and other fields. Their work adds principles to computing and to their own fields.

aeronautics and computing people developed a new field, computational fluid dynamics, which computed the complex movements of flowing air. They designed computational methods based on 3D grids to solve equations from fluid dynamics in the regions of space around an airframe. They exploited a category of fast *multigrid algorithms*, which solved very large airframes in minimal time on hypercube-connected parallel processors (Chan and Saad 1986, Denning 1987). These teams also developed new methods of refining grids dynamically to add precision in zones of rapid change of air pressure or speed. Some of these methods were recognized as new principles of computing. As a result, computational methods became a permanent part of fluid dynamics.

Computing domains are numerous. The Association for Computing Machinery (ACM) recognizes 42 domains of direct professional interest to its members, and there are dozens of additional application areas and collaborations with other fields (Denning and Frailey 2011). In this chapter we examine four computing domains—security, artificial intelligence, cloud computing, and big data—within a framework that analyzes four factors:

- Who is involved in the domain
- What domain problems, concerns, and interests are taken care of in the domain
- What computing principles are mobilized for the domain
- How domains have generated new principles for computing as well as the other participating fields

This kind of analysis can reveal other principles that could improve a design. It can help other domain participants understand the advantages and limitations of what computing offers them. It could also expose connections between technologies, which might be exploited for future innovations.

Before turning to the examples, it is worthwhile to take a closer look at the relationship between the computing domains and the great principles framework. This understanding will help with the analysis of the domains.

Domains and Principles

There are two basic, useful strategies for representing a field's body of knowledge. One enumerates the domains of the field, the other its principles. These different interpretations of the same knowledge space create different possibilities for actions. For this chapter, we use the term *domain* to mean a technology domain, namely a domain centered on a particular technology.

Educators use the term *body of knowledge* (BOK) to mean an organized description of the knowledge of a field. Educators often work with a BOK to design curricula that cover the essential knowledge of their field. The ACM offered its first computing BOK in 1968. It provided updates in 1989, 2001, and 2013. ACM listed nine core domains in 1989 (Denning et al. 1989), fourteen in 2001 (ACM Education Board 2001), and eighteen in 2013 (ACM Education Board 2013). They are core domains because all the other domains depend on their technologies in some way.

A principles framework, as in this book, is orthogonal to a domain-oriented framework. The same principle may appear in several domains, and a particular domain relies on several principles. The set of active principles (those used in at least one technology) evolves much more slowly than the technologies.

Although the two styles of framework are different, they are strongly connected. To visualize the connection, imagine a two-dimensional matrix. The rows are the topics from a domain-oriented framework, and the columns are the categories of principles. The interior of the matrix is the *knowledge space* of the field (see figure 2.2).

With this picture, we can say that the technology-oriented BOK enumerates the knowledge by rows of the matrix, whereas the principles-oriented BOK enumerates by columns. They see the same knowledge—from different perspectives and interpretations.

Imagine someone who wants to enumerate all the principles involved with a technology. That person can analyze the technology domain for its principles in each of the six categories—which corresponds to reading the principles from the row of the matrix (see figure 2.3). That is what we will do with the four example domains in the following sections.

The principles framework opens new inquiries. For example, someone could enumerate all the technologies that employ a particular principle or category of principles (see figure 2.4).

Security

Security as a domain has a long, rich history in computer science. Even in the earliest days, when batch processing was the norm, users were concerned about data entrusted to the machine. Was the machine in a physically secure place? Was the memory cleared before a new job was loaded? Could an operator's mistake or hardware failure lose data?

With the first multiprogrammed, time-sharing systems around 1960, operating system designers got heavily involved in information protection.

Principles categories

Domains	Communication	Computation	Coordination	Recollection	Evaluation	Design
Architecture						
Internet						
Security			key distr protocol zero knowl proof			
Virtual Memory						
Database						
Programming language						

Figure 2.2

The knowledge space of computing can be represented as the interior of a matrix whose columns are the categories of principles and rows the names of computing domains. The figure shows two principles from coordination used in the security domain: *key distribution protocols* (for securely distributing encryption keys) and *zero knowledge proofs* (for securely exchanging a secret between two parties).

They devised ways to partition main memory so that code and data of different programs could not mix; virtual memory was the most sophisticated mechanism. They invented the hierarchical file system to give users custodianship over their files and decide what access, if any, would be granted to other users. They invented password systems to keep unauthorized users out. They built structures to prevent Trojan horses and other malware from interrupting systems and corrupting data. They invented ways to control access so that confidential information could not flow into public files. They created policies for computer operators to protect data and guard against intrusions. From 1970 it was widely accepted that operating systems designers had a strong responsibility for information protection (Denning 1971, Saltzer and Schroeder 1975).

The ARPANET of the 1970s, Internet of the 1980s, and World Wide Web of the 1990s provided a worldwide network for information sharing and vast new opportunities for information loss and pilfering. Cryptography

	Communication	Computation	Coordination	Recollection	Evaluation	Design
Security	Secrecy authentication, covert channels	Complexity of encryption functions	Key distr protocol zero knowl proof	Confinement partitioning, Reference monitor	Protocol performance analysis	End-to-end layered functions, Virtual machines

Figure 2.3

The principles of security can be identified by reading the knowledge matrix across the security row. Like most other computing domains security draws principles from all six categories.

assumed a central role in security and authentication (Denning 1982). Designers responded to many new issues with database records protection, password protection, biometric authentication of users, antihacking protection, intrusion detection, protection from viruses and worms as well as malware, multilevel secure systems, information flow management, anonymous transactions, criteria for levels of trust in systems, forensics, auditing, data recovery, and security-enhancing practices for users. Law enforcement experts started seeing a rise in crimes and attacks against computing systems, and they began warning everyone to take serious steps to protect personal information. Unfortunately, few took these calls seriously. In the interest of expediency to deliver new systems rapidly, many developers downplayed security and assumed they could add protections later if security became an issue. Sadly, they bet wrong. Large numbers of highly vulnerable systems were deployed that lacked structural safeguards for information protection and employed lax policies in their operations.

As more and more financial data, personnel data, personal data, and corporate data became accessible online, the volume of attacks rose sharply. Defense experts worried about information warfare (Denning 1998). Privacy experts cried out for protections of personal information lest basic

	Communication	Computation	Coordination	Recollection	Evaluation	Design
Architecture			Hardware handshake			
Internet			TCP and IP protocols			
Security			Key distr protocol zero knowl proof			
Virtual memory			Page fault interrupt			
Database			Locking protocol			
Programming language			Semaphores monitors			

Figure 2.4
The technologies of coordination can be identified by reading the knowledge matrix down the coordination column. Almost all computing domains, including the six illustrated here, employ coordination principles.

freedoms be lost (Garfinkel 2001). In 1999 there were palpable fears of network collapse from the "Y2K" problem caused by encoding years with two digits instead of four. After that many people slowly awoke to the vulnerabilities of information networks and to the challenges of securing them. Experts in many countries began predicting devastating cyber attacks that could ruin economies and even endanger civilization (Schneier 2004, 2008, Clark 2012).

The people, problems, and computing principles of the security domain are displayed in table 2.1.

Artificial Intelligence

The idea of machines performing human intellectual tasks dates back five centuries. Blaise Pascal built a mechanical calculator in 1642. Charles Babbage proposed the Difference Engine in 1823 to calculate navigation and other arithmetic function tables automatically. In the late 1800s the "mechanical Turk" was a convincing hoax appearing to be an expert chess-playing automaton (Standage 2003). Indeed, many of the ideas that have

Table 2.1
Security Domain

Who	Members	Operating system designers, network engineers, cyber operators, military defense, law enforcement, forensics investigators, homeland security, public policy officials, diplomats, privacy advocates
What	Breakdowns, problems, concerns	Controlled sharing, memory protection, file protection, access control, information flow, trusted systems, secret communications, authentication, signatures, key distribution, preventing inference through data correlation
Computing principles	Communication	Cryptography, secrecy, authentication
	Computation	One-way functions, cryptographic complexity, hashing, formal verification
	Recollection	Access control, error confinement, information flow, multilevel secure storage, reference monitors
	Coordination	Key distribution, zero knowledge proofs, authentication protocols, signature protocols
	Evaluation	Performance and throughput of protocols, criteria for secure systems
	Design	Open design, least privilege, fail-safe defaults, psychological acceptability, end-to-end designs, layered functions, virtual machines
Principles from other fields		Information assurance practices, intrusion detection, biometric ID, forensic rules of evidence, inference from statistical databases

become the basis of artificial intelligence (AI) predated most of computer science (Russell and Norvig 2010).

In 1956 John McCarthy organized a workshop at Dartmouth with help from Claude Shannon and Nathaniel Rochester. Their workshop gave birth to the field of artificial intelligence. Their founding vision was that "every aspect of learning or any other feature of intelligence can in principle be so precisely described that a machine can be made to simulate it." This appeared plausible because so many intelligent tasks appeared to be following algorithms, and the brain itself appeared to be an electrical network capable of executing algorithms. Herbert Simon predicted that by 1967 a computer would be world chess champion, a computer would discover and prove an important new mathematical theorem, and many theories in psychology would be embodied in computer programs. His first dream was achieved 30 years late, and the other two have yet to be achieved.

Alan Turing (1950) crystalized many of the seeds of modern AI: the Turing test, machine learning, and even the idea that we might "grow" an intelligent machine through stages of development, like a child. Turing realized that "intelligence" is so ill defined that he could make no progress with the question of when a machine might be intelligent. His imitation game (the Turing test) asks not whether a machine *has* intelligence but instead whether it *behaves* intelligently. He predicted that by the year 2000 machines would be able to fool 70 percent of determined human interrogators for at least five minutes. That dream also has yet to be achieved.

Turing's behavioral focus was adopted into the founding dream of AI. By the 1970s, however, it became the brunt of sharp criticism. Many AI projects set out to design "expert systems," which would perform as well as human experts in many domains such as medical diagnosis. Hubert Dreyfus (1972, 1992) maintained that expert behavior was beyond the capability of rule-based machines. He was initially ridiculed, but time seems to have proved him right. Only a handful of expert systems worked competently, and none approached genuine experts. John Searle (1984) attacked the notion that conventional computing machines are capable of intelligence; he described a rule-based machine that might appear to carry on conversations in Chinese but did not embody any sort of understanding of Chinese. He attacked "strong AI"—the notion that the mind is a product of machine behavior—and favored "weak AI"—that simulations might imitate a behavior without any resemblance to the way a brain generates the behavior. Terry Winograd and Fernando Flores (1987) argued that AI was based on philosophical assumptions that could not explain or lead to intelligence.

By the mid-1980s it was clear to many that the initial dreams of AI were not going to be achieved any time soon. The research funding agencies began to withhold funds and to demand deliverable results. Many researchers did a lot of soul searching about the weaknesses of their field. AI pioneer Raj Reddy called that dark time the period of "AI winter."

A new field of AI emerged from that introspection. The focus shifted from trying to model the way the human mind works to simply building systems that could take over human cognitive work. Automated cognition systems need not work the same way the human mind works; they do not even need to mimic a human solving a problem. The field simultaneously adopted a strong emphasis on experimental methods to validate whether proposed automations were useful, reliable, and safe (Russell and Norvig 2010, Nilsson 2010). Recent publicity-garnering triumphs include the IBM Deep Blue chess program beating World Chess Champion Garry Kasparov in 1997, Google's driverless car in 2010, and IBM's Watson computer winning the TV game Jeopardy in 2011. The methods used in these programs were highly effective but did not resemble human thought or brain processes. Moreover, the methods were specialized to the single purpose and did not generalize.

Many researchers in computer science, cognitive science, medical science, and psychology continue to study how the brain works and how it generates a mind. The fascination with the singularity (Kurzweil 2005) and the Brain Activity Map Project (announced in 2013) are signs that this line of inquiry maintains its allure.

The reborn AI field has been so successful that it has raised a new set of concerns. In *Race against the Machine*, Erik Brynjolfsson and Andrew McAfee (2012) document how waves of automation are edging out knowledge-work jobs, just as mechanical automation in the previous century had edged out many manual labor jobs. Examples of knowledge automation abound: call centers, voice menu systems, online purchasing, online banking, government services, publishing, news distribution, music publishing, advertising, surveillance, terrorist hunting, and much more. The authors worry that we are sliding toward a society with too few jobs to sustain the population of workers and insufficient resources for public agencies to serve the jobless.

The people, problems, and computing principles of the artificial intelligence domain are displayed in table 2.2.

Cloud Computing

Cloud computing is a modern buzzphrase that hides a rich tradition of information sharing and distributed computing. It refers to networks of computing devices that give economies of scale by hiding the locations of servers and data stores. The term "cloud" came into use in the late 1990s, probably from a practice of showing "the network" as a cloud in technical and marketing presentations.

The idea of building systems that could share computing power among many users cheaply was embodied into MIT Project MAC in the mid-1960s. MAC was an acronym for "multiple-access computer" and sometimes for "man and computer." Project MAC built Multics, a powerful multiplexed system that distributed the expense of memory, disk, and CPU over a large community so that the cost of computing for any one user would be very small. J. C. R. Licklider, the visionary who supplied the initial inspiration, thought that computing power could be supplied like a utility: anyone could plug a terminal into a wall-socket (Licklider 1960).

The ARPANET, which started operation in late 1969, supported the utility ambition. It was designed for resource sharing—users anywhere in the

Table 2.2
Artificial Intelligence Domain

Who	Members	AI experts, AI practitioners, artificial lifers, planners, singularity followers, chess players, Jeopardy enthusiasts, Bayesian learners, machine learners, biologically inspired designers, cognitive scientists, human factors designers, psychologists, economists, law enforcers, roboticists
What	Breakdowns, problems, concerns	Automation of cognitive tasks, design and experimental evaluation of heuristics, evolutionary computing, genetic computing, neural computing, pattern recognition, automatic classification, speech recognition, natural language translation, artificial brains, superhuman intelligence, autonomous systems such as drones and cars
Computing principles	Communication	Noisy-channel model
	Computation	Heuristic algorithms, classification, Bayesian inference, machine learning, searching large state spaces, models of intelligence
	Recollection	Memory models, sparse distributed memory, neural network retrieval, locality learning algorithms
	Coordination	Training protocols, coordination theory
	Evaluation	Experimental methods for evaluating heuristics; precision, recall, accuracy
	Design	Storage of large data sets for use in supervised and unsupervised experiments
Principles from other fields		Brains generate minds, speech act theory, linguistics, neuroscience, statistical inference

network could connect with any host and use its services. No one had to replicate a shared service. The ARPANET designers soon realized that shared services would be sought by name rather than location and that location-independent addressing would be the only way to hide the many addressing conventions of local networks containing the services. Vint Cerf and Bob Kahn invented the TCP/IP protocols (1974) to exchange messages between any computers in the Internet knowing only their IP addresses but not their physical locations. The ARPANET standardized on the TCP/IP protocol in 1983.

In 1984, the ARPANET adopted the Domain Naming System (DNS), an online database that mapped symbolic host names to their IP addresses; for example "gmu.edu" maps to "129.174.1.38." This added another level of location independence, leaving only the names of servers visible to Internet users.

In the 1990s the World Wide Web allowed sharing of any information objects in the Internet (Berners-Lee 2000). Objects were named with their URLs (uniform resource locators), strings of the form "hostname/pathname," where pathname was the directory path of a file on the given host system. In the mid-1990s Robert Kahn designed a service called handle.net that mapped a unique identifier (a handle) to the URL of an object. He also designed the associated Digital Object Identifier (DOI) system for the Library of Congress and most publishers (Kahn and Wilensky 2006). The DOI was an even higher level of transparency for, once assigned, it designated a unique digital object in the Internet no matter where the object moved and how long ago it was created (Denning and Kahn 2010).

The architecture for distributing computing services to users has been continually refined over the years. Multics multiplexed the resources of a mainframe system among its users. In the 1970s Xerox PARC (Palo Alto Research Center) created the Alto system, which was a network of standalone graphic workstations linked on an Ethernet (Metcalfe and Boggs 1983). They called their architecture client-server because the user accessed services elsewhere on the network by a local interface called the client. The X-Window system, originated at MIT in 1984, was a generalized client-server system that allowed a new service provider to plug in its hardware and user interface without having to design client-server communication protocols. Most web services today use client-server architectures: the vendor makes the service available through an interface displayed on a standard web browser. Most services accessible in the cloud are client-server architectures whose server locations are completely hidden by the URL naming system.

The people, problems, and computing principles of cloud computing are summarized in table 2.3.

Big Data

Big data is another recent buzzphrase hiding a rich tradition in computing. It refers to the processing of massive data sets in the Internet, looking for population statistics, correlations, faint signals, and rare events. These analyses are used in a diverse range of applications in science, engineering, business, census-taking, and law enforcement.

Computer scientists have long been involved with problems of storing, retrieving, and processing data sets that exceeded the current technology.

Table 2.3
Cloud Computing Domain

Who	Members	Network designers, distributed computing designers, client-server architects, enterprise system designers, businesses, governments, economists
What	Breakdowns, problems, concerns	Location-independent services and data storage, redundancy, restricting cross-border flows, distributed computing models
Computing principles	Communication	Error-correcting codes, compressing sound and image files, location-based identification
	Computation	Map-Reduce methods, massively parallel computing
	Recollection	Replicating data, atomic transactions, transaction rollback, database structures, searching Internet, naming, digital object identifiers, digital object handles
	Coordination	Locking protocols, rollback protocols, file-transfer protocols, file-syncing protocols, hypertext protocols, domain name system, time stamping, version control
	Evaluation	Performance of massively parallel and massively distributive memory systems
	Design	Interface design, data warehouse architecture
Principles from other fields		Social networks, e-commerce, critical infrastructure modeling, statistical inference of location

What was once big is now small. The term "big data" is a recent moniker for an old problem, which now affects many communities. For example, as part of normal business, corporations amass petabytes of customer-related data, which they use to identify trends, target advertising, and track loyalty. Publicly funded science research projects are now required to make their data available for free to the public, and other projects are required to "mine" it for possible insights. Police use massive databases of telephone calls and credit card transactions to hunt and locate suspects and fugitives. All these groups actively seek data analysts, data scientists, and data system architects to help them do these jobs.

Computer scientists have contributed in two main ways. One has been new computationally efficient analytic methods, and the other has been systems and architectures that enable processing of massive amounts of data. For example, Richard Karp (1993) applied his knowledge of efficient combinatorial methods to algorithms for merging experimentally sampled gene data into genome maps. Tony Chan and Yousef Saad (1986) demonstrated that one of the first parallel architectures, the hypercube, was optimal for a large class of numerical algorithms, called multigrid algorithms, used in solving mathematical models applied to very large data spaces. Jeffrey Dean and Sanjay Ghemawat (2008) designed MapReduce, a new method for mobilizing thousands of parallel processors to solve very large data-processing problems.

Large data sets have always been a concern for businesses. They store data on customers, inventory, manufacturing, and accounting—everything companies need to operate while big and international. IBM became wealthy in the data-processing markets in the 1930s, many years before electronic computers, selling business machines such as card sorters and retrievers. In the 1950s IBM joined a growing number of computer companies that offered electronic data processing. IBM generated considerable publicity in 1956 when it introduced the first hard disk storage system, RAMAC 305. IBM claimed businesses could move warehouses of file cabinets on to a single disk and process the data with amazing speed. As data stores grew, the designers focused on methods to organize the data for fast access and easy maintenance. The two chief competing methods were the Integrated Data System (Bachman 1973) and the Relational Database System (Codd 1970, 1990). The IDS was simple, fast, and pragmatic in its approach to managing large sets of files while hiding the file structure and location on the disks. The RDS was based on the mathematical theory of sets; it had a clean conceptual model but took many years to perfect and achieve the kinds of efficiency seen in IDS. Starting in the 1970s, there has been an active community of researchers who meet annually to discuss issues in very large databases (VLDB).

Beginning in the 1950s, computing researchers helped librarians to organize data for fast retrieval of documents. Libraries were early users of these information retrieval systems. They developed search systems that could deal with fuzzy queries such as "find documents about information retrieval" but without necessarily containing the text string "information retrieval." Today's Internet is a large unstructured store in which keyword retrieval is very fast but imprecise and information retrieval is difficult (Dreyfus 2001).

The Gartner Group defined the modern "big data" domain in terms of four V's: problems with large *volumes* of data, which arrive at high *velocity*, are in a large *variety* of formats, and whose *veracity* is important to decisions based on it. As of 2014, data science courses, centers, and curricula were popping up at universities and research labs. The people involved are from

Table 2.4
Big Data Domain

Who	Members	Business, government agencies, enterprise designers, scientific data collectors, statisticians, large systems modelers
What	Breakdowns, problems, concerns	Finding correlated items in very large data sets, computational complexity, privacy issues, inference, forensics of data recovery, information retrieval
Computing principles	Communication	Reliable transmissions from thousands of sensors to repositories, detecting if data have been corrupted, altered, or lost, detecting if data has been placed in illegal jurisdictions
	Computation	Computational complexity of algorithms for data analysis
	Recollection	Storage, replication, error control, testing whether data still exist, testing for physical location of data, forensics data recovery from very large stores
	Coordination	Map-Reduce computing
	Evaluation	Predicting completion times of large searches and analyses in very large networks
	Design	Replication of data, indexing data, structuring for optimal retrieval
Principles from other fields		Natural language processing, statistic inference, mood inference, crowdsourcing, forensics practices

many disciplines including analysts from operations research and statistics, architectures from computer science and information systems, and visualizers from modeling and simulation. The associated "data science" domain is concerned with the scientific basis for analysis and processing of very large data sets.

The people, problems, and computing principles of the big data domain are summarized in table 2.4.

Conclusion

The great principles framework is a useful way to identify bundles of principles making up a technology. It is also useful to identify computing principles that underpin computing domains, in which people from computing and other fields interact to solve persistent problems of concern in their communities.

3 Information

The semantic aspects of communication are irrelevant to the engineering problem.
—Claude E. Shannon

Software is not just an interaction device, it generates a space in which the user lives.
—Terry Winograd

The study of information has advanced rapidly since mathematician and communications engineer Claude Shannon developed information theory in the 1940s. A key tenet of his theory is that information and meaning are distinct, making it possible for machines to process information without regard to its meaning. And yet the whole purpose of communication and computing is to convey and produce meaningful results. How can this be?

Software designers, scientists, and consumers look to software to generate virtual worlds, social networks, music, new discoveries, financial projections, love letters, inspiring images, and much more. But the meaning of the information output by these systems seems to depend on the observer. For example, a tabulation of stock prices may look like numerical gibberish to a financial amateur but a source of riches to a professional investor. How can we formulate an information science if its fundamental object is at least partly subjective?

These questions look paradoxical because information theory says that *meaning* is irrelevant to computational machinery, a statement that personal experience with computational systems seems to contradict. Moreover, the concept of information seems fuzzy and abstract to many people, making it hard for them to understand how information systems really work. Our objective in this chapter is to show that information is quite real, existing as physically observable patterns (see figure 3.1). We examine what information theory has to say about representing and transmitting

Figure 3.1
In 1956 IBM introduced the world's first magnetic disk information-storage system, the RAMAC 350. A promotional film for the machine showed hallways of file cabinets with frazzled secretaries walking along them. The RAMAC 350, the film showed, stored the entire content of the cabinets in about 5 cubic meters and allowed near-instantaneous searches of the data. To contemporary viewers the film also demonstrates that the struggle to make the seemingly abstract concept of information tangible is not new. (Photograph courtesy of IBM)

information, how it combines with computability theory, and where its limits are. This examination shows why classical information theory cannot explain meaning and generation of new information. We describe a model of meaning-preserving transformations that resolves the apparent paradoxes.

Representing Information

We humans are incredibly flexible about how we communicate information. Here are four examples. The first two illustrate explicit meaning:

1. We point to an object and tell our friends what that object means—and now that object "carries" information because that meaning is triggered in our friends' brains whenever they see the object.
2. We discover and name recurrences, which are patterns of events that repeat. When we see the pattern, we can predict the outcome. The pattern carries information about the outcome. Discovering recurrences in nature is an objective of science, and putting recurrences to work as technologies is an objective of engineering.

The next two examples illustrate implicit, or tacit, meaning:

3. Communities develop recurrent practices that communicate information. For example, many drivers communicate their intention to merge into freeway traffic by inching sideways with a blinker on. No written rule of the road tells them to do this.
4. Everyday habits and conventions of human practice are unnamed recurrences that carry information. For example, a "come here" wave in most cultures communicates a request to move closer to you.

Scientists and engineers routinely build technologies that deal with explicit information, which is an association between a physical representation and an intended meaning. For example, an electromagnetic signal encodes someone's speech. We create information by declaring an association between a representation and its meaning. We process information by storing the representations in memory and applying transformation rules to them.

Social scientists and philosophers have been grappling with implicit information for millennia—often without reaching much consensus. Engineers have the easier task with explicit information.

The field of artificial intelligence tries to push the boundary between explicit meaning and implicit meaning. Engineers in this area look for ways to represent information that is only tacitly recognized, yet easily understood, by human users.

Whether explicit or implicit, all information exists by human agreement. We know what a representation or a recurrence means because someone either explicitly told us how to interpret it or we implicitly learned it by experience.

Computer and communication engineers specialize in systems that transmit information encoded as electromagnetic signals. For example, a microphone generates an electric signal as someone speaks, a magnetic disk records a copy of the signal, and a speaker generates a sound wave from that signal. A radio transmitter superimposes an audio signal on a radio frequency (RF) signal so that the RF amplitude tracks the audio signal; and a receiver subtracts out the RF signal to extract the audio. Engineers must be very precise and unambiguous about how they encode representations and their intended meanings. Otherwise, the physical systems they build will not work.

Computer and communication engineers settled on the bit (short for binary digit) as their basic unit of information. Claude Shannon introduced the term "bit" in the mid-1940s at the start of the computer age. Although decimal hardware components were possible and were used in some early

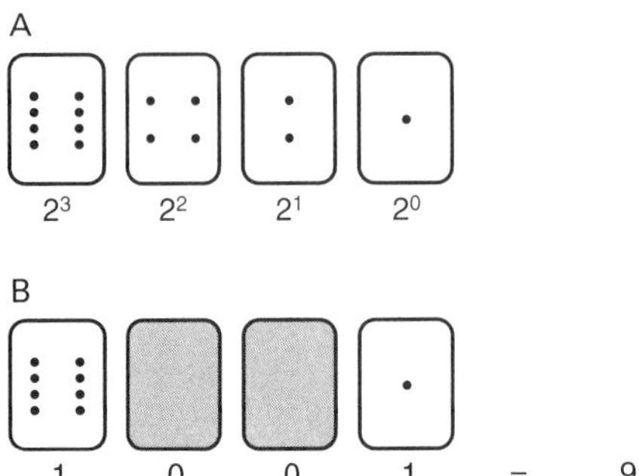

Figure 3.2
Children learn binary numbers quickly with cards. (A) Each card has twice as many dots as the card on its right. Four children line up and the instructor asks them to display various numbers by holding up their cards. Thus, (B) the first and fourth children hold up their cards while the second and third hide theirs, making the number 9. Children grasp binary numbers very quickly this way. Because any signal can be digitized into binary numbers and any text file encoded with binary numbers, bits have become a universal way to represent information and quantify the amount of it. (Courtesy of Tim Bell and Mike Fellows, csunplugged.org/videos)

computers, binary components became the standard because they are far more reliable. Shannon discovered that the functions of binary computer circuits could be expressed by logic formulas whose variables could only have the values true or false; thus, bit patterns could represent computer circuits. The numbers processed by the circuits were themselves encoded in a binary system (see figure 3.2). Since the 1950s, computers have been binary through and through, in their logic circuits and their data.

Shannon also demonstrated that the continuous signals used in practical communication systems could be digitized, in many cases with negligible error. We will return to this shortly.

Because all forms of data—numbers, signals, logic formulas, and text—can be represented as patterns of bits, the bit has become the standard unit of measure for information quantity. It shows up in modern terms such as "24-bit color," "100-megabit connection," "32-bit computer," and "256-bit encryption key." In the 1960s, computer makers coined the term *byte* as a group of eight bits needed to represent a single letter, number, or punctuation mark in the extended ASCII code. Over the years the size of data sets processed by computers has grown exponentially, and new Greek prefixes have been unearthed to designate them (see table 3.1). Each prefix corresponds to 1000 times as much data than the previous prefix (or 1024 times

Table 3.1
Names for Sizes of Data Sets

Name (symbol)	Decimal	Binary
byte (B)	8 bits	2^3 bits
kilobyte (KB)	10^3 bytes	2^{10} bytes
megabyte (MB)	10^6 bytes	2^{20} bytes
gigabyte (GB)	10^9 bytes	2^{30} bytes
terabyte (TB)	10^{12} bytes	2^{40} bytes
petabyte	10^{15} bytes	2^{50} bytes
exabyte	10^{18} bytes	2^{60} bytes
zettabyte	10^{21} bytes	2^{70} bytes
yottabyte	10^{24} bytes	2^{80} bytes

larger expressed as a power of 2, 2^{10}). In the 1960s, disk and RAM memories were measured in kilobytes. By the 1980s, they were measured in gigabytes, and NASA worried about how to store the 1 terabyte of data collected every day from satellites. In 2014 the term "big data" was used for petabyte data sets, and the Internet carried over a zettabyte every year. The Cisco Corporation (2012) forecast continued exponential growth in the size of the network and the amount of data it carries.

Communication Systems

The simplest kind of information system is a *communication system.* In a 1948 paper titled "A Mathematical Theory of Communication," Shannon offered the first theoretical model of such a system (Shannon 1948) (see figure 3.3). At its essence is the following process. A source sends a message. An encoder generates a distinct signal for the message, as prescribed in a codebook. A channel is the medium that carries signals from the source to the receiver. A decoder on the receiver end converts the signals back to their original form, using the same codebook—and the message has arrived. Shannon's model applies to any system that encodes, decodes, transports, stores, or retrieves signals or data. It has even served as a model of scientific discovery by treating nature as a source of facts (messages) and the channel as the discovery process (Dretske 1981).

Noise is an important element of the communication model. Noise is any disturbance in the channel that alters a signal, causing the decoder to output the wrong message. Examples of noise abound in communication technologies: fog and darkness interrupt ship-to-ship semaphore

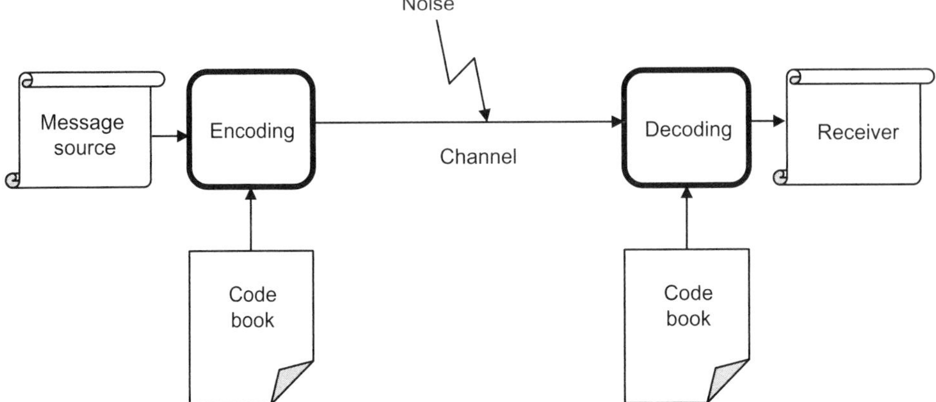

Figure 3.3
Claude Shannon (1916–2001) described a model information system that is now the basis of information theory. The message source represents the set of all messages that could be sent. The channel is the physical medium for storing and carrying signals. Encoding converts messages into signals, and decoding converts signals back into messages. The codebook contains the rules for converting messages to signals and back again, and noise is any disruption that alters the signals.

communications; excessive distance between telegraph operators degrades the signal strength; lightning strikes disrupt AM radio transmissions; scratches render DVDs unreadable; and environmental sounds drown out speech.

Note that in communication systems, coding is not the same as encryption. Encryption is an additional step that converts messages from the source into cipher text before that text goes to the encoder, so that only receivers who have the cipher keys can read them. The job of the communication system in this case is to deliver the cipher text accurately to the receiver, which can then remove the cipher if it has the key.

As mentioned above, Shannon standardized his mathematical model on bits. He argued that any signal can be represented as a pattern of bits, a process called digitization—literally, the conversion of analog information into digits. Digitization does not result in an exact replica of the information; it is an approximation that frequently loses some of the information. Some examples are obvious, such as pixelated photographs in which objects have ragged edges; others are subtler. Quantities from physical phenomena, such as the orbital position of a Mars lander, cannot be represented exactly in the finite arithmetic of the computer. Rounding errors can accumulate over many computational steps, placing the accuracy of the overall computation in doubt and putting the Mars lander at risk. Even worse, some computational steps can magnify errors; for example, the difference between two almost equal numbers can round to zero and then cause a major error when divided into another number. Designers of mathematical software have devised many clever techniques to prevent digitization errors from wrecking their results.

Harry Nyquist, a contemporary of Shannon, pointed out an important exception to this general rule: communication systems need not suffer from digitization errors (Nyquist 1928). Every continuous, bandwidth-limited signal can be digitized without any loss of information by sampling at a rate of at least twice the highest frequency. Audio compact discs (CDs), for example, record 44,100 samples per second (44.1 KHz) without significant loss of quality, because very few humans can hear sounds whose frequencies are greater than 22,000 Hz.

Shannon argued that, because we can digitally sample any signal and because real communication systems are bandwidth limited, we lose nothing if we restrict the communication model to binary sequences. This simplified the mathematics and still allowed the conclusions to work for any real channel.

A simple code serves as a running example to illustrate various features of the communication model. Consider a message source that transmits only one of four messages, which we designate as A, B, C, and D. We assign two-bit codes to these letters:

A: 11
B: 10
C: 01
D: 00

A code representing just four possible messages is not far removed from nature. The DNA in our cells is a natural message source that uses just four letters—G, A, T, and C are the first letters of the four nucleotides in DNA.

If the source wants to transmit the sequence "CAB" it sends the bits "011110" down the channel. The receiver reverses the process by looking up each pair of received bits in the codebook and reporting the corresponding letter.

In any discussion of codes we quickly encounter a trade-off between the size of the code (number of bits in the code words) and the difficulty of overcoming noise in the channel. Short codes are more efficient, transmit faster, and require less storage. However, short codes are easily disrupted by noise. A single-bit error in the channel will change one code word into another. For example, if the channel switched the first bit of A to 0, the receiver would receive 01, and decode it as C, not A. We add parity bits to alert the receiver to errors. The parity of a bit pattern is "even" if the number of 1s is even, and is "odd" if the number of 1s is odd. Here is the original code modified for even parity by adding a third bit:

A: 110
B: 101
C: 011
D: 000

Now an error that changes the first bit of the code for A to 0 delivers 010 to the receiver. The receiver recognizes that an error has occurred because 010 is not a valid code. In general, a one-bit error will cause the affected code word to have an odd number of 1s, flagging it as a noncode pattern.

However, the single parity bit does not indicate which bit was affected. For example, the receiver knows that 010 is not a valid code, but it cannot tell which of three codes (A, C, or D) was altered by the single bit error. By adding more redundancy, we can build decoders that not only detect that an error has occurred but can identify which message was corrupted. Consider this example, in which the original code modified by adding three extra bits:

A: 11111
B: 10010
C: 01001
D: 00100

This code was constructed to satisfy the principle that, with the extra bits, each code word differs from every other one by at least three bits. Now a one-bit error causes the received code word to differ by one bit from the correct code word and by two or more bits from the other code words. The decoder can thus detect and correct the corrupted code: it is the one with only a one-bit difference.

Communication engineer Richard Hamming first articulated (in 1950) the principle of sufficient distance between code words. Distance is the number of bits that differ, a measure that became known as "Hamming distance." Hamming noted that, to correct k errors, the code must have sufficient bits that the minimum distance between code words is at least $2k+1$. He also invented a family of codes, now known as Hamming codes, that embedded k parity bits into code words of length $2^k - 1$ bits, and gave a simple method of building circuits that converted corrupted bits back to their original values. One of the most popular Hamming codes is the (7,4)-code, which embeds three parity bits and four data bits into each seven-bit code word. Hamming codes are widely used in computers to correct errors in moving data between processors and memory.

Hamming codes work well when the noise is randomly distributed over the bits. In some signals, however, the noise comes in bursts. For instance, a solar flare can disrupt a deep-space signal for several seconds, or a scratch can disrupt a series of neighboring pits etched on an optical disk. These are called *bursty* errors. Another type of code, the Reed-Solomon code, was invented to detect and remove bursty errors. It is mathematically more complex but is, like the Hamming code, easily implemented by fast digital circuits.

Unlike signals, bits do not have a physical reality. A bit is a notation that represents which of two observable properties holds. For example, an engineer might assign bit "1" to mean that a laser beam reflects from a spot on the surface of a DVD and a "0" to mean that there is no reflection. Or the "1" might mean that the output of a transistor is 5 volts, and a "0" might mean it is 3 volts. Or a "1" might mean that a particular frequency, say 400 Hz, is present in a musical recording, whereas a "0" means it is not. Bits are abstractions that we use to specify what we want the systems to do. Engineers arrange the physical "stuff" (materials) so that it behaves as specified.

Because information in a physical system is always represented by physical states, it takes time and energy to read, write, and transform it. Communication and computation can never be free of the constraints of the physical world. Computer chip engineers know that effects such as heat accumulation and feature size (the average size of the various elements contained on a chip) place real limits on how small they can make their circuits. And the time cost for every operation places limits on how many instructions can be computed in the time available. Although new algorithms have yielded dramatic improvements in finding optimal results for common difficult problems, the larger cases are often still intractable because time needed for all the physical operations exceeds our capacity to wait. For example, finding the two prime factors that make up a 600-digit key for the widely used RSA encryption system would take centuries on the fastest known computers.

Our ability to store and compute information has increased exponentially over the years. In the same year Shannon published his essay, and in the same place—Bell Labs—the newly invented transistor began to replace vacuum tubes in electronic computers. Circuit designers were able to compress the size of transistors, putting about twice as many into the same physical space at no additional cost every 18–24 months. They have been doing this year after year for nearly 50 years, giving us 100 times more computational power with every decade. This trend is known as Moore's law after Intel cofounder Gordon Moore, who first described it in a 1965 paper (Moore 1965).

Moore's law has given us two effects. One is amazing computational abilities that would appear as magic to the 1940s pioneers of computing science. The other is a flood of information, as James Gleick (2011) calls it. The first effect—ever smaller physical mechanisms for transmitting and storing information—leads directly to the second, an overwhelming abundance of information. People do not function well when feeling overwhelmed and unable to make sense of information.

Those vast computational abilities have given rise to the popular notion that computation manipulates ethereal bits, not atoms, and consequently there is no physical limit on the size and power of computational structures (Negroponte 1996). From the standpoint of physics, this notion is simply wrong. An abstract bit can do nothing until it is recorded in a physical medium, where a machine can get at it. The recording process brings us back to the world of atoms: we cannot have computation without them. We can make computation, transmission, and storage breathtakingly small and fast, but we will never completely eliminate their time and energy costs.

Measuring Information

Because he wanted to know the length of the shortest code for a message source, Shannon devised a measure of the information inherent in a message source. The number of bits in a code cannot serve as such a measurement because, as we saw above, a single source can be represented by any number of different codes. He concluded that a good measure would be the size of the shortest possible code for a set of messages. A code with fewer bits would fail to transmit all the information in the messages.

He rejected measures that depended on the meanings human observers assign to codes and, instead, sought mechanisms for encoding, transmitting, and decoding that worked the same every time, regardless of the context in which they were used. Postal services follow a similar principle: their distribution and delivery systems do not depend in any way on the contents of the envelopes they transport. Shannon's remarkable insight was this: *He equated the reception of information with the reduction of uncertainty.* He defined information as the minimum number of yes-no questions needed to determine which of many possible messages a source was sending. The more we know about what a source might send, the less information we gain when we see what it sends.

Imagine that you know someone will respond only Y (yes) or N (no) to a question, but you have no way of knowing in advance which answer the speaker will give. The speaker resolves your uncertainty by saying Y or N. Shannon would say that the speaker just gave you one bit of information (either 1 or 0), which selects the actual response from the two possible responses. When there are more than two choices, more bits will be needed to distinguish the message that was sent.

Suppose that we want to find the page containing a friend's name in a phone book. How many bits do we need to encode the page number? A clever method answers this question. We open the book in the middle and ask which half holds the name, which is easy to do since the contents are alphabetized. We then split that half in half using the same question. We repeat this step until only one page remains. The friend's name should appear on that page. The repeated question ("Which half?" or equivalently, "Is it in the left half?") takes us rapidly to the location. With a 512-page phone book, the first question leaves us with 256 pages to search, the second question leaves 128 pages, then 64, 32, 16, 8, 4, 2, and, finally, 1. It takes nine "which-half" questions to find the page containing the word. Therefore, when we learn the page number that contains our friend's name, we have received nine bits of information.

In constructing a code, people take account of the probabilities of occurrence of possible messages. Samuel Morse, who devised Morse code to use with the electric telegraph he co-invented in the 1830s, assigned the shortest code—a single dot—to the letter *e* because he knew that *e* is the most common letter in English (about 12 percent of all letters used). He assigned the longest code to the letter *j* because it is one of the least common letters (about 0.15 percent). These choices minimized the average length of a transmission. Figure 3.4 shows how the questions one must ask to identify a message can define a code for the message and how prior knowledge of the probability of occurrence of various messages can lead to shorter codes.

Suppose that we have a set of code words of lengths L_i and probabilities P_i. The average length (L) of the code is

$$L = \sum_i L_i \cdot P_i$$

For the code in figure 3.4, this formula gives 2 bits for the average length of the first code and 1.75 bits for the second.

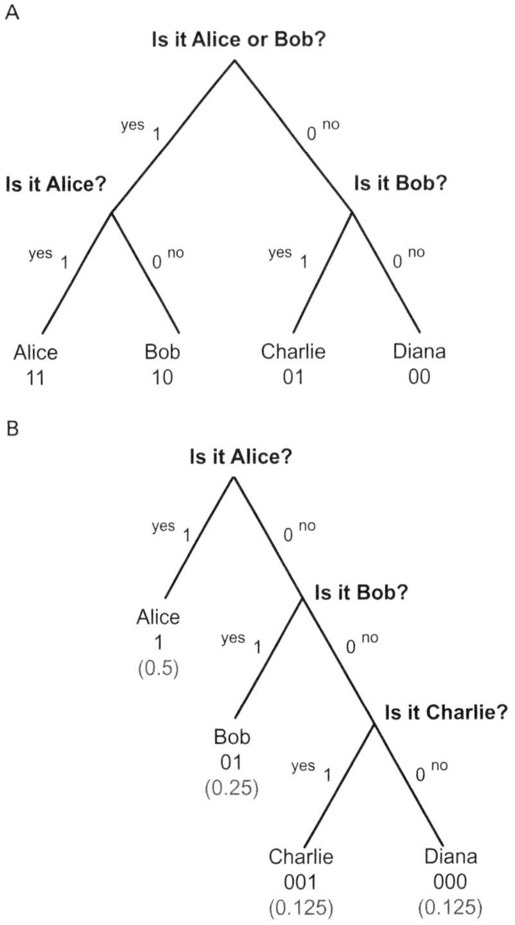

Figure 3.4
Shannon defined the amount of information contained in a message as the number of yes-no questions needed to select the message from the source. The questions reduce uncertainty about which message is sent. Imagine, for instance, that we need to find which of four persons has been selected to do a task. Using a simple decision tree (*left*), we ask, "Is it Alice or Bob?" If the answer is yes, the selection will be in the left half of the tree. One additional question, "Is it Alice?" reveals the answer. The code for each individual is the path describing the yes-no patterns that lead to him or her. If we know the probability that an individual will be selected (*at right, parenthetical numbers*), we can make a graduated decision tree that results in codes of variable length. For instance, if Alice is most likely to be chosen, we assign a code of 1. Bob, the next most likely, gets 01, and Charlie and Diana, who have equal probability, both get three-bit codes.

What are the lengths of the code words in the optimal code, that is, the one that minimizes *L?* Shannon answered that question in an appendix to his 1948 paper; he showed that the optimal length of a code word is the negative base-2 logarithm of the code word's probability, that is, $-\log_2 P_i$. Therefore, the average length of the optimal code is

$$H = -\sum_i P_i \cdot \log_2 P_i$$

This formula has the same form as the entropy formula in thermodynamics and a similar interpretation. *Entropy* is a measure of disorder or uncertainty about the state of a system. The more disordered a set of states is, the higher the entropy. The greatest disorder occurs when all states are equally likely to occur. The greatest order occurs when one state is certain and the others do not occur at all.

Shannon considered entropy to be the measure of the inherent information in a source. A source consists of a set of possible messages and their probabilities of occurrence. The entropy, which depends only on the probabilities of the messages, not on their codes, tells us the average length of the shortest possible code. Any shorter code would be ambiguous and could not be uniquely decoded. Take the following example:

A: 1
B: 0
C: 01
D: 10

If these messages have probabilities of 0.5, 0.25, 0.125, and 0.125, respectively, the resulting code will have an average length of 1.25 bits. However, a receiver would not be able to tell whether 1001 stands for ABBA, ABC, DBA, or DC. The entropy of the messages (calculated using the formula above) is $H = 1.75$, which defines the threshold between decipherable and indecipherable codes. The average length of this code, 1.25 bits, is below that threshold. The code is indecipherable.

The Huffman code is a fast way to compute a code within one bit of the entropy (figure 3.5).

Another way to put this is that the entropy threshold defines the boundary between reliable and unreliable channels. If the source sends a new message every T seconds, and the shortest code has average length H, the source is generating a demand of H/T bits per second. If the channel bandwidth is H/T or higher, then all the bits offered by the sender can flow to the receiver. If the channel bandwidth is lower than H/T, some bits will be lost, and the receiver will be unable to recover the original messages.

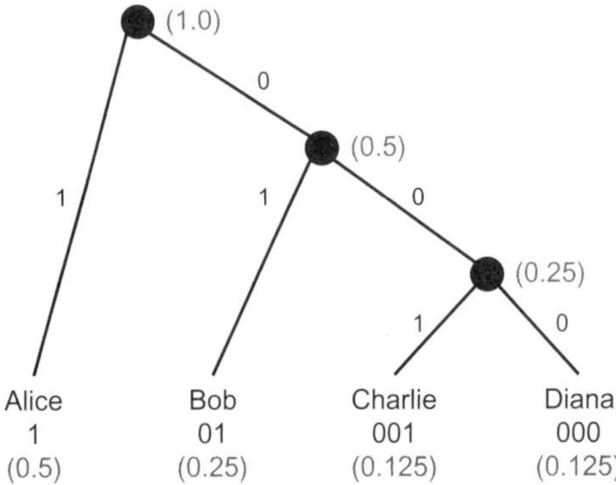

Figure 3.5
In 1951 David Huffman at MIT devised an algorithm for generating a code of minimum average length given the message probabilities. His method starts by treating each message as its own singleton tree. It then repeatedly combines the two smallest probability trees into a larger tree whose probability is the sum of its components. The whole tree is complete in n steps for n messages. In this example Charlie and Diana are combined first, then that tree is combined with Bob, and finally that tree is combined with Alice. The paths in the tree define the binary codes for each message. Huffman's method generates a code whose average length is within one bit of the entropy threshold. It generates the first code in figure 3.3 when all the messages are equally likely and the second code when they have the given unequal probabilities.

File compression is an important application of information theory. It reduces storage space and transmission time. Most computer programs represent text with standard codes. These include the traditional fixed-length code ASCII and the modern variable-length code Unicode. In both cases each individual letter is always encoded with the same code. A text file can often be shortened significantly by finding repeating patterns and replacing them with even shorter codes than the originals in the context of that file. For example, a file containing many instances of the letter "e" could be shortened by replacing them all with a new, shorter code. The length of the new code depends on how often "e" occurs in the file—the new code might be 3 bits in one file with frequent "e" and 5 bits in another with less frequent "e." The file compression algorithm generates a table that shows how to convert the new codes back to their originals. The file formats ".zip" and ".rar" employ this strategy. These strategies are designed to never "compress" below the limit given by entropy. If they did, the original document would not be guaranteed to be recoverable. These strategies are called *lossless compression*.

Another strategy is *lossy compression*. Lossy approaches offer much greater compression factors but cannot entirely recover the original file. For example, MP3 audio compression reduces file size by a factor of 10 after discarding frequencies that most people are unlikely to hear, but there is no way to recover the original discarded frequencies. JPEG image compression discards bits that generate colors barely discernible by the human eye, but there is no way to recover the original bits. Such compression schemes enable the economical sale to consumers of DVDs, online movies, and music recordings. The small loss in perceived quality incurred by these methods is usually considered a good trade-off for the large reduction in file size.

Transforming Information

A pure communication system simply transmits information from one place to another. But computers do more: they transform information. Transformation opens many new possibilities, most notably the production of what seems to be new information. Simple transformations include squaring a number, calculating a specified number of decimal digits of π, and arranging a list of numbers in ascending order. Each takes a pattern of information as input and creates a pattern of information as output.

Because a binary pattern can be interpreted as a number, a transformation looks mathematically like a function that maps input numbers to output numbers. Functions that can be computed by machines are called *computable functions*. Turing and his contemporaries used this notion to define computation. Turing showed that a simple abstract computer, the Turing machine, has enough power to implement any computable function (Turing 1937). The Turing machine follows a program of extremely simple instructions that implement the transformation. Because every instruction is obviously implementable by a machine, it appears that computers transform binary patterns without regard to their meaning. This is analogous to Shannon's insistence that communication channels can be designed to transmit information reliably without regard to its meaning.

When we dig a little deeper into how a machine transforms inputs, however, we can see an important aspect of the design of a program that we call *meaning-preserving*. Consider the addition of two numbers, a and b. What does it mean to add two numbers? It means that we follow a series of steps given by an addition algorithm. The steps concern adding successive pairs of digits from a and b and propagating a carry to the next higher pair of digits. We have clear rules for adding pairs of numbers from the set $\{0,1,2,\ldots,9\}$

and producing carries of 0 or 1. As we design a program for the algorithm, we pay careful attention that each and every instruction produces exactly the incremental result it is supposed to. If we succeed, we can have confidence that the machine adds two numbers properly. If we fail, we say that the machine is broken.

In other words, the design process itself transfers the idea of addition from our heads into instruction patterns that perform addition. The meaning of addition is preserved in the design of the machine and its algorithms.

This is true for any other computable function. We transfer our idea of what it means for that function to produce its output into a program that controls the machine to do precisely that. We transfer our idea of the meaning of the function into the design of the machine.

From this perspective the notion that machines and communication systems process without regard to the meaning of the binary data is shaky. Algorithms and machines have meanings implanted in them by engineers and programmers. We design machines so that the meaning of every incremental step, and the output, is what we intend, given that the input has the meaning we intend. We design carefully and precisely so that we do not have to worry about the machine corrupting the meaning of what we intended it to do.

Computers combine computable functions with communication channels. A channel brings the input pattern to the machinery that computes the function; another channel brings the output pattern to its destination. In these scenarios the channels and the computers seem to do nothing more than move and manipulate bits. Yet human observers say that the computation has given them new information. This happens no matter if the machine produces more output bits than input, or fewer. For example, the π-computing function mentioned earlier would generate 900 digits of π as output in response to a three-digit input "900," an expansion factor of 300. A sorting function delivers the same bits as the input in a different order. An averaging function can produce a small number of digits expressing the average of a large amount of data.

Representations of numbers and operations of machines both rely on physical processes. Each operation of the machine takes a small amount of time and energy to complete. Many of the functions we want to compute require so many steps that there is not enough time to return answers within any deadline we can live with. The physics of computing imposes severe limits on what can be computed.

The logic of computing also imposes limits. The most famous is that there are functions we might want to compute but cannot. Turing's example in 1936 was the halting problem—no program exists that can inspect the code of any given program and tell whether it contains an infinite loop on a particular input. A modern example is malware detection—no program exists that can tell whether any given program has a malicious procedure embedded in it. We return to this topic in chapter 6 when we examine the physical and logical limits of computation.

Even when we restrict our attention to computable functions that return answers soon enough to be useful, we find interesting questions. When a function computes bits we have not seen before, are those bits new information (see figure 3.6)? Or are they just the consequence of existing information? Does DNA contain information? Many biologists say it does. If it is a message, what are the source and destination? If we decode DNA, do we gain information? The decoded DNA might be used to find a cure for a genetic disorder, or it might identify the perpetrator at a crime scene. Does

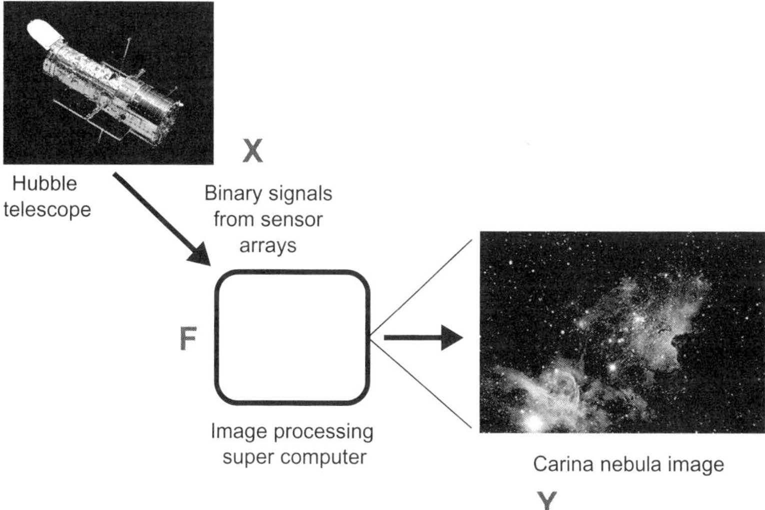

Figure 3.6
The Hubble space telescope's photon-gathering sensor arrays encode terabytes of data for transmission to Earth. The data are then processed into images. Computing theory would characterize the image processing as a function $Y = F(X)$ that yields output image Y when applied to the input data X. The machine implementing the function --- and the signals sent to it and generated by it --- do not depend in any way on the meaning of the information from the telescope. Yet human observers see Y, the output, as a beautiful image—of the Carina nebula in the instance illustrated. (Images courtesy of NASA)

matching the DNA to a database merely uncover existing information, or does it generate new information? Questions like these cannot be answered with classical information theory.

Interaction Systems

Many computer programs are interaction systems: they can receive new input and generate new output at many points, and, barring intervention or breakdown, they may go on doing this without end. Interaction systems are everywhere. Every operating system is an interaction system, as are a car's GPS system, Facebook, an online merchant's web server, or the Internet's domain name system (DNS). The Internet itself is a global interaction system for exchanging data and coordinating actions. The distinguishing feature of interaction systems is that they operate continually; they have no programmed end. In contrast, function systems are finished when they produce their answers.[1]

For years computer scientists intensely debated whether interactive computation is more powerful than function computation (Goldin et al. 2010). In recent years experts have come to agree that interactive computation is more powerful. The contemporary conundrum of how to meaningfully label digitized images illustrates why. The solution to this problem lies in interaction: a game structures the interaction between humans and machines to perform a function that no human or machine could do alone (see figure 3.7). Interaction systems can generate outputs that no known machine-computable function can.

Resolving the Paradoxes

In the discussion above, we have noted a series of seeming paradoxes concerning information:

1. Engineers design communication systems that operate without understanding the meaning of the information. How then can the human recipients receive meaning?
2. Engineers design computer systems that transform information without understanding the meaning of program or data binary patterns. How can these systems generate new information?
3. Programmers design programs that operate without understanding the bits they process. On what basis do human users interpret program outputs as meaningful?

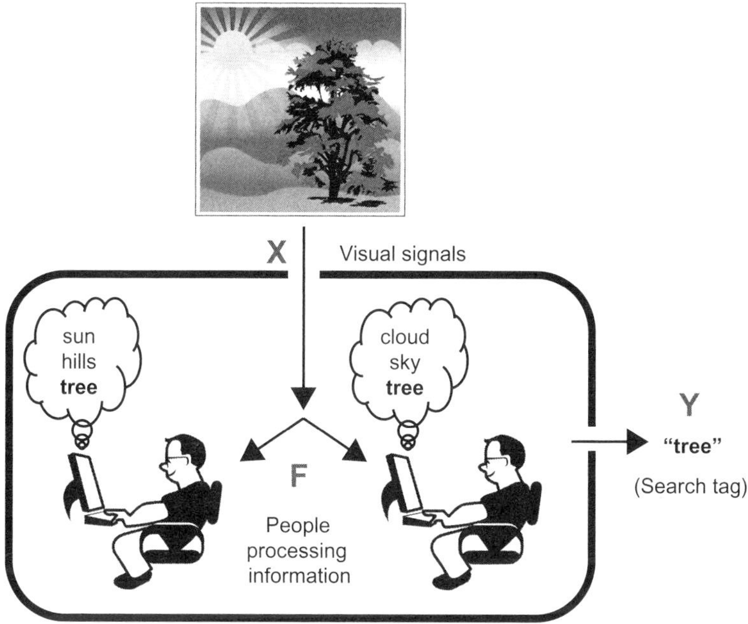

Figure 3.7
In a 2004 paper Luis von Ahn and Laura Dabbish of Carnegie Mellon University described a novel computer game, ESP. Players are paired and shown an image. They type words that describe the image with the goal of finding a word their (unknown and unseen) partner has also used. The common word becomes a new search tag for the image. The game teams humans with machines to compute a function (image recognition) that no one knows how to compute by machine alone. Like other functions, it transforms information, but now the meaning interactively supplied by the players shapes portions of the transformation.

4. Does making an association (as in placing a web link [Berners-Lee 2000]) create new information?
5. If a computer program by design generates deceptive information, are its outputs information at all?
6. Where is the information in an encrypted message?
7. If a computer program makes a discovery in science, did it create new information or merely pass on existing information that humans did not perceive before?

Various common notions about information do not answer these questions. For example, saying that symbols "carry" information only raises new questions. Where is the carried information? How do insertion and extraction work? Another example is the idea that meanings are embedded in social conventions and are triggered by the outputs of machines. That idea only helps with the third question but not the others. Still another example is the "sign-referent" model (Rocchi 2012), which associates signs with their meanings but works only for explicit information.

The notion of meaning-preserving transformation resolves all these paradoxes. Humans intentionally design software programs to support practices, create links, hide information,[2] or find new information. The meanings are all the result of designers arranging a machine's actions so that human users will interpret them as intended. When a machine does not produce the intended behaviors, its designers and users say it is broken.

The paradoxes may have arisen in the first place because computer scientists have always tended to anthropomorphize machines; for example, we say that a machine understands its inputs or is creative in its outputs. When others look inside our programs and machines, they see only mechanical steps. They do not see "understanding" or even "creativity" in the steps. The understanding and meaning come from the designer, who arranges the patterns of the machine to produce the intended meaning when it is used.

Information and Discovery

What do we mean when we say that a computer discovers a new pattern? Consider a computer program that finds a trend in data. The program is presented with a set of input-output pairs (x,y) observed in past performances of an experiment. Using statistical regression, the program finds the best parameters a and b for a straight line fitting the data: $y = ax + b$. The program's output is a formal description of a straight line. The output is meaningful for human users who know how to use straight lines to make predictions. It is easy to make another program that uses the straight line with parameters a and b to predict the output y that will be generated for a new value x.

What has happened here is that a designer has used mathematical knowledge to calculate the parameters of a best-fit line from a set of data. The steps in the calculation are mechanical. The output is meaningful to those who understand straight-line models of trends in data. The meaning comes from the designer, not the processing of the data.

Someone who does not know about straight-line trends in data would not know what the output of the program meant. But this does not mean that the meaning of the output is subjective. It means only that the designer did not intend to produce any meaning for those users.

In the 1980s researchers began to use powerful computers to sift through large data sets seeking to discover patterns. They used Bayesian inference, a sophisticated method of analyzing data to infer the most likely set of conditions that would generate the data. Bayesian inference is based on Bayes's formula for conditional probabilities from statistics:

$$P(H \mid E) = \frac{P(E \mid H) \cdot P(H)}{P(E)}$$

It says that the probability of a hypothesis H given evidence E can be computed from the probability of the evidence given the hypothesis, multiplied by the probability of the hypothesis, and divided by the probability of the evidence. Figure 3.8 gives an example for a simple case of doctor trying to diagnose whether a patient has the flu given that the patient has a headache.

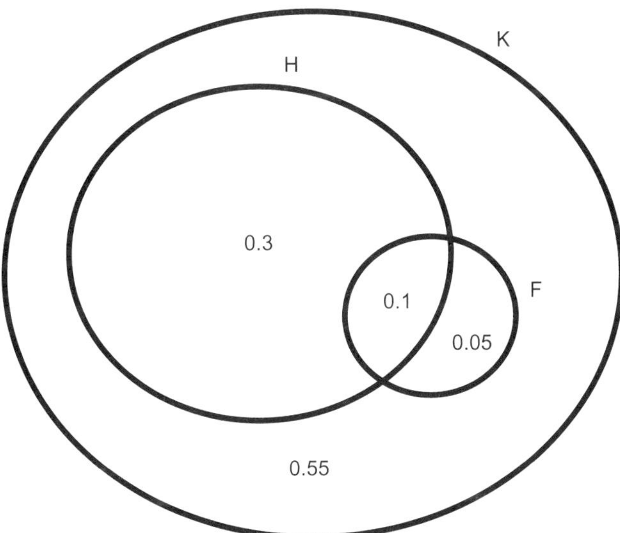

Figure 3.8
A Venn diagram illustrates how a difficult-to-judge hypothesis can be assessed by Bayes's rule. A population K contains a subset F of people who have flu and a subset H of people with headaches. A doctor sees a patient who complains of a headache and worries about flu. According to Bayes's rule $P(F|H) = P(H|F) \cdot P(F)/P(H)$. The medical databanks tell the doctor that the probability of someone having a headache is $P(H) = 0.4$, the probability that someone has flu is $P(F) = 0.2$, and the probability of a headache among flu patients is $P(H|F) = 2/3$. Then $P(F|H) = (2/3) \cdot 0.2/0.4 = 1/3$, or one chance in three. With no information, the probability of flu is 0.2, but given the information about headache, the probability rises to 0.33.

A discovery in this context is a new hypothesis. The program can generate a series of hypotheses and evaluate each one using Bayes's rule to calculate its probability given the evidence at hand. The most probable hypothesis is selected as the "discovery."

In this case, the designer is combining the knowledge of Bayes's rule with knowledge of search methods to find a most probable hypothesis for the given data. The program's output is intended for users who can understand the hypothesis and the data it "explains." The users will decide if the hypothesis is a discovery.

In classical information theory we would say that Bayesian inference works by determining the content of a message source based on data observed from the source. For communication of messages, it was reasonable for Shannon to assume that the content of the source was known a priori. For scientific discovery, the set of possibilities within the source is initially unknown; the inference process makes them and their probabilities known. Bayesian inference is an automated method of transforming observed data from a source into knowledge of the content of the source.

Conclusions

Human beings have been encoding signals for transmission in different media channels since time immemorial. In the 1940s Shannon's theory of information gave us four great principles:

- Every communication system can be modeled as a noisy channel carrying encoded signals representing messages from a source.
- The entropy of a source gives the length of the shortest decipherable code for the source, and the Huffman code is within one bit of the entropy.
- Sufficient redundant bits can be added to any code to overcome noise in the channel and guarantee 100 percent accurate reception.
- Files can be compressed to smaller sizes by substituting shorter codes for patterns in the file.

These principles enabled communication and computer engineers to design digital systems so that no information would be lost in transit and errors introduced by noise could be removed.

Some entrepreneurs who did not understand Shannon's theory predicted a new, vastly enlarged economy based on "bits not atoms." Their dream cannot come true because real communication and computing systems are powered from representations recorded as physical signals and states. Computations and transmissions always take time and consume energy. We spend a lot of energy on computations: the connections and data centers of the Internet consume nearly 6 percent of the world's electricity. We cannot wish intractable problems away by postulating that their solution methods are done by bits not atoms. The atoms behind the bits are matter that matters.

As our ability to store information multiplied exponentially, as Moore's law had predicted it would, we are increasingly pressed to say what all that information means. By definition Shannon's information theory cannot resolve the question. That is a seeming paradox: How can systems process information without regard to its meaning and simultaneously generate meaning in the experience of their users?

The meaning-preserving transformation reconciles the meaningless mechanics of machines with the human experience that machines generate meaning. The designer of a program arranges the instructions so that the output will produce an intended meaning in a community of users; each individual instruction moves the partially computed result incrementally closer to the intended output. Let us celebrate the role of designers, who give us software and hardware that makes sense to us.

Acknowledgment

This chapter is adapted from "The Information Paradox" by Peter Denning and Tim Bell (2012), which appeared in *American Scientist*.

4 Machines

A person with paper, pencil, eraser, and subject to strict discipline, is a universal machine.

—Alan Turing

Machines may be the true humanizing influence. They do the work that makes life possible; human beings do the things that make life worthwhile.

—Isaac Asimov

Computer scientists are fond of abstractions. An abstraction is a mental model that captures the essential features of a thing and suppresses all other features. Computer scientists often describe programming as designing a hierarchy of abstractions represented as "abstract objects" operated on by designated functions. This notion has become so popular that computer science is often touted as the field that has learned best how to manage abstractions.

Computing abstractions differ in an important way from the mathematical abstractions common in other fields: computing abstractions perform actions. The terminology of abstractions often obscures the *principle of stuff*: the reality that computational actions are implemented as physical processes controlled by programs.

Consider for instance a musical song. On a computer, a song is represented by an MP3 file, which contains a digitized version of the music from the publisher. To listen to the song, we activate a program "play" on the file. The "play" program encodes the millions of bits from the file in disk storage as signals that travel to the earphones, where sound-generator circuits vibrate diaphragms. At the abstract (user) level, the play program and the MP3 file appear as single objects: apply "play" to "song" and you hear music. The implementation is quite complicated, involving many steps, each of which depends on a physical process.

In this chapter, we examine how to organize physical machines that compute functions. The allowable moves of the machine are expressed as single instructions, such as adding two numbers. A program is a series of instructions arranged in a precise way to cause the machine to evaluate the desired function. Instructions and data are encoded as binary patterns stored in a memory. When fetched into a processor, instructions cause the hardware to transform input data into output data.

In the earliest days of electronic computing, programmers wrote programs directly as binary codes arranged in sequences on paper tapes or cards. Programming languages quickly superseded binary coding because they were much less error prone. A special program called a compiler automatically translated statements of the language into binary machine code. In the next chapter, on programming, we discuss how a compiler does this.

The organization of a computing machine is often called its architecture.[1] An architectural specification covers the central processing unit (CPU), which executes instructions; the random-access memory (RAM), which contains the program code and the data,[2] and the data structures used to organize program components in memory.

Machines

A machine is an apparatus for using or applying energy to perform a particular task. Machines are usually powered by mechanical, chemical, thermal, or electrical means. Electronic machines are powered by electricity with no moving parts—for example, radio, television, mobile phones, and tablet computers.

An automaton is a self-operating machine. The cuckoo on a clock was once considered an automaton. So was The Turk chess player of the late 1700s (Standage 2003) (see figure 4.1). From the 1940s, computer scientists have thought of automata as abstract mathematical models of computers, and from the 1950s they believed automata embodied into software or robots have the potential for self-conscious thought.

Machines to aid calculation date back thousands of years. From 2700 BCE onward, merchants in Mesopotamia, Egypt, Persia, Greece, Rome, and China used the abacus to calculate sums. The Greeks showed how to measure the height of a tree by measuring its shadow and taking ratios with the shadow of a stick of known height; the stick and its operating procedure were a simple computing device. Another measuring stick, the slide rule, was invented around 1620 after John Napier published the concept of a logarithm; often called a slip-stick, the slide rule was a standard computing

Figure 4.1
In his 1784 book *Inanimate Reason*, Karl Gottlieb van Windisch described The Turk, a chess-playing machine. Beginning in 1770 for the next 84 years, its various owners promoted it as an automaton that would play chess with anyone, winning most matches. It was an elaborate hoax. An expert chess player hid inside the cabinet, observed the pieces with mirrors, and used levers to move his pieces on the board. The illusion appealed to a deep human belief, perhaps a fear, that the human brain is a machine and most intelligent acts are actually mechanical moves. In 1997 the chess computer IBM Big Blue beat grandmaster Garry Kasparov. The reaction was not that the machine had become intelligent but rather that the machine searched faster than Kasparov.

machine used by engineers until the 1970s, when the electronic calculator displaced it. In 1642 Blaise Pascal built a computing machine that added and subtracted numbers, and he presented algorithms for multiplication and division as repeated additions or subtractions. Charles Babbage designed the Difference Engine (1822–1842) to compute numerical tables of arithmetic functions; existing tables, calculated tediously by hand, were riddled with errors and posed great risks to navigators and other users. In 1911 the Marchant Company began selling mechanical calculators built from gears, pulleys, and levers that could add, subtract, multiply, and divide. In 1922, the German engineer Arthur Scherbius invented the Engima machine for generating ciphers; the Poles broke the code in 1932 and passed the information to the British, who used it to build the Bletchley code-breaking machine in the early 1940s. In the late 1920s Vannevar Bush built the differential analyzer to solve differential equations by mechanical integration.

In World War II the US Army commissioned teams of women at Aberdeen Proving Grounds to calculate ballistic tables for artillery. Gunners used the tables to determine the best gun direction and angle given the wind and range of the target. Following programs written on paper, the women operated mechanical calculators (such as the Marchant machines) to prepare these ballistic tables. Because the teams were error-prone and could not keep up with the volume of ballistic tables needed for the growing inventory of ordnance, the Army decided to replace the human calculators with electronic machines. They commissioned the first computing machine project, the ENIAC, at the University of Pennsylvania in 1943. The ENIAC could compute ballistic tables a thousand times faster than the human teams. Although the machine was not ready until 1946, after the war ended, the military made heavy use of computers after that.

It is interesting to note that in the 1920s, the term "computer" meant a person who calculated numbers. Thus, to distinguish them from actual, human computers, the first electronic computing machines were billed as "automatic computers." The acronyms of the first electronic computers in the 1940s ended in "-AC" to signify this.

In 1937 Alan Turing defined a computer as a machine capable of calculating a mathematical function, and he discovered functions that cannot be calculated by any computer. He used the term *computable* for functions that could be calculated by computers. A function is computable if there exists a finite set of instructions that can generate its output value for any given input value (see figure 4.2). For example, addition is computable because we can specify a finite set of instructions that produce the sum $x + y$ given any numbers x and y. An unanswered mathematical question in Turing's

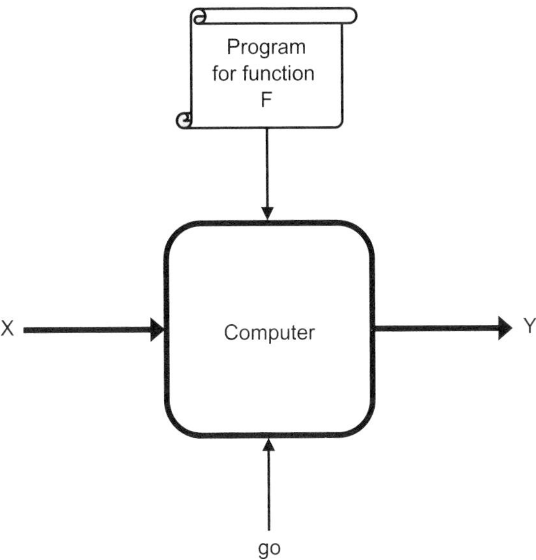

Figure 4.2
A computer is a machine that takes an input binary pattern X and calculates an output binary pattern Y. The computer is controlled by instructions from a program designed to calculate a specific function F. When a signal arrives on the "go" input, the computer starts to work and after a while stops with output $Y = F(X)$. The time required before the computer stops depends on the function and the program. Some programs may contain infinite loops, in which cases the computer will never stop. We can define a function $H(F,X)$ that yields value 1 if program F halts for input X and 0 if it does not halt. Alan Turing proved that H cannot be implemented by any computer.

time was how we could describe the set of computable functions. We examine this question more deeply in chapter 6 on computation.

Turing argued that every computational method to calculate any computable function was based on the very simple operations of reading symbols, setting a control state depending what has been read, and writing symbols. He created an abstract machine, now called a Turing machine, which consisted of a control unit moving along an infinite tape, reading and writing symbols in the squares of the tape. The specification of the control unit was the machine's program. Programs used loops to repeat steps as many times as needed. He also described a universal machine capable of simulating any other Turing machine given its program. And finally he showed the existence of functions that are well defined but not computable, such as the problem of determining whether a Turing machine will halt (come to a stop without going into an infinite loop). Although several others in his day also produced designs for computational machines and demonstrated them equivalent to Turing machines, Turing's design became the reference model because it most closely resembled the functions of real electronic computers, particularly the processor (control unit) and memory (tape).

The definition of computer as a machine that transforms an input pattern into an output pattern and then stops is not the only mode for using computers. Interaction is common. An interactive machine receives numerous inputs and generates numerous outputs and never stops. We noted in chapter 3 that an interactive machine, in cooperation with a human, could compute functions that a stopping computer could not.

Computing Machines

A computer is a machine controlled by a program that computes an output value from a given input value. Now we take a closer look at how we can build a machine that works this way.

A *stored-program computer* is electronic hardware that implements an instruction set. An *instruction* is a single arithmetic or logical operation carried out by the machine. An *operation* is a very simple, elementary function. Typical operations take two inputs and produce one output. For example ADD sums two numbers and EQ compares whether two numbers are equal; thus ADD(3,5)=8 and EQ(3,5)=0 (false). Instruction sets also contain branch instructions that control which instruction is next after the current one.

A *program* is a set of instructions arranged in a pattern that causes the desired function to be calculated. *Programming* is the art of designing a program and providing convincing evidence that the program computes its function correctly.

A *computing system* is a combination of program and machine. The program causes the machine to calculate a function. We can also say that the computing system calculates a function.

To make all this work, our computing system needs:

1. Precise specification of the set of instructions implemented by the hardware.
2. A precise method to represent a program as a series of instructions.
3. A memory that stores the program and the data on which it operates.
4. A control unit that reads and executes instructions of a program in the order prescribed by the program.

A CPU (central processing unit) is a hardware device that reads instructions from a program and executes them, one at a time, in the order prescribed by the program.

A RAM (random access memory) is a hardware device that holds data values in locations that can be read or written by the CPU. RAM is organized as a linear array of locations. Each location holds an elemental quantity of data, typically an 8-bit byte or a 32-bit word. The locations are numbered 0, 1, ..., $2^n - 1$, where n is the number of bits in an address. RAM is called "random access" because it can access any random location in the same amount of time. Locations hold only binary patterns (of 8 or 32 bits). The RAM does not attempt to interpret patterns; it simply stores and retrieves them reliably. The time required for the memory to respond to a CPU read or write request is the *memory cycle time*, today typically just a few nanoseconds. A block diagram of the CPU and RAM is shown in figure 4.3, and one of the interface between CPU and RAM in figure 4.4.

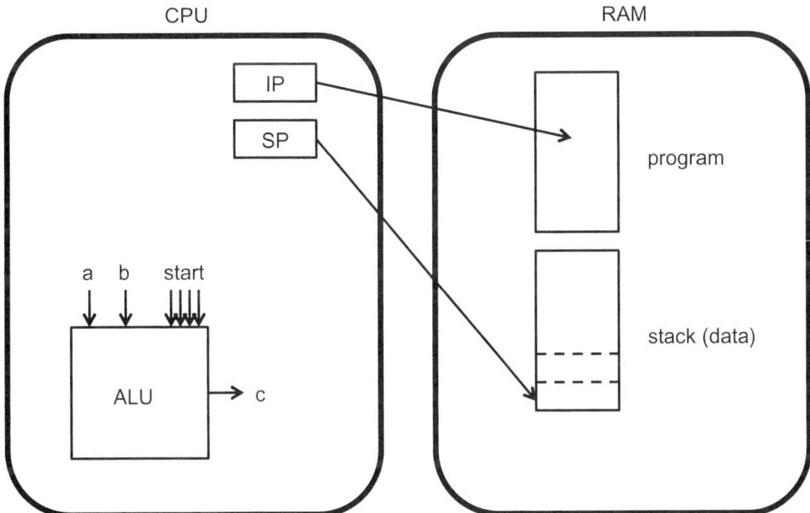

Figure 4.3
The hardware of a computing system consists of a central processing unit (CPU) and a random access memory (RAM). The program and its data are in the RAM. The data are arranged as a stack, which means that new values are added only to the top of the stack and values are retrieved only from the top. The CPU contains two special registers. The instruction pointer (IP) is the RAM address (in the program) of the next instruction to be executed. The stack pointer is the RAM address of the top of the stack. The CPU also contains an arithmetic-logic unit (ALU), which takes two input numbers (a and b) and produces one output number (c). A series of start lines signals the ALU which operation to perform, for example, add, multiply, or test equality.

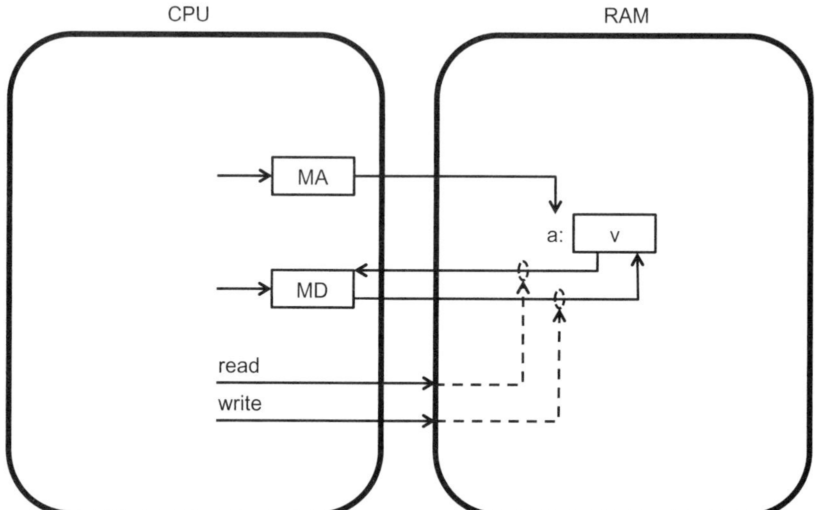

Figure 4.4
The CPU-RAM interface consists of several components. The objective is to read or write a particular location (*a*) in the RAM; a read operation transmits the value *v* in the selected location to the CPU, and a write operation transmits a new value from the CPU to the selected location. The memory address register (MA) tells which location is selected. The memory data register (MD) holds the value. The read signal line tells the memory hardware to select an address (in MA) and copy its value to the CPU (in MD). The write signal line tells the memory hardware to copy the value from the CPU (in MD) to the location selected (by MA). The time required to do these operations is called the memory cycle time, under 10 nanoseconds in modern RAMs.

Real computers have memory other than RAM, for example a disk. Disk access times are random variables, depending on seek and rotation delays of moving magnetic media. The additional problems of moving data among multiple types of memory are considered in chapter 7 on memory.

The CPU uses the instruction pointer (IP) register to keep track of which instruction is next to execute. It executes instructions of a program by repeating the following cycle until it comes to an exit instruction in the program:

1. **fetch** instruction is addressed by IP and set IP=IP+1
2. **decode** by reading the operation code contained in the instruction
3. **execute** by carrying out the operation
4. **check** for interrupts: error conditions that might have arisen during the previous steps

The CPU contains a clock that issues a signal once every clock tick. The clock signal propagates through the CPU and activates selected circuits. A typical clock tick interval is around 0.5 nanosecond. It takes four ticks to sequence the CPU through the four steps of an instruction cycle. The length of the clock tick interval is chosen to allow all the circuits involved in a step of the instruction cycle to settle into a new state. If the clock tick is too short, some circuits will not have had time to settle, and the CPU will malfunction. Figure 4.5 illustrates how the CPU decodes and executes instructions, and figure 4.6 illustrates how the ADD component of the CPU's Arithmetic-Logic Unit (ALU) works.

The conclusion from this brief introduction is that we can design electronic circuits that will cause a machine to calculate a function by executing a sequence of instructions. The design outlined here was created for the first electronic computing machines in the 1940s—at the University of Pennsylvania, MIT, Princeton, and Cambridge. John von Neumann, a mathematician working with some of the engineers, wrote up descriptions of the design. Because of his writings, the design is often called "von Neumann architecture," although the design was actually invented by the engineers J. Presper Eckert, John Mauchly, Herman Goldstein, Arthur Burks, and others.

Many other architectures are possible for computers. The common feature is that they completely automate the process of following programs of instructions to calculate functions.

Programs and Their Representations

The previous discussion might give the impression that a program is any sequence of instructions from the machine's instruction set. That is not so. Programs have to obey precise rules of structure. There can be absolutely no ambiguity about what each individual instruction does and what the whole pattern does. Otherwise, we could not attain reliable computers that give the same answer for the same input every time.

Let us outline a design for programs. Generally when we calculate numbers we do three kinds of things:[3]

1. Perform instructions in a strict sequential order (sequencing).
2. Make a choice between two alternative calculations based on the outcome, true or false, of a test (choice).
3. Repeat a calculation many times until a test says to stop (iteration).

Notice that the iteration pattern opens the possibility of an infinite loop because the test might never be satisfied.

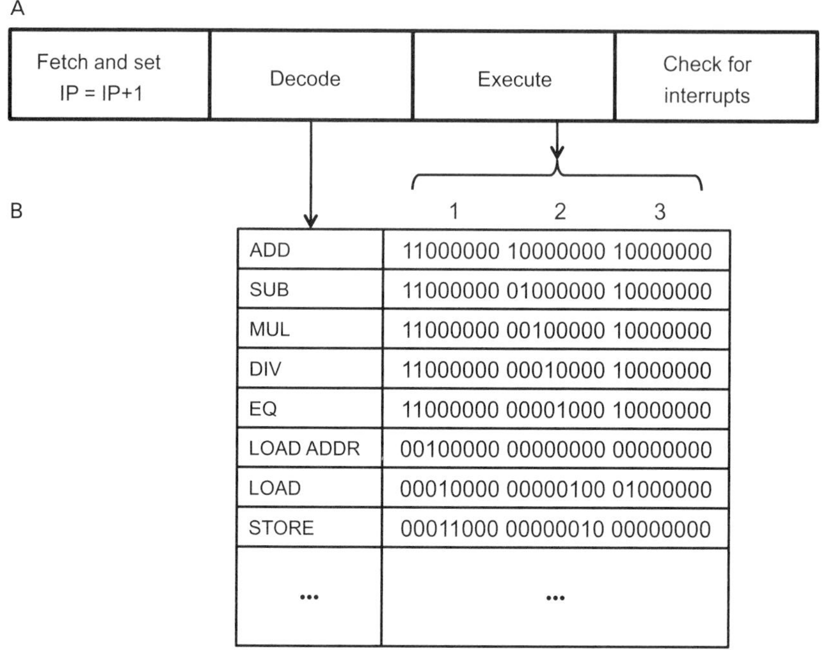

Figure 4.5

CPU instruction cycle consists of four phases (A). At each clock tick, the CPU advances to the next phase. The first phase gets a copy of the current instruction from address IP (instruction pointer) in RAM and sets IP to the next instruction. The second phase takes the operation code bits from the current instruction and interrogates a local control memory to get a control word for that instruction. In this example the control word is broken in three eight-bit blocks, corresponding to three subticks that occur between two regular clock ticks. We designate bits by their block and position; thus, bit 1.1 is bit 1 of the first block. At a subtick, each of the eight bits in a control word block activates a logic circuit; up to eight things can happen in parallel. The first five example instructions assume that the two operands are in registers R1 and R2. Bit 1.1 copies R1 to the "a" input of the ALU, and bit 1.2 copies R2 to the "b" input of the ALU. The first five bits of the second block send an appropriate trigger signal to the ALU telling it to add (2.1), subtract (2.2), multiply (2.3), divide (2.4), or test-for-equal (2.5). The first bit of the third block (3.1) copies the ALU output to register R1. The other three instructions activate different paths. LOAD ADDR activates 1.3, which says "copy the address bits from the instruction word to R1." LOAD activates 1.4, 2.6, and 3.2, which say: "copy R1 to MA (memory address register)," "activate memory read," and "copy the MD (memory data) to R1." Finally, the STORE instruction assumes R1 contains an address and R2 a value; it activates 1.4 and 1.5 in parallel and then 2.7, meaning: "copy R1 to MA," "copy R2 to MD," "activate memory write."

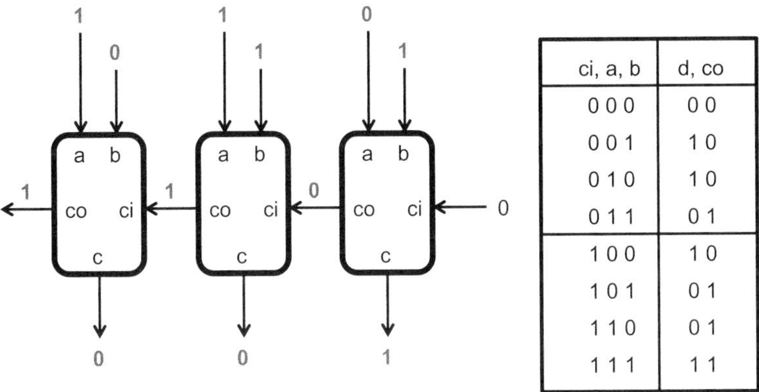

ci, a, b	d, co
0 0 0	0 0
0 0 1	1 0
0 1 0	1 0
0 1 1	0 1
1 0 0	1 0
1 0 1	0 1
1 1 0	0 1
1 1 1	1 1

Figure 4.6
To add numbers, we follow a simple algorithm that sums the 1s digits, then the 10s digits, then the 100s digits, and so on, and occasionally transfers a carry of 1 to the next higher stage if a digit sum is bigger than 9. For example, to add 17 and 26, we start by adding the 1s digits 7 and 6, giving a sum digit 3 with carry 1. Then we add the 10s digits 1 and 2 plus the carry, giving a sum digit 4 with carry 0. The answer is 43. The same algorithm simplifies for the binary number system because sums can be only 0 or 1. The figure depicts a three-bit binary adder (*left*). The inputs are numbers *a* and *b*, and output is number *c*. The carry transfers (*co* = carry out, *ci* = carry in) from one stage to the next higher. The right stage sums the 1s bit, the next stage the 2s bits, and the third stage the 4s bits. Some bit combinations produce a carry; for example 1 + 1 = 0 with carry 1. The table (*right*) shows the output combinations of a stage for all possible input combinations. We use the carry from the leftmost stage (*co*) as a fourth bit of the output because some sums are greater than 7 (the largest number that can be represented in three bits). The largest sum would be 111 (= 7) + 111 (= 7) or 1110 (= 14). Each stage is implemented with a few transistors. The sum is available as soon as all the stages settle; the worst-case settling time occurs when a carry propagates the entire length of the chain. The same structure is used for larger numbers; thus, a 32-bit machine represents numbers with 32 bits and uses 32-stage adders. In most computers the adder is a component of a larger arithmetic logic unit (ALU) that performs add, subtract, multiply, divide, and logical test operations such as equal, not equal, or less than.

A *programming language* is a set of syntax rules describing a precise notation for each of the above structures. There are thousands of programming languages. Despite the diversity of possible computer languages, they all have a single purpose: to describe how a computing machine can be made to evaluate a specific function.

When we design programs, we think of a pointer moving through the program steps and the machine doing each designated instruction, one at a time. The pointer is called the instruction pointer (IP). The CPU implements the IP as a register containing the address of the RAM location of the next instruction to be executed (see figure 4.3). When we are done with an instruction, we normally go to the next instruction in sequence (IP+1) unless a control instruction redirects IP. For example, an instruction "GO 17" sets the IP to 17, so that the CPU next executes the instruction at memory location 17.

The next step in our story about machines that execute programs is to show how to design an instruction set that supports any program conforming to the three-part structure above. That is the subject of the next section.

Stack Machine: A Simple Model of a Computer System

For a thousand years students of algebra have been told that arithmetic operators have orders of precedence: all multiplications and divisions are done before additions and subtractions. A series of operators of the same order are evaluated left to right. These rules ensure that all expressions evaluate the same, no matter who does the evaluation. For example, 1 + 2 * 6/4 – 2 would be evaluated by applying operators one at a time starting with the highest precedence:

1 + 2 * 6/4 – 2

1 + 12/4 – 2

1 + 3 – 2

4 – 2

2

More advanced students also learned that there is a third precedence level, exponents and logarithms, which are performed before multiplications and divisions.

Students of algebra are also taught that algebraic terms can be grouped within parentheses to force groupings not implied by the rules of precedence.

For example, grouping the last two terms in the previous expression results in a different outcome:

1 + 2 * 6/(4 – 2)

1 + 12/(4 – 2)

1 + 12/2

1 + 6

7

In 1924 Polish logician Jan Lukasiewicz invented a new notation, now called Reverse Polish notation (RPN), which followed the rules of precedence and avoided parentheses.[4] The idea was to follow two numbers by the operator that combines them in the expression. In his notation the two expressions above respectively become

1 2 6 * 4 / + 2 –

1 2 6 * 4 2 – / +

Early in the days of computer science someone noticed that Polish notation expressions could be evaluated on a stack. A stack is a last-in-first-out memory structure. You read the Polish expression from left to right, pushing numbers on the stack as you encounter them; and you perform operators on the top two numbers, replacing them with the result. For example, the series of stack configurations for the first expression is as follows (with top of stack on the right):

1	(Push 1 onto the stack.)
1 2	(Push 2 onto the stack.)
1 2 6	(Push 6 onto the stack.)
1 12	(Pop 2 and 6, multiply them, then push product 12.)
1 12 4	(Push 4 onto the stack.)
1 3	(Pop 12 and 4, divide 12 by 4, then push quotient 3.)
4	(Pop 1 and 3, add them, then push sum 4.)
4 2	(Push 2 onto the stack.)
2	(Pop 4 and 2, subtract, then push difference 2.)

The Burroughs B5000 machine (1961) organized its memory around a stack and achieved a highly efficient method of evaluating expressions (Organick 1973). The English Electric KDF9 (1963) used a stack structure. The Hewlett Packard scientific calculator HP-67 (1972) used the same structure because it reduced keystrokes and errors when evaluating complicated

Table 4.1
Instruction Set of Stack Machine

Type	Op Code	Name	Before	After	Memory Effects
Arithmetic and logical operators	ADD	Add	S a b	S c	
	SUB	Subtract			
	MUL	Multiply			
	DIV	Divide			
	EQ	Test for equal			
	NE	Test for not equal			
Memory interface	LA a	Load address a	S	S a	v = Mem[a]
	L	Load	S a	S v	leaving Mem[a]=v
	ST	Store	S a v	S	
Sequencing	GO	Go	S a	S	leaving IP=a
	GOF	Go on false	S a v	S	leaving IP=a if v=0
Completion	EXIT	Exit	empty	empty	

expressions. Modern HP calculators continue to use the stack structure. Numerous programming languages, beginning with Algol (1958), were designed on the assumption that the underlying machine had a stack memory. Modern multicore computing chips use stack memory for subroutine calls. Modern compilers use CPU machine registers to simulate pushdown stacks for evaluating expressions. The stack memory structure is ubiquitous.

Table 4.1 is an instruction set for a CPU-RAM configuration as depicted earlier in figure 4.3. "Op Code" is an abbreviation for the name of the instruction. The effect of executing the instruction is shown in the "Before" and "After" columns, which show the stack configuration just before and just after the instruction is executed. The letter "S" represents the state of the stack prior to the current instruction. Mem[*a*] means the contents stored in memory location *a*. Essential side effects of changing the instruction pointer and changing the contents of a memory location are shown in the "Memory Effects" column.

Figure 4.7 is an example of a program in this instruction set evaluating an assignment statement that sets a variable *X* to the value of an expression.

Procedures and Exceptions

The machine's instruction set contains instructions that control the sequencing of the CPU as it moves through a program. Programs in higher-level languages require more sophisticated sequencing control because they allow programmers to write their own functions beyond those in the

X = A*(B+C)

	LA X	LA A	L	LA B	L	LA C	L	ADD	MUL	ST
	X	X	X	X	X	X	X	X	X	
		A	4	4	4	4	4	4	20	
				B	3	3	3	5		
						C	2			

Figure 4.7
This series of snapshots shows the stack as it executes a program implementing the statement X=A*(B+C) when A=4, B=3, and C=2; when the program is done, memory location X=20 and the stack is empty.

instruction set and to write functions that deal with errors and other events requiring special attention. The basic structure for both cases is the procedure call and return mechanism. The purpose of the procedure mechanism is to transfer the CPU to the first instruction of another program and, when the called program is done, to return the CPU to its calling point.

The designers of the first stored program computers realized that programmers would want to add functions of their own design, implemented as new subprograms that can be invoked with the same ease as machine instructions. A subprogram mechanism allows a programmer to call a subprogram from wherever it is needed rather than rewrite its code at that point in the program. It also allows experts to create libraries of standard functions, such as trigonometry or algebra, which can be used reliably by anyone else.

Originally, in the 1950s, reusable subprograms were called *subroutines*. That name eventually gave way to "procedure" in the 1960s under the influence of the Algol language. A *procedure* is a subprogram that implements a single, usually simple, function.

The key idea of procedures is that a procedure is "active" only between the moment it is called and the moment it returns, and the data it needs while active are in a private segment of memory called an *activation record* (AR). A call allocates memory for the procedure's activation record, and a return reclaims it. When procedure calls are nested—meaning that an active procedure can call another procedure, including itself—there will be multiple activation records, one for each call. They will be linked together in the order of call so that when one returns, its caller can resume from where it made the call (see figure 4.8). Because returns occur in reverse order of calls, activation records are pushed on the normal stack on calls and deleted on returns (see figure 4.9).

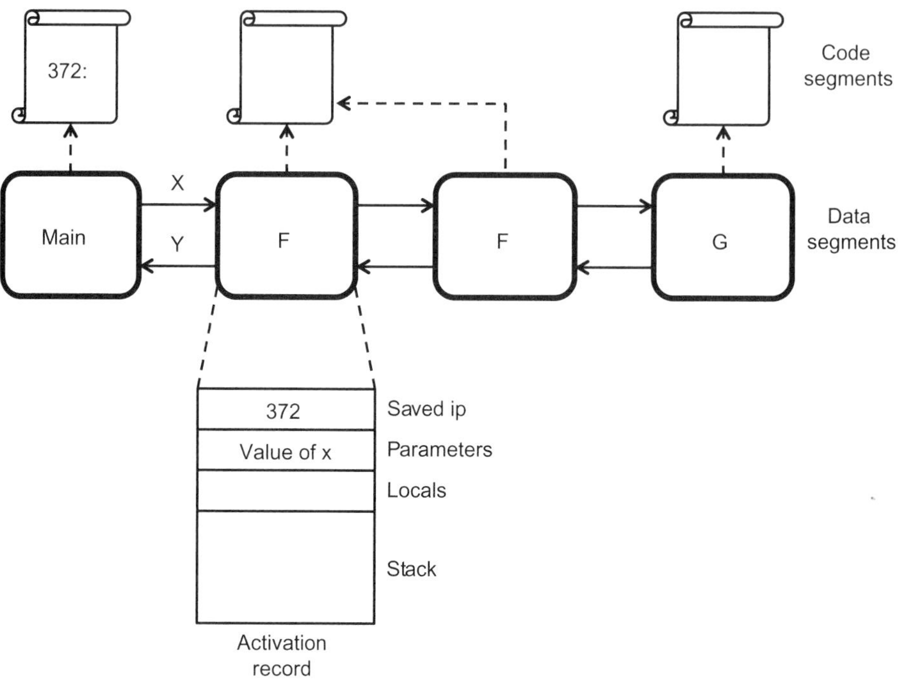

Figure 4.8
Programming languages accommodate procedures (separate subprograms) implementing functions. The *MAIN* program is treated as a procedure called by the operating system. In this example the *MAIN* program has called procedure *F*, then *F* called itself, and then the second *F* called *G*. While procedure *G* is active and executing, procedures *MAIN* and both calls to *F* are active but suspended. The right arrows represent the call actions and passing of parameters; for example, *MAIN* called *F* with parameter *X*. The left arrows represent the returns of values; for example the value *Y=F(X)*. Each procedure is implemented with a code segment and a data segment. The dashed arrows represent links to the procedure's code. When a procedure *F* calls itself, each instance gets its own data segment, and all instances link to the same code segment for *F*. The data segment is implemented as an activation record that contains the saved instruction pointer (IP), the parameters of the call, local variables used only by the procedure, and a stack area used only by the procedure. The saved IP belongs to the caller; for example, the instruction at address 372 in the *MAIN* code segment called *F*, and when *F* is done the CPU instruction pointer is restored to 372. Because procedure activations are not known until a program is executed, the storage for activation records must be handled dynamically. A stack can be used for this purpose because deactivations (returns) occur in reverse order from activations (calls).

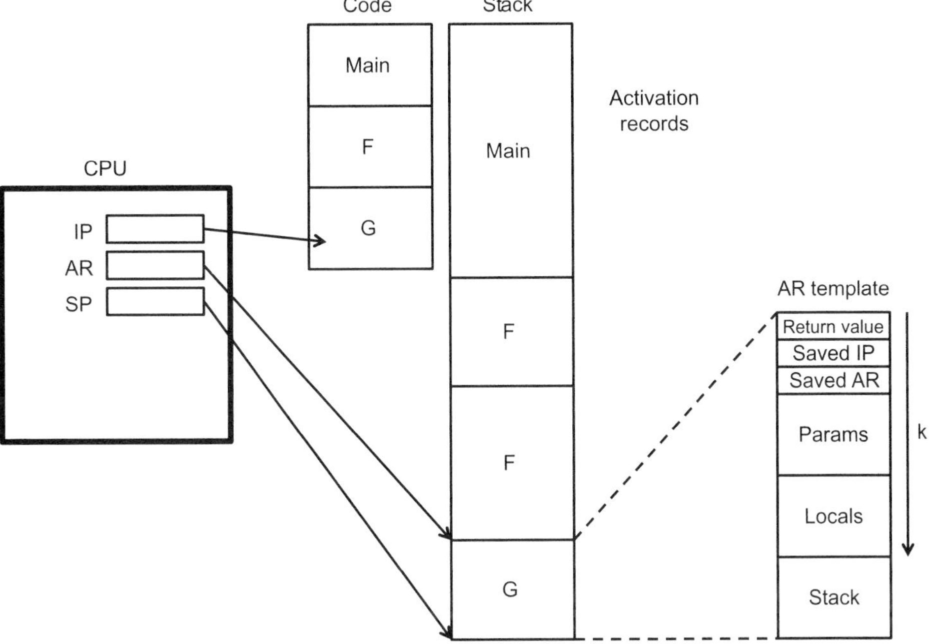

Figure 4.9
With a few modifications of the CPU, the activation records of an executing program (as in figure 4.8) can be stored on the program's stack. Procedure call pushes an activation record for the called procedure on top of the stack, and return pops it from the stack. The register AR points to the beginning of the current activation record. Just prior to the call, the caller code builds the new AR on the stack by loading values of parameters and local variables on the stack. At the call, the IP and AR registers are diverted to the called procedure, and their former values are restored at the return. Inside the called procedure, parameters and local values are found relative to the base of the activation record; for example, the first parameter is at address AR+3. The caller resumes with the value computed by the called procedure on top of the stack.

Consider an example of a call on the function LOG(Y). The purpose of the procedure call is to execute the code that computes $\log_2 Y$ and leave the result on top of the stack. To do this the CALL instruction diverts the CPU to the code for LOG. The LOG code computes the result and places it in the reserved slot at the start of the AR. When the LOG code finishes, it executes a RET (return) instruction, which resumes the CPU at the next instruction after its CALL. These five steps give more details of how this happens:

1. The caller builds a new activation record for LOG in accordance with the LOG AR template. The template reserves one slot for the parameter (Y) and two slots for internal local variables. This is accomplished by a series of k = 6 load operations to fill in those slots.
2. The caller places the target address for LOG on top of the stack. At this point the base of the new activation record is precisely k slots below the stack pointer; in other words, the new AR base is to be SP – k.
3. The caller executes the instruction CALL k, which does all of the following: save IP and AR registers in their reserved slots (at addresses SP – k + 1 and SP – k + 2, respectively), set register AR = SP – k, and pop the top of stack into register IP.
4. Now the CPU executes the code of the LOG function. That code will find the value of the parameter Y at location AR+3, and the two internal variables at AR+4 and AR+5. The code saves the computed value of LOG(Y) into the slot served for the return value, which is at address AR.
5. The called procedure executes the RET instruction, which sets SP to AR and restores the values of IP and AR from their saved locations. Now the caller resumes executing instructions after its call and the value of LOG(Y) is on top of the stack.

The procedure architecture described above allows recursive procedures, which are programs that can call themselves.[5] Lisp and Algol, first specified in 1958, were the first programming languages to incorporate recursion. Their designers did this because they wanted a language capable of expressing and executing any algorithm. Lisp expressed algorithms using Church's lambda calculus, and Algol expressed them with procedure notation consistent with recursive functions. Around 1960, Edsger Dijkstra proposed organizing the memory as a stack and built the first working Algol compiler. By comparison, Lisp compilers were much more difficult; it was not until the 1970s that efficient ones were available. Many programming languages since that time have provided for recursive procedures.

The procedure architecture turned out to be immensely useful not just for programming functions but also for dealing with errors during computations. For instance, what happens if a program attempts to divide by zero? Mathematically the result is undefined, and the program cannot give an answer. Rather than allow an undefined value to propagate through the program, CPU designers built the arithmetic-logic unit (ALU) to signal when this error condition occurs. They modified the CPU instruction cycle to check for this signal; it is the fourth step of the instruction cycle described a few pages back. If the "divide by zero" error condition was set, the CPU used a procedure call to divert to a special subprogram that would either remove the error or abort the program. The action of diverting the CPU to the error handler was called an "interrupt." Organick (1973) characterized an interrupt as an "unexpected procedure call."

A divide-by-zero error is not the only reason for interrupting the CPU. Designers used the words *exceptional condition* for any event that requires immediate attention from the CPU. Exceptional conditions can be of two kinds: errors and external signals. An error is a condition in a program that would cause incorrect or undefined behavior. Examples of errors that can be detected by sensors in the CPU are divide-by-zero, arithmetic overflow and underflow, page fault, protection violation, or array reference out of bounds. An external signal indicates that a high-priority event has occurred. Examples of external signals are timer alarm, disk completion, mouse click, or network packet arrival. For any exception, the CPU is interrupted from whatever it was doing and put to work on dealing with the error or responding to the external signal. With the addition of an "interrupt vector," the CPU can automatically and rapidly invoke interrupt handler procedure *k* when the sensors report that exception *k* has occurred (see figure 4.10).

Choice Uncertainty

The interrupt mechanism opens the door to *metastability*, a subtle and potentially devastating error. What happens when an exception signal occurs at the same time the CPU is trying to read the flipflop that records the signal? The clock controls when the CPU looks for interrupts, but not when the external signal arrives.

Here is what happens. Suppose the circuits use 3 volts to represent 0 and 5 volts to represent 1. The arrival of the external signal triggers the interrupt flipflop to transition from the 0 to the 1 state, meaning that the flipflop's output voltage changes from 3 to 5 volts. Because that transition takes time, there is a small interval where the voltage is in between 3 and 5 volts but not close enough to either be reliably counted as 0 or 1. Electronics engineers call such an output a "half signal." A half-signal input can cause a

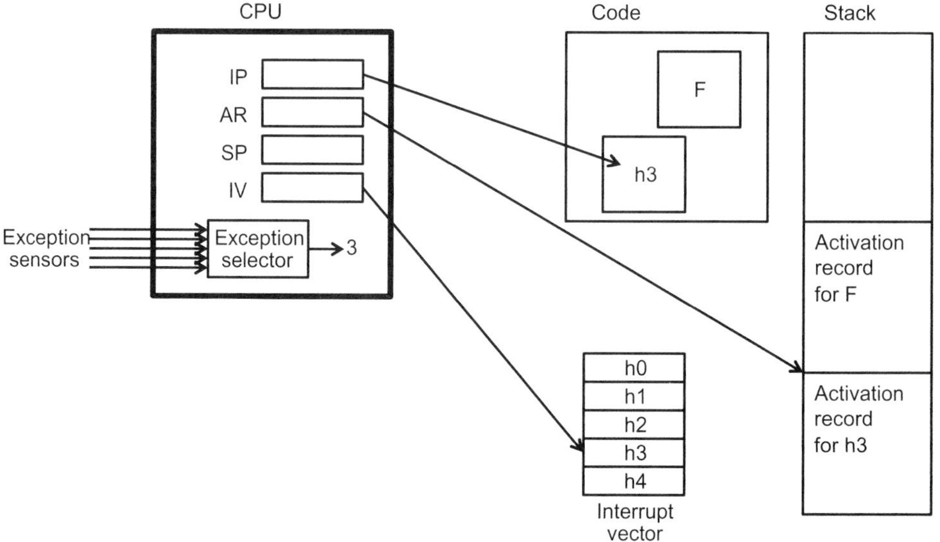

Figure 4.10
An interrupt mechanism enables the CPU to interrupt the current task and execute a procedure (handler) that resolves an error or responds to a high-priority external signal. Sensor circuits in the CPU and elsewhere in the computer system detect when any exceptions exist. A selector circuit selects the exception of highest priority and outputs its number (or 0 if there is no exception). At the end of each instruction cycle the CPU checks for exceptions, and, if there is one, the CPU suspends normal instruction execution. Instead it uses the exception number (here number 3) to index an interrupt vector, which is a list of entry-point addresses for each of the handlers, and makes a procedure call (here on h3). The AR (here for h3) is pushed on the stack and the normal instruction cycle resumes. When the handler is done, its return instruction restores the interrupted program, which continues from where it was interrupted.

flipflop to enter a *metastable state* with the output voltage poised midway between the two stable states. That midpoint is like a ball poised perfectly on the peak of a roof: it can sit there for an unknown amount of time until air molecules or roof vibrations cause it to lose its balance.

Metastability creates a risk of malfunction of any circuit that reads the flipflop's output. If the half signal persists beyond the next clock tick, the next circuit will receive an input that cannot be interpreted as 0 or 1, and its behavior may be unpredictable.

The metastability problem was well known to hardware engineers. Chaney and Molnor (1973) and Kinniment and Woods (1976) describe

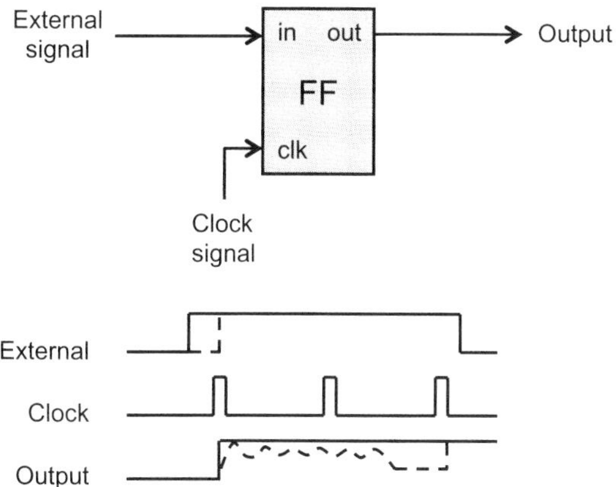

Figure 4.11
An experimental setup enables observing flipflop (FF) metastability. Each clock pulse signal triggers the FF state to match the input signal. If the input signal is changing when the clock pulse arrives (dashed external line), FF may enter an indefinite state that lasts several clock intervals (dashed output lines). In a digital computer, the indefinite output becomes the input of other logic circuits at the next clock pulse, causing half-signal malfunctions.

experiments to measure the likelihood and duration of metastable events. By synchronizing clock frequency with external signal frequency, they attempted to induce a metastable event on every external signal change. They saw frequent metastable events on their oscilloscope, some of which persisted 5, 10, or even 20 clock intervals (see figure 4.11). Other engineers had known for a long time that chooser circuits, also known as *arbiters* because their job was to arbitrarily choose one of two simultaneous signals, were hard to build (Seitz 1980, Denning 1985, Ginosar 2003).

Since that time, chip makers have been concerned about the chances of metastable states in their circuits. Sutherland and Ebergen (2002) reported that contemporary flipflops switched in about 100 picoseconds (100×10^{-12} seconds) and that a metastable state lasting 400 picoseconds or more occurred once every 10 hours of operation. Xilinx.com, a chip maker, reported that its modern flipflops had essentially no chance of showing a metastable state when clock frequencies were 200 MHz or less, but faster clocks incurred metastable events (Alfke 2005). In experiments with interrupt signals arriving 50 million times a second, they observed a metastable state about once a minute at clock frequency 300 MHz and about once every 2 milliseconds at clock frequency 400 MHz. In a computer system generating 500 interrupts per second, about 1/100,000 of their experimental rate, these extrapolate to one interrupt-caused metastable state about every 2 weeks at 300 MHz and about every 3 minutes at 400 MHz.

Now you can see the problem. There is a chance that the interrupt flipflop is metastable at the time when the CPU asks for the state, and that throws the next bank of flipflops controlling the CPU cycle into a metastable state. If those flipflops have not settled down by the next clock tick, the behavior of the CPU is unpredictable. The experimental results show that there is a good chance this can happen.

This problem plagued many early computer systems. Before engineers understood it, all they would see was that at random times the CPU would stop. They described these mysterious freezes as "cosmic ray crashes" because they seemed to be random disruptions of transistor function. Only a full-power-off reboot would restart the CPU. Because they could occur every few hours or days, these freezes could be quite troublesome.

Around 1970 David Wheeler, a hardware engineer at the Computing Laboratory of the University of Cambridge, UK, discovered the reason for these mysterious freezes: half signals appearing at the output of the interrupt flipflop. He designed a new kind of flipflop, which he called a threshold flipflop, and a protocol for using it that eliminated the danger of CPU freeze on interrogating the interrupt flipflop (see figure 4.12).

Situations like the interrupt flipflop confront hardware engineers in many other parts of a computer. Circuits that must choose between near-simultaneous events are everywhere. For example, at the same time, two CPUs access the same memory location, two transactions lock the same record of a database, two computers broadcast on Ethernet, two packets arrive together at the network card, an autonomous agent receives two requests, or a robot subsystem perceives two alternatives at the same time. In all these cases if we demand that a decision be made between the choices by the next clock tick, there is still a chance that the chooser circuits have not settled. If we want to wait for the circuits to settle, we need to stop the clock.

We can summarize these findings about chooser circuits with the choice uncertainty principle: "No choice between near-simultaneous events can be made unambiguously within a preset deadline"[6] (Lamport 1984, Denning 2007b). The source of the uncertainty is the metastable state that can be induced in the chooser by conflicting forces generated when two distinct signals change at the same time.[7]

Choice uncertainty is not about how a system reacts to an observer but how an observer reacts to a system. It also applies to choices we humans

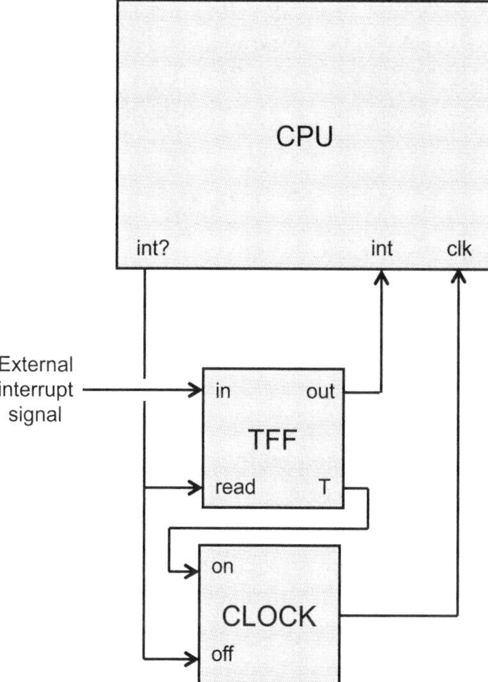

Figure 4.12
The threshold flipflop (TFF) guarantees that the CPU's interrupt input ("int") will be stable when interrogated at the end of an instruction cycle. When the CPU asks for the value of the external interrupt signal ("int?"), it triggers the TFF to record the current external signal in its state, and it turns the clock off. As soon as its state returns to "0" or "1," the TFF sends a pulse on the *T* output, which turns the clock back on. The clock suspension is only as long as necessary to assure that TFF is again stable. David Wheeler proposed the idea of temporarily shutting off the clock when checking interrupts in the Cambridge CAP computer in the 1970s.

make. What happens when the options are presented together and we are given a short time to choose? Sometimes we are still in indecision when the deadline comes, and we lose the opportunity presented to us. We do not have the option, as did Wheeler, to turn off the clock until we can decide. Individuals and groups can persist in an indecisive state for seconds, hours, days, months, or even years.

The possibility of indefinite indecision is often attributed to the fourteenth-century philosopher Jean Buridan, who described the paradox of the hungry dog that, being placed midway between two equal portions of food, starved (Lamport 1984, Denning 1985). If he were discussing this today with cognitive scientists, Buridan might say that the brain can be immobilized in a metastable state when presented with equally attractive alternatives.

Conclusions

Our purpose has been to show, in convincing detail, that it is possible to build an electronic machine that will calculate any function for which someone can find a computational method. The machine consists of a processor (CPU) and memory (RAM). In a repeating instruction cycle, the processor executes a sequence of machine instructions stored in RAM, operating on data also stored in RAM. The machine instructions implement simple operations including arithmetic, memory read and write, and control sequencing. Each instruction is implemented by a circuit in the CPU. We showed how to design a simple instruction set for the case where the data part of RAM is organized as a stack. Instructions for basic operations, choices, and iterations give the machine universal computing power.

The procedure-calling mechanism permits separately written programs to be invoked as procedure calls at any point within any program. On detecting exceptional conditions, operating systems use the procedure mechanism to interrupt programs.

We concluded with the choice uncertainty problem, which is that chooser circuits may be thrown into a metastable state by simultaneous inputs and be unable to make a choice by a deadline such as the next clock tick. The problem arises from the physics of circuits and can be avoided if the clock is turned off until the circuits settle.

The study of machines reemphasizes the central importance of physical "stuff" in computation. All the instructions and data of a machine are recorded as patterns of 0 and 1 in physical circuits and media. The 0 and 1 are the names of states of the media. Instructions manipulate these stored states in precise, prescribed ways. Programs record the steps of computational methods as series of instructions arranged in precise patterns. The machine reads the program instructions and carries them out on the data. All this is done automatically. The circuits simply obey laws of electricity and physics; they have no understanding of the meanings of the signals passing through them.

The stack structure cited here is only one of several models for executing programs. Each model has its own rules and machine structures. But they all do the same thing: control electronic circuits that calculate output values from input values.

5 Programming

People who are more than casually interested in computers should have at least some idea of what the underlying hardware is like. Otherwise the programs they write will be pretty weird.

—Donald Knuth

Programming is one of the most difficult branches of applied mathematics; the poorer mathematicians had better remain pure mathematicians.

—Edsger Dijkstra

Ada Lovelace, it is said, was the first computer programmer. In 1843 she wrote in her "Notes on Babbage's Analytic Engine" an algorithm that would cause the machine to calculate a sequence of Bernoulli numbers. Babbage never completed his machine; Lovelace never ran her program.

For input of programs and data, Babbage planned to use punched cards such as those used at the time for Jacquard looms. Historians might wonder if those who specified card sequences for the looms were programmers; they encoded methods for execution by a machine and, unlike Lovelace, got to see them run. Modern programmers would say no, loom programs are not computer programs: looms could not compute mathematical functions.

Historians might also wonder if mathematicians who devised algorithms were programmers—for example, Newton's elimination method for solving simultaneous equations (1670) or Napier's method for calculating logarithms (1614). Modern programmers would again say no because these algorithms were not encoded for a particular machine.

Almost 100 years passed between Lovelace's program and the first programs that ran on electronic digital computers. The first programmers of this generation were the women who specified algorithms for the ENIAC as patterns of cables on patch panels (1949) (see figure 1.3 of chapter 1). Two years later the programmers of EDSAC and EDVAC—the first stored-program computers—wrote algorithms as binary numbers passed to the computer on paper tapes. The women who calculated ballistic tables for the Army during World War II were also programmers, although their programs were not instructions for a machine but for themselves to operate mechanical calculators. In effect, they were human processing units.

From the beginning, programmers found that they spent a considerable amount of time looking for errors in their own programs (Wilkes 1985). Errors are a universal occurrence; even the best programmers make them. Computer designers soon began to design programming languages and methods of dynamic error checking that would help in the fight against errors. That fight continues today. Designing error-free software is not only a reliability problem, it is a safety and security problem.

Our purpose in this chapter is to demonstrate that, in spite of the large numbers of languages, the basic idea of a translator—automatically converting source programs into instructions for the machine—is the same for all languages. Moreover, there are programs called compiler generators that take a language description and output a compiler for the language. Automatic generators have removed the barrier to implementing new languages when and as they are needed.

Programs, Programmers, and Programming Languages

A *program* is an expression of an algorithm, encoded for execution on a machine. A *programming language* is an artificial language with its own rules of syntax, used for expressing programs. A *programmer* is a person who uses programming languages to design programs and works to get them to run without error on machines.[1]

Programming languages have proliferated since the first commercial languages were introduced in the late 1950s. How many are there? In 2014 Wikipedia had a list of over 500 programming languages that are or have been used for commercial software production. If you count languages invented and their minor variants, upgrades, and updates, the number is likely to be many thousands.[2] Each was designed for a specific purpose, usually to facilitate design of computations in a particular domain. Thousands of domains use computing; hence, a claim of thousands of languages is no surprise.

Table 5.1 is a sampling of prominent languages. Three of the original four are still used today. Only Algol does not survive as a language; however, many other languages inherited their syntax from Algol.

One of the major innovations of the Algol language project was the use of a formal grammar to specify the syntax of the language. The grammar

Table 5.1
A Few Widely Used Programming Languages

Language	Date	Purpose
Fortran	1957	Efficient processing of equations of mathematical models
Algol	1958	General algorithmic language supporting recursive procedures
Lisp	1958	Manipulate lists representing lambda-expressions from the Church calculus (the first language used in AI)
Cobol	1959	Support operations in business, finance, and administration
APL	1962	Special purpose language for manipulating arrays of numbers representing functions
JCL, Shell	1966	Language to control processing of jobs in an operating system; successors are the shell languages of Multics (1968) and Unix (1972)
PL/I	1966	General algorithmic language based on Algol and including features for business data processing and system programming; most of Multics and OS/360 was in PL/I
Simula	1967	Discrete event simulation using classes of objects; the first object-oriented programming language
Pascal	1970	Algol-like language supporting structured programming; popular language for teaching programming to beginners
Smalltalk	1971	General object-oriented programming with message passing from Simula; standardized in 1980
Prolog	1972	Find whether a given query is a logical consequence of the terms declared in the program's database (used in AI, natural language processing, and theorem proving)
C	1973	System programming, first used in the Unix kernel, later Linux
CLU	1974	Object oriented language built on abstract data types
Ada	1983	US Department of Defense language to replace the hundreds of languages then used by DOD and to provide reliable programs
Sisal	1983	Express algorithms as functional compositions amenable to high-speed execution on parallel processors
Perl	1987	Scripting language commonly used in web sites
Java	1995	Object-oriented language whose programs could run on any machine with a web browser
Python	2000	General-purpose programming supporting imperative, functional, and object-oriented styles and emphasizing readability

was called Backus-Naur form, or BNF for short, after its developers John Backus and Peter Naur (Backus 1959, Knuth 1964). The grammar facilitated agreement on what the language structures meant and on how to generate machine code that would execute those structures faithfully. The grammar was also the basis of a method for building a compiler program. Subsequent research led to very efficient compilers and also to compiler-generators, which would create a compiler automatically given the grammar. We discuss the principles of compilers shortly.

Here is an example of a BNF specification for the portion of a programming language that uses assignment statements to associate the values of arithmetic expressions with numbers and variables:

```
<assign>    ::= <var> = <A>
<A>         ::= <A><aop><A> | <M>
<M>         ::= <M><mop><M> | <F>
<F>         ::= (<A>) | x
<aop>       ::= + | -
<mop>       ::= * | /
```

The syntactic elements are named in < > brackets. The elements <A>, <M>, and <F> stand for additive, multiplicative, and factor expressions, respectively; and the elements <aop> and <mop> stand for additive and multiplicative operators, respectively. The double-colon-equal symbol (::=) means "is defined as." The vertical bar (|) separates alternatives. The letter x stands for any alphanumeric variable name or numeric constant (see figure 5.1). This grammar honors arithmetic precedence by pushing multiplicative operations lower than additive ones, which forces the multiplicatives to be evaluated before the additives. In a later section we show how a compiler uses these syntax trees to generate machine code that implements the expression.

Programming as a Practice

Programming is the practice of encoding algorithms for execution on a machine. A programmer's work consists of two main parts:

1. Design an expression of a solution method for a problem and encode it for a machine
2. Verify that a machine controlled by the program properly solves the problem

Programmers use many tools to support them in this work. Design tools include programming languages and graphical editors that force compliance

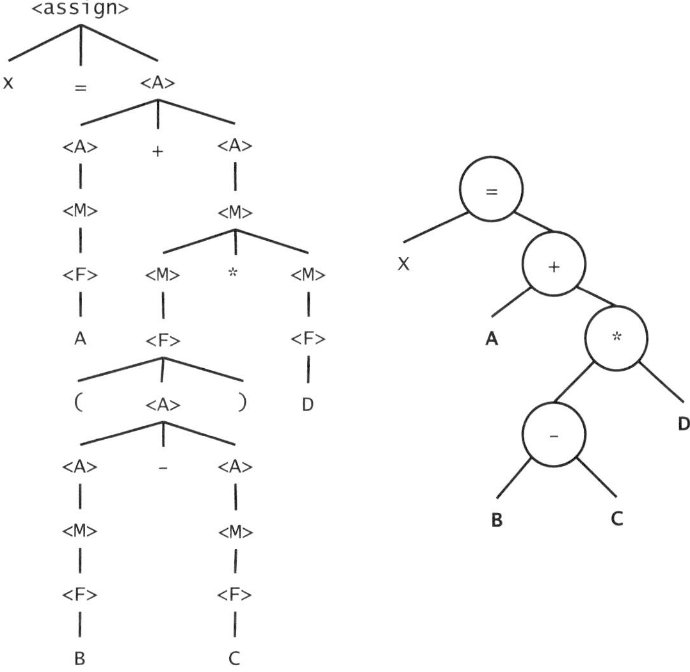

Figure 5.1
The assignment statement X=A+(B-C)*D can be represented by two kinds of syntax tree. The one at the left applies the grammar of the text to build a tree explaining the syntax of the expression. The one at the right is a simplified form obtained by retaining only the operators and operands. The parentheses are not needed once the structure is known because the grammar honors arithmetic precedence.

with the language syntax. Compilers, linkers, and interpreters convert a program into a computation on a machine. Testing and debugging tools help locate and remove errors. Library and version control tools help keep programs up to date and enable their reuse. Programmers are artisans in using these tools.

Programmers develop varying levels of skill at programming. Novice programmers find themselves spending a lot of time trying to understand the syntax of their programming languages and generally accepted basic algorithms. Competent programmers can perform a range of standard programming tasks and satisfy customers without requiring a supervisor to watch over them. Virtuoso programmers can program large systems well and can mentally move from high-level system views to low-level machine code views with great facility. Productivity—measured, for example, as lines of code written and verified—varies hugely among programmers. Many proficient programmers are ten times more productive than entry-level competent programmers, and a few virtuosi are as much as fifty times as productive.

Some programmers have become legendary because they made programs that changed the world. John MacCormick (2012) celebrates nine algorithms that were the work of such programmers—names such as Len Adleman, Sergey Brin, Jim Gray, Tom Mitchell, Larry Page, Ron Rivest, and Adi Shamir. Many of their key conceptual tricks have become new principles for computation.

In addition to programs many systems have become legendary in their influence—for example, operating systems such as VM/370, Multics, Unix, Windows, and MacOS; database systems such as Oracle; networking systems such as Akamai web caching system; TCP/IP protocol suite; Domain Naming System (DNS); and Digital Object Identifier (DOI) system used by publishers. Some of their developers are legendary—names such as Vint Cerf, Fernando Corbato, Bill Gates, Bill Joy, Bob Kahn, Alan Kay, Butler Lampson, Paul Mockapetris, Roger Needham, Jon Postel, Rick Rashid, Dennis Ritchie, Jerry Saltzer, and Ken Thompson.

Many programs are embodied into large systems that required hundreds or thousands of programmers. Operating systems and large applications such as Microsoft Office are examples. How to organize that many programmers to maximize productivity, minimize errors, and meet deadlines is not simply a talent selection process; it presents major challenges in project coordination and testing that have dogged the software industry for fifty years. Fred Brooks, who was the manager of the IBM 360 operating system project in the 1960s, recorded many insights into large-project organization in his famous book *The Mythical Man Month* (Brooks 1995). We discuss principles for the design of large systems later in chapter 10 on Design.

The Error Problem

Since its beginnings in the 1940s, software has had a reputation of being extremely error prone. Programmers have always been frustrated by the intricacy of programs for even the simplest tasks, the amount of time they need to locate mistakes in their own programs, and the challenges of protecting their software and data from external errors (see figure 5.2).

Most physical systems obey continuum laws that guarantee that a small change in one variable produces a small corresponding change in other (dependent) variables. Thus, the system can naturally tolerate a small error. Many biological systems, including human and animal immune systems,

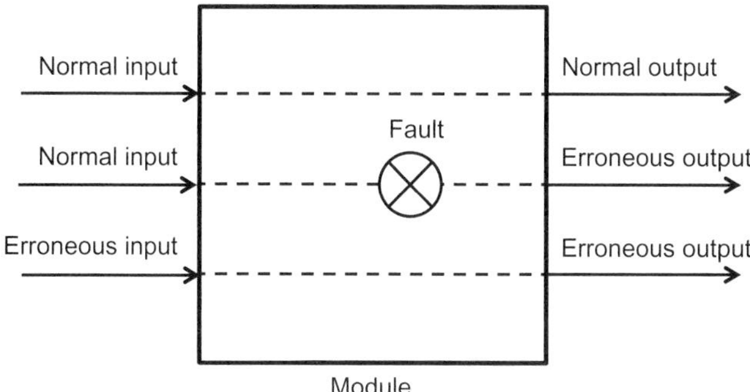

Figure 5.2
Errors in the output of a software module can arise in two ways: as a consequence of a fault (defect) in the module or as a consequence of an erroneous input. Finding defects and detecting erroneous inputs can be dauntingly complex.

contain self-detection and repair mechanisms that respond to such errors through feedback and correct them.

In contrast, the virtual worlds created by software tend to be highly sensitive to errors. A single bit changed in a program can drastically change the algorithm represented by the program. Moreover, it is easy to create software whose actions conflict with physical laws, leading to errors when the software interacts with the world. The quest to reduce or eliminate errors has not been easy given the vulnerabilities inherent in the chain of transformations that designers must master (see figure 5.3).

The desire to reduce errors has motivated programming language designers to adopt error-reducing structures. Over the years these have included types, subroutines, separate modules, exceptions, objects, packages, syntax editors, debuggers, and languages that reduce the "semantic gap" between the expressive power of a language and the problems of the domain. Even with these improvements, errors are still a major problem in programming.

The desire to reduce errors motivated software engineers (professional systems programmers) to adopt the traditional four-stage engineering design process: (1) requirements, (2) specifications, (3) prototypes, and (4) testing. In the requirements stage, engineers consult with users and others familiar with the domain of use to learn all the behaviors that the system should have and should not have. In the specifications stage, engineers create formal descriptions in a precise language for the system's functions that meet the requirements. In the prototype stage, engineers implement a partially working system. In the testing stage, engineers subject the prototype to various tests to see whether it behaves according to the specifications

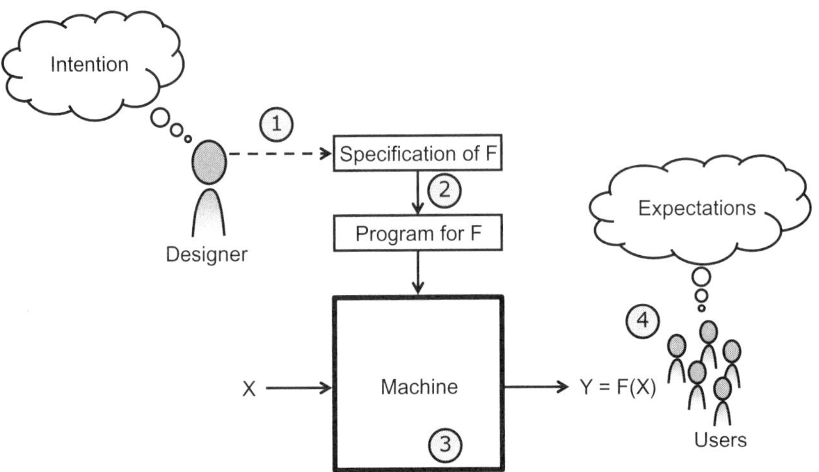

Figure 5.3
The process of transforming a designer's intention into a machine is fraught with opportunities for error. There are four. (1) The specification does not accurately represent the designer's intention or is based on misunderstandings of user expectations. (2) The programmer makes mistakes, for example, by introducing bugs or poor approximations, and the compiler might contain bugs or Trojan horses that cause the machine code not to be equivalent to the source program. (3) The machine itself contains bugs, defects, malfunctions, intrusions by other buggy machines or attackers, and other factors that cause it to misbehave while executing its basic operations. (4) The users' expectations of what the machine's job is differs from what they see the machine doing. Automatic verifiers try to eliminate type 2 errors. Fault-tolerant system designs help reduce type 3 errors. Prototyping and getting user feedback help reduce types 1 and 4 errors.

and meets user expectations. Engineers view this process as imprecise and are constantly iterating and backing up as they learn new things. For example, while writing a specification, they may learn that a requirement is ambiguous, and they must consult with users to resolve the ambiguity. While implementing a prototype, they may learn that a specification leads to a major inefficiency, requiring a change of specification or requirement. While testing, they may discover a performance problem or uncover a bug, requiring that they double check their implementation, review the specifications, or consult again with users. These steps can become unwieldy with large systems consisting of many modules and built by large teams. Sophisticated decision tracking, coordination, and version control systems are used to keep track of all the changes, steps forward, and steps backward.

Even when this process is run by experienced engineers, it is distressingly common for projects to overrun their budgets or deadlines. Typical estimates are that 60 percent of software projects fail by being over budget, late, or missing an important function; and about 30 percent are canceled because of poor execution.[3] Although the reasons for failure are often put to management misestimating cost and time, the sheer complexity of many systems also challenges even the most experienced engineers. There are strong economic reasons for finding sound design principles.

Automatic Translation

A critical component of programming is the conversion of the program as an expression into a form executable on a machine. There have been two approaches to this, the compiler and the interpreter. A *compiler* is a program that takes an input file containing string of symbols representing a program, parses it into a syntax tree according to the grammar of the language, and generates machine code that implements the operations called for by the syntax tree. An *interpreter* is a program that also parses the input but, instead of generating machine code, it calls system operations as soon as the parser identifies them; the system operations are subroutines already compiled into machine code. Over the years the distinction between the two forms of execution has blurred. Perhaps the most important one is that a compiler runs once and produces executable machine code that can be run many times, whereas an interpreter is run on every execution.

Let us begin with an examination of a compiler's function. The objective is to translate a program into a set of machine instructions that implement exactly what the program specifies (and nothing else). To accomplish this we need two things. First, the programming language grammar (BNF) must be unambiguous, meaning that there is exactly one syntax tree for any given valid input string. Second, the translation process should map a syntax tree to a unique machine code sequence.[4]

For simplicity, we assume that parsing BNF grammars leads to a syntax tree with operators at the internal nodes and variable names or constants at the leaf nodes (the simplified tree in figure 5.1 illustrates this). We also assume that the programming language allows for the basic structures mentioned in chapter 4 on Machines: assignment of a value to a variable, sequencing statements, choosing between statements, and iterating statements. These structures are sufficient to program any algorithm; if we can translate them, we can translate any program.

Figures 5.4–5.7 illustrate the translations for assignment statements and expressions, sequencing, choice, and iteration. The left part of each figure is a syntax tree for the structure, and the right part is a template of machine instructions that implement the tree.

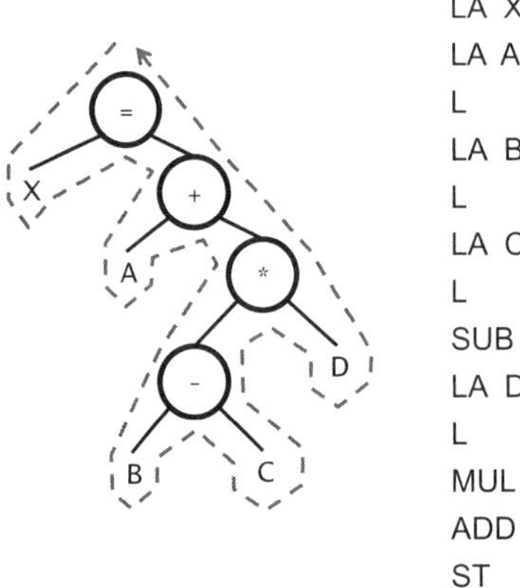

Figure 5.4
This diagram summarizes the work of a compiler to generate code for the assignment statement X=A+(B-C)*D of figure 5.1. The compiler first parses the statement into a tree with the operators at the internal nodes and operands at the leaves. It then makes a counterclockwise traversal (dotted line), and outputs a stack instruction for every leaf or operator the last time it passes that leaf or operator. The result (*right*) is an instruction sequence that properly evaluates the statement on a stack machine (see chapter 4).

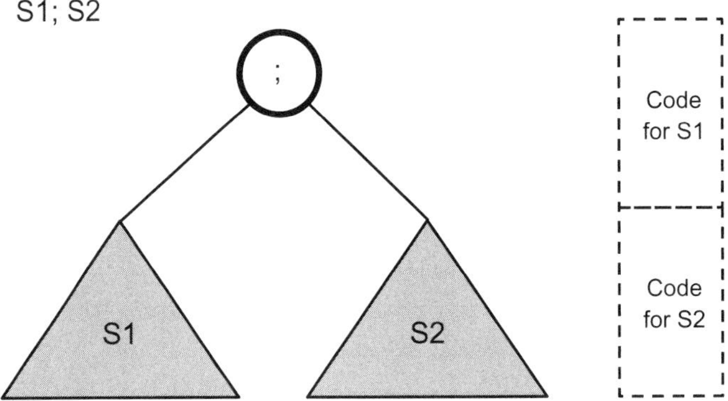

Figure 5.5
This diagram summarizes the work of a compiler to generate code for a sequence of statements. The compiler first parses the two statements into their trees and joins the two with a semicolon operator (denoting sequencing). It then makes a counterclockwise traversal and generates the code pattern at the right, which simply puts the code for S1 before the code for S2.

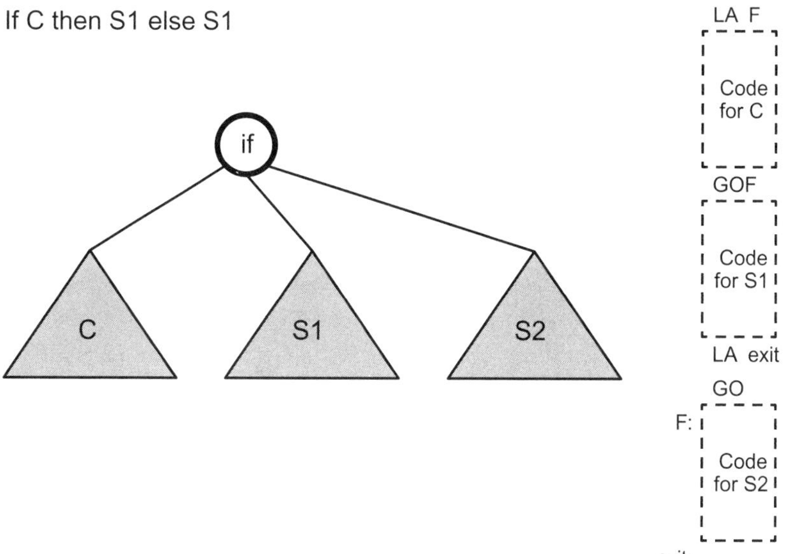

Figure 5.6
This diagram summarizes the work of a compiler to generate code for a selection statement. The compiler first parses the three components (condition expression C, and statements S1 and S2) into their trees and then joins the three with an "if" operator. It then makes a counterclockwise traversal and generates the code pattern at the right. After each code segment it inserts jump instructions to make sure that S1 code executes when C is true and S2 code executes when C is false. The instruction GOF (go on false) assumes that a true-false value followed by target address are on stack, which is accomplished by the "LA F" and code segment for C.

The method of converting a tree to instructions is called "tree traversal." We imagine following a path (see figure 5.4) counterclockwise around the tree, visiting every node; the path visits a leaf node once and a k-way operator node $k + 1$ times; it outputs instructions the last time it passes a node.

The compiler method outlined above has one drawback. There can be a large "semantic gap" between the expressive level of the source language and the machine code. A large gap leaves more to the compiler writer's interpretation, which may not agree with the language designer's intended meaning. That increases the possibility of errors in the code.[5]

Language designers have sought to narrow the semantic gap by extending the instruction set of the base machine. The extended instructions are implemented as separately compiled and validated procedures. Now the

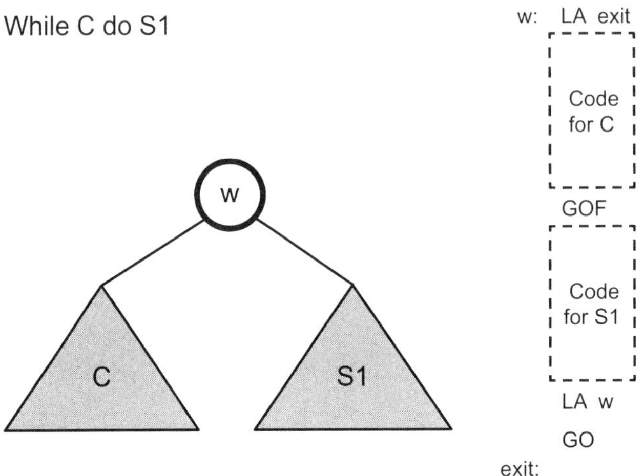

Figure 5.7
This diagram summarizes the work of a compiler to generate code for an iteration statement. The compiler first parses the two components (condition expression C and statement S1) into their trees and joins them with a "while" operator. It then makes the counterclockwise traversal and generates the code pattern at the right. After each code segment it inserts jump instructions to make sure that S1 code executes while C is true and exits as soon as C is false.

compiler can translate some language operators to the extended instructions, reducing a possible source of translation error (see figure 5.8).

The Java Virtual Machine (JVM) is a prominent example of this approach. The instructions of the JVM, called "bytecodes," implement actions on Java objects. The Java compiler translates a Java program only into bytecodes and not base machine instructions. The JVM instruction set is implemented as a set of procedures, one for each bytecode, compiled for the base machine. This two-level design enables the portability of Java programs. The JVM can be implemented within any operating system by coding the bytecode procedures with the instructions of the base machine. Thus, bytecode output by a Java compiler can be executed on any JVM in any operating system. A user on any machine can create and compile a Java program and distribute it to any other machine via a web site.

Operating systems are great examples of virtual machines. Operating systems manage multiple kinds of objects including processes, virtual memories, message channels, files, input-output, and directories. A subsystem manages each kind of object; for example, the file system manages files by

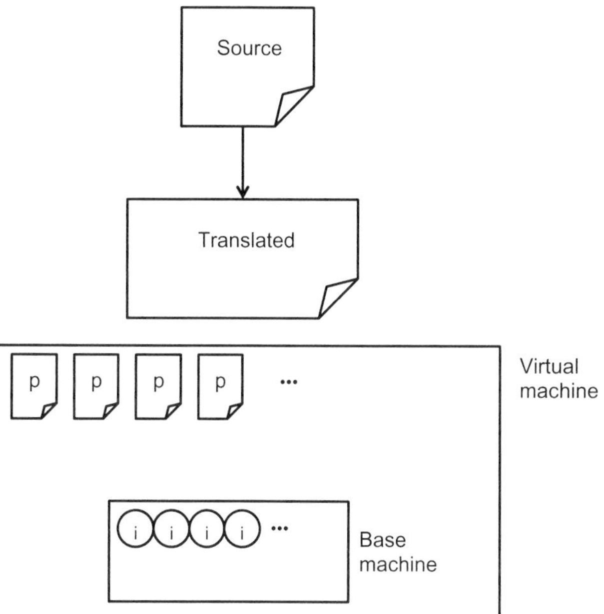

Figure 5.8
A virtual machine is a common mode of execution. Here we show a base machine with a set of instructions (*nodes labeled i*). A virtual machine is an extension of the base machine created by adding new operations as procedures executable on the base machine (*nodes labeled p*). The translator of the source code can use operator nodes in the syntax tree corresponding to the virtual machine's virtual operations. The Java language is based on this kind of execution environment. The Java compiler translates the source into "bytecode," a series of instructions for the Java virtual machine (JVM). The JVM is implemented separately for each operating system (base machine) by programming its operations in the base system's machine code. This enables great portability of Java programs because it is relatively easy to implement JVMs for any operating system.

providing standard operations to create, delete, open, close, read, and write files. The file system virtual machine provides these six extended instructions, which are much more reliable and secure than user-defined file operations. In operating system parlance, the file system manages "file objects" by making "system calls" on the six operations. Input and output of programs are usually passed as files. The compiler can translate input or output operations in the source to the proper file system operations. System calls are much easier and more reliable than subroutines linked from a library.

Operating systems have a component called the "shell" that implements a job control language. Users interact with the shell to issue commands saying what programs they want run and where their input and output are. The shell parses a command into a syntax tree and uses the tree to determine which system calls are needed (see figure 5.9). Unlike a compiler, the shell uses its parser just once to process a command. This is a good example of the interpretive mode of language translation.

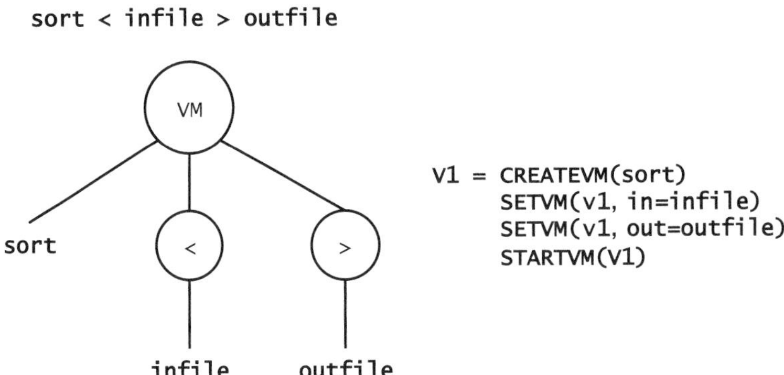

Figure 5.9
The Unix shell language lets a user type the name of a program, such as sort, which gets its input from an "infile" specified by the user and places its output into an "outfile" specified by the user. The user types this as a line shown at the top left. The "<" symbol means to use the next name as an input file and the ">" means to use the next name as output file. The parser creates a syntax tree as at the bottom left with "VM" for virtual machine as the operator node. In traversing the tree, the shell interpreter generates the four operating system calls shown at the right. The first creates a virtual machine running the "sort" program. The second sets the input of the virtual machine to the "infile." The third sets the output of the virtual machine to the "outfile." The fourth initiates the execution of the virtual machine. When the virtual machine is done (sort terminates), the script is done, and the user may now type a next command.

Conclusions

Programming is the action of designers preparing computational solutions to problems. Good programming is an artisan skill developed with good training and years of practice.

Programming languages are designed for particular domains. They allow programmers in the domain to express computational solutions in terms familiar in the domain. Because programming languages are defined with Backus-Naur Form (BNF) syntax, and we know how to build parsers for any BNF grammar, it is easy to generate compilers for new languages. These tailored languages reduce the semantic gap between the programmer's intentions and the expressive power of the language.

Programmers have a concern for errors that sometimes borders on the paranoid. The process of building a computational solution to a problem is fraught with errors, which can occur at any of four key points: expressing intentions and desires accurately, programming accurately, compiling accurately, and executing accurately. Here, "accurate" means preserving the original intention of the designer. System designers have provided an impressive array of technologies to help programmers avoid errors and write dependable, reliable, usable, safe, and secure programs.

The part of the process that translates source program statements into machine code can be fully automated. Once the mappings are set and verified, programmers can have great confidence that their machine codes do exactly what the language statements say and nothing more or less. To illustrate, we showed how a compiler translates the standard structures of assignment, sequencing, choice, and iteration into machine codes.

When there is a large semantic gap between the language and the machine, the language designer and compiler writer have to deal with possible errors of interpretation that creep into the translations. The compiler writer could use a pattern of machine code that the programmer would say does not implement the intention properly. One way to reduce this kind of error is to close the semantic gap by extending the base machine with virtual machine instructions. The virtual machine instructions perform operations that closely mirror the actions intended by users of objects. For example, the operations create, delete, open, close, read, and write of a file system are virtual instructions that execute those operations on files. The compiler is greatly simplified if it can translate file input and output into file system calls rather than compile them into machine code.

The compiler is one mode of translation. Another is the interpreter, which parses a statement in a language and then dynamically calls the operators in the syntax tree as they are processed. Many languages such as logic languages, list-processing languages, and command languages are more efficient when translated in interpretive mode. The main reason for this is that the operations require very dynamic use of storage, and a dynamic run time system can adapt quickly through such means as garbage collection.

With these designs we can be certain that the machine code implements exactly what the program calls for and nothing else. If we could not be certain of this, we could not use programming languages effectively.

6 Computation

The information highway is about the global movement of weightless bits at the speed of light.

—Nicolas Negroponte (1996)

This sentence is false.

—Alfred Tarski

Computations are sequences of constantly changing constellations of bits. Each change affects only a few bits, takes a little time, and uses a little energy.

Computational work is measured by the time (or energy or space) required to get a computation to its completion. How much time (or energy or space) does a computing machine need to complete a task? Can we predict the computational work of a task or a family of related tasks?

Such performance questions have challenged designers of computational tasks since the 1930s. Designers ask four questions:

1. Is there an algorithm for the task?
2. How long does the algorithm take?
3. Is there a faster algorithm?
4. What is it?

These questions have led to an amazing search to understand the "complexity" of computation, that is, the number of time steps needed to calculate the values of computable functions. Table 6.1 is a summary of the four main categories of functions discovered in this search. These categories will be our guide in the rest of this chapter.

The table refers to decision problems, which are functions that decide whether something is true (1) or false (0) about the values presented to them. Computer scientists use decision problems to calibrate the difficulty

Table 6.1
Categories of Functions by Difficulty of Computing Them

Category	Description	Technical Name	Order of Difficulty
Easy	Decision problems for which fast algorithms are known	Polynomial (P) or tractable	$O(log\ n)$ and $O(n^k)$ for constant k
Hard, with easy verification	Decision problems for which no fast algorithm is known, but a proposed solution can be quickly verified; typically involve searches over large sets	Nondeterministic polynomial (NP) and NP-complete	$O(2^n)$, $O(n!)$, or worse
Very hard	Decision problems for which no fast algorithm or verifier is known	Intractable	$O(2^{f(n)})$ where $f(n)$ is exponential or worse
Impossible	Decision problems for which no algorithm at all can exist	Noncomputable or undecidable	

of various problems. Nothing is lost by this apparent restriction. For any function $F(x)$, there is an associated decision function $DF(x,y)$ that returns 1 when $F(x) = y$ and 0 otherwise. This decision function is no more difficult to solve than the general function, and sometimes the decision function is much easier than the general function. However, if the decision function is hard, the original function will be at least as hard.

The terms "easy" and "hard" are relative. Easy means that we can decide the problem in a reasonable time for instances that fit on available computers. Hard means that we can decide only limited, rather small instances in a reasonable time. Very hard, or intractable, means that the fastest supercomputers would take centuries to decide instances of interest to us. In the middle, between very hard and easy, is a large set of over 3000 practical problems from many fields (technically called NP-complete problems) that are hard to decide but whose solutions can be verified easily. If anyone finds a fast algorithm for any one of them, that algorithm can be adapted to solve all the others fast. Whether or not such a fast algorithm exists is considered to be one of the foremost open questions in mathematics and computing.

The order of difficulty in the table is the growth rate in the number of steps in the solution as a function of the size of the input (n). Thus $O(n)$ means that the computation time grows linearly with the size of the input. $O(2^n)$ means that the computation time grows exponentially. The meanings of these difficulty measures are explained as we go along.

Sidebar 6.1
Sidebar—Turing Machines

The Turing machine (1937) has long been the reference model for computation, winning out over competing models such as Post's rewriting systems, Church's lambda calculus, and Gödel's recursive functions. It achieved this status because it most closely resembled automatic computers and could compute any function any of the other models could.

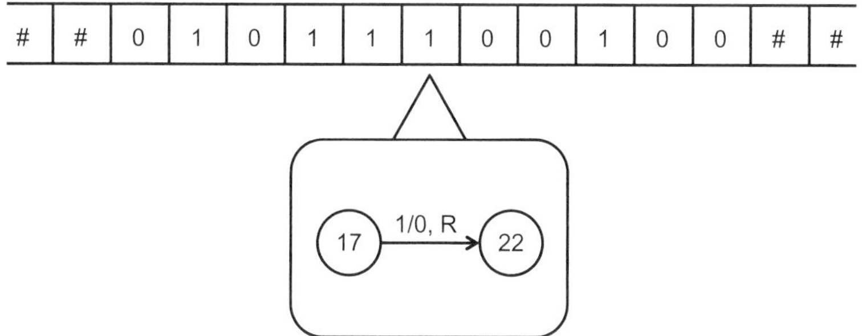

A Turing machine consists of a finite-state control unit that moves along a two-dimensional infinite tape. The tape squares contain any of the symbols 0, 1, or #, where # is a blank. The control unit is specified as a set of tuples of the form (*q, a/b, LR, q'*), where *q* and *q'* are control states, *a* and *b* are tape symbols, and *LR* is a direction indicator. Thus, (17, 1/0, R, 22) means "if in state 17 and the current square contains 1, write 0, move right one square, and enter state 22." One state is designated as the halting state. If and when the machine enters that state, it halts and its output is the contents of the tape.

Turing also described a universal machine, which could simulate any other machine described by its set of tuples. The universality of the machine led to the Church-Turing thesis, the hypothesis that any other computational model can be represented as a Turing machine. No new computational model has yet been found that violates this thesis. Many functions, such as the halting decider, are not Turing computable. Other functions such as image labeling (figure 3.7 in chapter 3) are computable by human-machine partnerships, but no Turing computable method is currently known.

The Turing machine is a convenient reference model for computational complexity. An algorithm's complexity is measured as the number of Turing machine moves needed to execute that algorithm on an input. The inherently sequential Turing machine is ideal for counting moves and determining an upper bound on how long the machine would take to reach a halting state.

(*Continued*)

The notion of a verifier corresponds to a "nondeterministic" Turing machine. In such a machine multiple tuples may apply for a given state and current tape symbol. For example, the machine might contain (17, 1/1, L, 24) in addition to the tuple (17, 1/0, R, 22) given above. Which tuple should the machine apply? The machine must make a choice because the next state is not uniquely determined by the current state and tape symbol. A nondeterministic machine computes an output if there is a series of choices that leads to a halting state with that output on the tape. A nondeterministic machine can be converted to a deterministic one by building a tree of copies of the program corresponding to each possible choice; such a tree can quickly become overwhelmingly large.

A verifier simply confirms that a given computational path through the nondeterministic machine leads to the proposed output. That is often much easier than enumerating all the choices and checking whether each one produces the desired output.

Modern complexity theory does not refer directly to Turing machines but still works with precise definition of programs and the numbers of steps they take to complete their functions.

Easy Functions

Let us begin with a few examples of easy computations and the measures we use to estimate their completion times.

Example 1. Simple Linear Search

Find the page number of the first page of this book on which the name "Turing" occurs. One way to do this is to represent the book as a string of characters with embedded marks for page boundaries. We then take the search string "Turing" and slide it along the book string one character at a time to see whether "Turing" matches the current chunk of book string. If we find a match, we stop and output the most recent page number we encountered.

Comparing the search string to a current substring of the book takes a fixed time proportional to the length of the search string. Let us say that the length of the search string is s. For every character in the book, we can compare the search string to the book substring beginning at that character. If the book size is b characters, the total search time will not exceed $An + B$ for some constants A and B and $n = sb$. We call this time "order n" because for large n the time grows proportional to n. We use the shorthand notation $O(n)$ to mean "order n." This search method is called linear search.

Example 2. Binary Search

Simple linear search may not be the fastest. Suppose that the book contains an alphabetized index of every word along with all the page numbers on which the word appears. Now we can do a binary search on the index: we repeatedly ask whether the search string is in the lower or upper half of the portion of the index we are searching. At each stage our search narrows to half as many items as the previous stage. This means that we need $\log_2 n$ splits until we come to a list of size 1, which is either the search string or not (see figure 6.1).

Thus, the work to find the string "Turing" in the index is proportional to $A \log_2 n + B$, for some constants A and B. We call this time "order log n" because for large n the time grows proportional to log n. We use the shorthand notation $O(\log n)$ to mean "order log n." Binary search is much faster than linear search. For example, a book with 2^{20} (about 1 million)

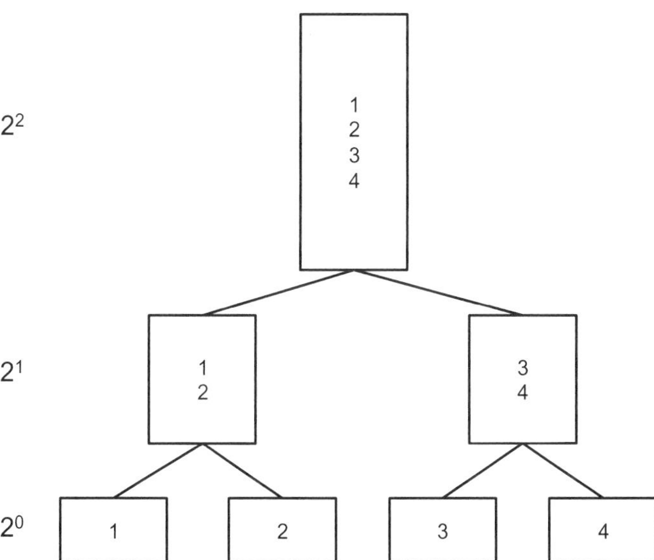

Figure 6.1

The binary split principle takes a larger set through a series of splits down to a singleton set. Here the set {1,2,3,4} is split in half, then each half is split again, and then again. The levels are numbered 0, 1, 2, . . . with 0 at the bottom of the tree. If $n = 2^k$, the depth of the tree is $k = \log_2 n$. The logarithm can be thought of as the number of divisions by the base (here, 2) until the quotient is 1. Many computational problems are approached by using this "divide and conquer" strategy. For this reason the logarithm appears frequently in the order notation of computational work.

characters will take time of order 2^{20} on linear search versus 20 for binary search—an advantage of 50,000. For large files, the advantage is huge. We next need to ask how much work it takes to build the index in the first place.

Example 3. Sorting

Building an index is an example of sorting. Sorting means to arrange a list of items in an order. For example, a list of words can be sorted into alphabetic order; a list of numbers can be sorted into increasing or decreasing order. Some lists may contain duplicates. A book-indexing algorithm extends sorting slightly by providing back pointers to the original positions of each word.

One method of sorting is *successive maxima*. We scan the list of n items to find the maximum element in it, and then we exchange the last element with the maximum. We then repeat this for the first $n - 1$ items, then the first $n - 2$ items, and so on. The number of comparisons needed to accomplish this is $n(n + 1)/2$, which is order n^2, or $O(n^2)$ (see figure 6.2).

Is there a faster method of sorting? Yes, but it is not immediately obvious to the novice (see figure 6.3). It applies the principle of binary splitting to divide the original list into two parts, which are then sorted by dividing each of them into two parts. This is repeated about log n times (see figure 6.3). At each level, all n items are examined. The total work is $O(n \log n)$.

Can we do any better? No. We can imagine a perfect algorithm that includes a procedure F that tells you the position in the sorted list of each item in the original list; that is, $F(i)$ is the sorted position of item i. F has to generate the bit string representing the sorted position. If there are n items, each bit string is of at least length log n; therefore, function F requires time $O(\log n)$. This is repeated for each of the n items, giving a total of $O(n \log n)$ for the whole list.

What can we see from these examples?

- First, some problems can be solved faster than others. A binary search is faster than a linear search or sorting.
- Second, it may not be obvious how to find a faster algorithm or whether there is any faster algorithm. It was easy to find the successive maximum sort but not so obvious to find the Quicksort. And it is even less obvious that $O(n \log n)$ is actually the fastest possible way to sort.
- Third, designers are always dealing with trade-offs. For example, when searching is frequent, a designer will pay the cost of the index to enable binary search.

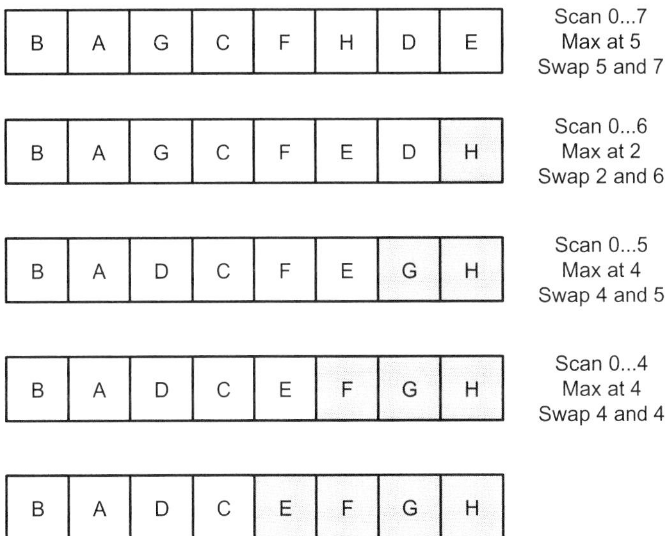

Figure 6.2
A sorted list can be constructed from an unsorted one by the method of successive maxima. Here an array of eight items in positions 0–7 are to be sorted. In the first pass (*first row*), the maximum element is found by examining all the positions; it is "H" at position 5. The elements at position 5 and 7 are exchanged, leaving the maximum at position 7. This is repeated on the shorter list (*second row*) of items 0–6, and again for 0–5 and so on. It finishes with the 0–1 row. The total number of comparisons is 8+7+...+1. The sum of the first n integers is $n(n + 1)/2$; for this problem, that comes to 36 comparisons. This method is order $O(n^2)$.

The examples above illustrate $O(\log n)$, $O(n)$, and $O(n^2)$. Here is an example of an algorithm that is $O(n^3)$.

Example 4. Matrix Multiply

A matrix is a square array of numbers, with n rows and n columns for a total of n^2 elements. In linear algebra we represent a set of equations as the product of a vector of unknowns and a matrix of coefficients. We express the solution to the equations as the multiplication of matrices. The matrix multiplication operation is very fundamental and is used in software of many applications; one of the most common is in graphics, such as on tablet computers and smartphones, where rotations and projections of objects are computed with matrix multiply operations. The software does this so fast that we do not perceive the representation; we only "see" the object on the screen or observe it rotating. Users do not ordinarily see matrix multiplications because they are buried in software

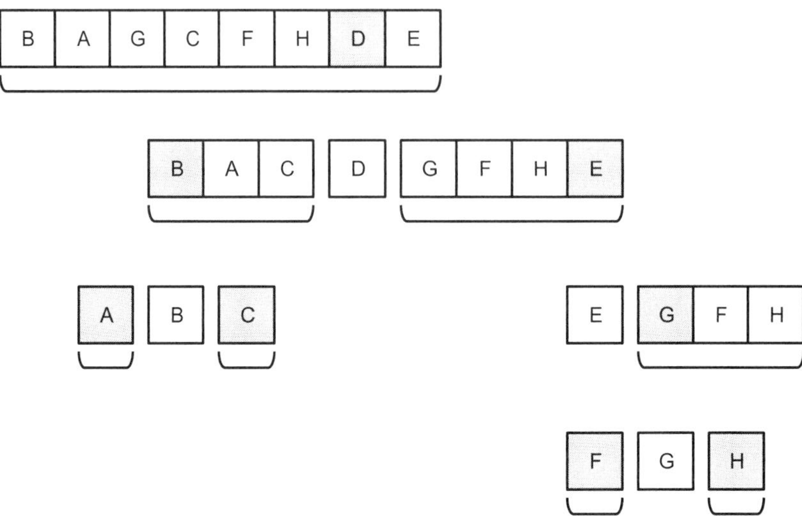

Figure 6.3
Quicksort attempts to divide a sorted list in half so that all elements in the left part are smaller than all elements in the right part. To do this, we select an element at random in the first list (D) and then move elements less than or equal to D to the left and larger to the right (second row). Now there is a list of size 3 to D's left and of size 4 to D's right. The left list is sorted by the same principle, where B was the random choice. The right list is sorted by the same principle, where E was the random choice. This is repeated all the way down to singleton lists. In a real implementation the sublists are indicated by pairs of pointers into the original list, and swapping is used to move items to the left or right. Thus, when the singleton lists are encountered, they are already in their proper places. If each selection of a random element divides the list in two, Quicksort would require about $\log_2 n$ passes, and each pass would examine all the elements, for a total time of order $O(n \log_2 n)$.

libraries, but they are ubiquitous. The nominal time to multiply two $n \times n$ matrices by the standard method shown in linear algebra books is $O(n^3)$ (see figure 6.4).[1]

The four examples we have just seen are all common problems for which we know fast solutions. Their computational work is of order $O(n^k)$ for a constant k. $O(\log n)$ is covered because it is even faster than $O(n)$.

Computer scientists have lumped all the problems that can be solved with algorithms of $O(n^k)$ for all k as "polynomial" because the computational work is measured by a polynomial in n with lead term n^k. They have established the convention that polynomial order problems are "easy" because

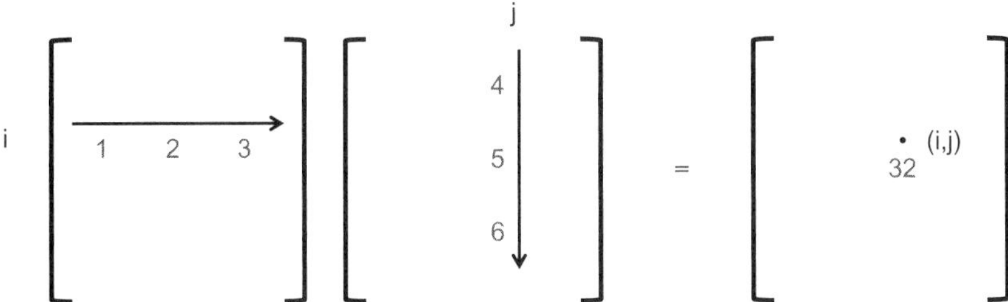

Figure 6.4
The square-matrix multiply algorithm combines two square ($n \times n$) matrices into a single matrix of the same size. The standard rule for computing the element at position (i,j) in the result matrix is "multiply row i of the first matrix by column j of the second." The multiplication of the two lists is defined as the sum of the products of the individual pairs. In the example shown, $n = 3$, and we multiply the list $(1,2,3) \cdot (4,5,6) = (1 \cdot 4) + (2 \cdot 5) + (3 \cdot 6) = 4 + 10 + 18 = 32$. This is called the "dot product." Each dot product takes n multiplies and $n - 1$ additions for a total of $2n - 1$ operations. This must be repeated n^2 times, one for each element of the result. The total work is $n^2(2n - 1) = 2n^3 - n^2$, which is $O(n^3)$.

they work well in most practical cases. There are many other problems whose solution methods are much slower. We consider these next.

Exponentially Hard Functions

Any problem relying on an enumeration is potentially harder. Suppose you have to examine each state of a state space to find out if it satisfies a property. You can make a list of all states with the property, but the time will be proportional to the size of the state space. For large state spaces, that will be a long time.

Example 5. All Ten-Digit Numbers
It seems easy to print out all the ten-digit numbers. Because there are 10^{10} of them, the algorithm would be

For $i=0 \ldots 10^{10}-1$, print i

That algorithm takes time $O(10^{10})$. How much time is that? On a fast modern chip running at 1 GHz (10^9 operations per second), it is about 10 seconds. How much paper would we need? Assume we print in very small font, getting 500 numbers to a page in five columns of 100. With two-sided printing we get 1000 (10^3) numbers to a sheet; hence, we need $10^{10}/10^3 = 10^7$ sheets. A box of twenty reams of paper contains 10,000 sheets; we need

$10^7/10^4 = 10^3$ boxes. At 3 cubic feet per box, we need a storeroom 10×30 and 10 feet high. That printout will not fit on a desktop.

Even if we had the storeroom, the situation is much worse. A fast printer can produce one sheet per second. The whole job would take 10^7 seconds, which is about 4 months.

The difficulty is not the algorithm but the time required to enumerate all the states. In the powers-of-10 table in chapter 3 on Information, we saw that a relatively small exponent can generate extremely large numbers. Any algorithm that requires exponential time is guaranteed to be hard.

Example 6. Pack the Knapsack

The knapsack problem is an old problem in operations research.[2] We are given a knapsack of a given size. We are also given a set of n objects of sizes $\{s_1,\ldots,s_n\}$ and their associated values $\{v_1,\ldots,v_n\}$. We want to find the maximum-value subset of the objects that fits in the knapsack.

The knapsack problem models many practical situations. One is the obvious camper with a limited pack having to decide which items to take on the hike. Another is a shipping department that has to fill its trucks with maximum-value loads. Still another is an assembly line manager trying to schedule jobs against a deadline and maximize profit.

This problem is difficult because with large n, there are many possible subsets; in fact there are 2^n of them (see figure 6.5). It could take a very long time to enumerate them all, compute their sizes and values, and then select the subset of maximum value from among those that fit. Such a search method will require time $O(2^n)$. For example, with ten items, the search examines 1000 subsets, with twenty items 1 million subsets, and with thirty items 1 billion subsets. No one has found an algorithm better than this. Neither has anyone proved that no faster algorithm exists.

Exponential searches can be sidestepped with heuristics. A common heuristic for the knapsack problem computes the value/space ratio for each item, then packs items into the knapsack in order of decreasing ratio until no more will fit. The sorting component dominates the linear search component and determines the heuristic's running time, $O(n \log n)$. Unfortunately, the heuristic is not guaranteed to find the best subset (see figure 6.5).

Example 7. Visit All the Cities

Every package delivery service is interested in this problem: What is the shortest tour of n cities for the delivery truck? This is commonly known as the traveling salesman problem. We can find the shortest tour with a

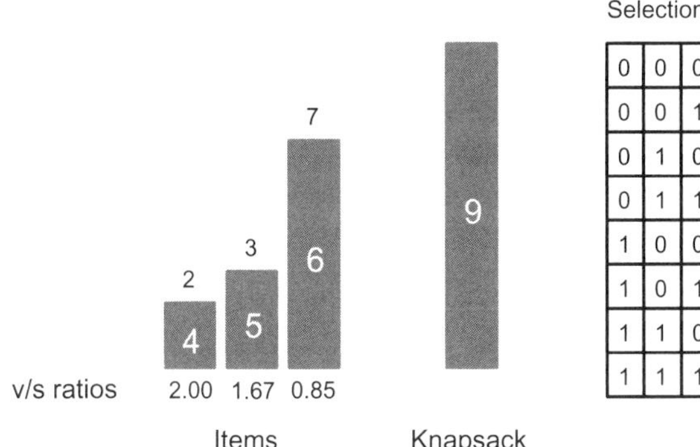

Selections			Total size	Total value
0	0	0	0	0
0	0	1	7	6
0	1	0	3	5
0	1	1	10	
1	0	0	2	4
1	0	1	9	10
1	1	0	5	9
1	1	1	12	

Figure 6.5
The knapsack problem aims to find a maximum-value subset of n items that fits into a given-size knapsack. In this example, we have three items of sizes {2,3,7} and respective values {4,5,6}. The knapsack is of size 9. The table shows an enumeration of the eight subsets of three objects in the left columns, where 1 means the item is included in the subset and 0 means it is excluded. The next column is the total size of the subset. The final column shows the values of the subsets that fit (their total sizes are 9 or less). The subset of items {1,3} is the solution. A heuristic approach is to label each item with its value/space ratio, then to put them into the knapsack in the decreasing order of the ratios until no more items fit. This strategy yields the subset {1,2} (second last row), which is close, but not the maximum value.

search: first, enumerate all the possible tours as permutations of the cities; second, calculate the length of each tour. The solution is the shortest tour.

How long would it take to accomplish this? Each tour can be constructed by choosing a first city (n choices), then a second ($n - 1$ choices), and so on until all n cities are chosen. The total number of choices is $n! = (n)(n - 1)(n - 2) \ldots (2)(1)$. This method is of order $O(n!)$. Sterling's approximation for large factorial is $n^n e^{-n}\sqrt{(2\pi n)}$, which can be astronomically large for relatively small values of n. For example 100! is on the order of 10^{158}. If we had a fast processor at clock rate 10 GHz, and if we could evaluate one tour per clock tick, we could evaluate 10^{10} tours a second, or about 10^{17} tours a year (there are 3.14×10^7 seconds/year), or about 10^{19} tours a century. The entire computation would take 10^{139} centuries. By comparison, the life of the universe is about 10^7 centuries. That is intractable!

As with the knapsack problem, heuristic methods have done very well. In 2004 a group in Sweden deployed a battery of heuristics to find the optimal tour of the 24,978 cities in Sweden. It took them about a century of CPU time spread over ninety-six processors.[3]

Example 8. Factoring a Composite Number

A composite number is the product of two or more prime numbers. In cryptography many important algorithms depend on composite numbers that are the product of exactly two primes. The RSA cryptosystem, for example, uses two large primes as its secret key and their product as the basis of the public key (Rivest et al. 1978). The public key is safe because no one knows a fast algorithm for factoring such a number into its two primes. All the known algorithms for integer factoring require a search over about $2^{n/2}$ possible divisors, making them exponentially hard. RSA is the only public key cryptosystem known to be secure. However, with a fast factoring algorithm, the two primes could be quickly extracted from a public key and the RSA cryptosystem would be useless.

At the current state of the art in hardware and factoring algorithms, 2056-bit public keys are secure, but may be crackable by 2020; 4096-bit public keys would be uncrackable forever. In 1994 Peter Shor found a quantum algorithm that factors in polynomial time. If and when a quantum computer is built, the RSA system could become obsolete.

These examples show that unless we can find a way to the answer without enumerating and searching the whole space, we can easily find ourselves facing a computation that cannot be done in the remaining lifetime of the universe.

The root cause is exponential (or worse) growth in the size of the search space. In chapter 2 we gave a table of the powers of 1000 and their prefix names including giga, tera, peta, exa, and zetta. Even our names cannot keep up with the growth. We now carry a zettabyte of data each year on the Internet, and there is only one remaining prefix (yatto), which will be surpassed in a few more years.

The conclusion is that problems of order $O(2^n)$ or $O(n!)$ are incomprehensibly harder in computational work than any of the polynomial problems. We call these exponentially hard problems.

From a practical standpoint, these problems are not solvable even for relatively small inputs. The only way around this is to use heuristics, approximations that search only a very small subset of the state space. We know of heuristics that give fast solutions, but we usually do not know how close to optimal they are. The Swedish group was fortunate that their heuristics found a traveling salesman tour they could prove is optimal.

Unfortunately, the only known algorithms guaranteed to solve exponentially hard problems are enumeration methods. These problems are common and pervasive. Researchers have searched for years to find faster algorithms for them, so far to no avail.

Hard but Verifiable Problems

Exponentially hard decision problems have an interesting feature: a solution can be verified quickly. Consider the knapsack problem stated as a decision problem: Is there a solution of value at least k? This decision form is no easier than the original problem. However, it takes linear time to demonstrate whether or not a proposed solution has value at least k—just add up the sizes and value of the selected items. Similarly with the cities problem, it takes linear time to demonstrate whether or not a proposed tour exceeds k.

We have already seen that computer scientists have introduced the notation "P" for the set of problems that can be decided in polynomial time. The P stands for polynomial. Any problem in P can be decided in time $O(n^k)$ for constant k.

Computer scientists have introduced the notation "NP" for the set of problems that can be *verified* in polynomial time. The NP stands for nondeterministic polynomial. Nondeterministic is a technical name for being able to magically guess the correct solution and verify it in polynomial time. All the algorithms we know for NP problems have computation time exponential or worse, and yet for each one a single guess can be verified in $O(n^k)$ time.

We need a little notation to discuss NP problems. For any problem A in NP, there is a polynomial algorithm V_A in P, its verifier. $V_A(x,y)$ verifies that $A(x) = y$. $V_A(x,y)$ is a decision problem because its output is 0 or 1 (see figure 6.6).

Note that a verifier can be used to find a solution to A. Suppose we want to compute $A(x)$ for a given x and we know that solution contains at most n bits. We can enumerate all the binary numbers $y = 0, 1, \ldots, 2^n - 1$ and compute $V_A(x,y)$. If any one verifies, we have found $A(x)$. This search procedure is $O(2^n)$ and is therefore exponentially hard. A direct algorithm for $A(x)$ might be faster than this search procedure. The verifier search procedure is not necessarily the best solution method.

NP Completeness

That problems in NP have polynomial-time verifiers once kindled hope that there might be undiscovered ways to solve NP problems in polynomial

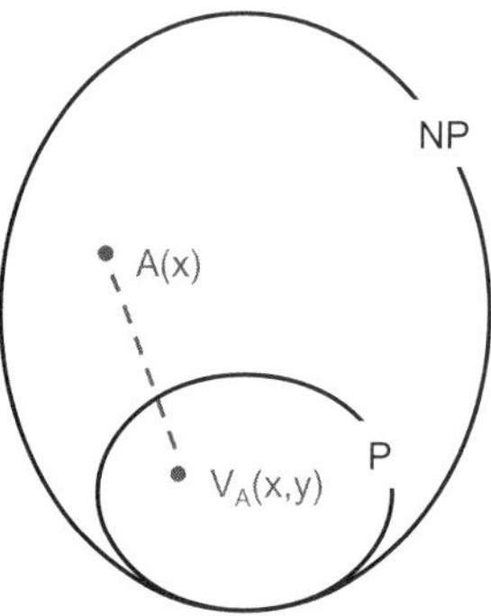

Figure 6.6
This Venn diagram shows the relation between the decision-problem classes P (polynomial) and NP (nondeterministic polynomial). Every decision problem $A(x)$ in NP has a verifier $V_A(x,y)$ in P that answers the question "Is $A(x) = y$?" Most problems whose best-known algorithms are exponentially hard are in NP because we can verify a proposed solution quickly. It is not known whether there are undiscovered methods for solving NP problems quickly. That is the P = NP question, which is one of the most important open problems in mathematics and computer science.

time. We will soon see that if this were so for even one member of a special class of NP problems, then every problem in NP could be solved in polynomial time. That would make P = NP. It has never been proved whether or not P = NP. That question is one of the most important open questions in mathematics and computer science (Cormen et al 2009).

Scientists and engineers often solve new problems by "reducing" them to previous problems for which they already have the answer. For example, electronic engineers use general circuit simulators to tell if the circuits they are designing work properly. It is easier to describe the new circuit with a description language for the simulator than it is to build a special simulator for that circuit alone.

Algorithm researchers use the same notion to discover relationships between problem-solving methods. Suppose that we can transform an instance of a problem that method *A* might solve into a form that method *B* can solve. We can then use *B* to get the answer to *A*. This is called a reduction of *A* to *B*. A reduction shows that the target method *B* is at least as powerful as *A*.

We insist, of course, that the reducing transformation be fast—that is, polynomial. If the conversion takes exponential time, then there is no point in trying to use B because the transformation would eliminate all hope of a fast (polynomial time) solution to A.

What if we could find a *single* problem B in NP to which every A in NP reduces in polynomial time? The solver for such a problem would work for every problem in NP. This could make our search for a fast algorithm for NP problems easier: if we find a fast algorithm for a master problem B, we can use it to solve every NP problem A fast.

In 1971 Steve Cook introduced the term "NP complete" for the master problems in NP. He noted that if there are multiple master problems, each would reduce to the others, and a fast algorithm for any one of them would yield a fast algorithm for every problem in NP.

Steve Cook's first NP complete problem was called circuit satisfiability (CSAT). A simple Boolean circuit is a set of interconnected logic gates (AND, OR, NOT) without a loop. It takes an input x—a set of 0 and 1 signals on its input wires—and produces an output 0 or 1. The circuits of a CPU are examples of complicated Boolean circuits with multiple outputs.

Let C be a circuit with n input wires. A configuration of those inputs can be represented as an n-bit binary number x. Then $C(x)$ is either 0 or 1. The CSAT question is: Is there an x that makes $C(x) = 1$?

CSAT is clearly in NP because we can rapidly verify whether a given x produces output 1 by tracing signals in the circuit. However, the best algorithm known for answering the satisfiability question enumerates all the possible x's and tests each one; it is $O(2^n)$.

Cook's method of reducing any problem A in NP to CSAT was based on its verifier V_A. The verifier $V_A(x,y)$ is 1 if $A(x) = y$. Here is an outline of the reduction transformation.

Generate a circuit for $CV_A(x,y)$ corresponding to the verifier $V_A(x,y)$. This circuit mimics the operation of the CPU with a series of stages, each capable of executing one instruction of the verifier algorithm. A stage maps an entire machine configuration (program, memory, CPU stateword, x, y) before an instruction execution to the configuration after an instruction execution. The mapping is done with a copy of the entire CPU circuit. Because the verifier algorithm completes in $O(n^k)$ steps, where n = size(x) + size(y), its circuit has $O(n^k)$ stages. This circuit is enormously complicated. It has to represent each bit of memory and CPU state as a signal on a wire between stages, and the number of stages can be huge.

Once have the $V_A(x,y)$ simulator circuit, we modify it slightly into a circuit $C_x(y)$ by fixing the x values to those given at input and leaving only the

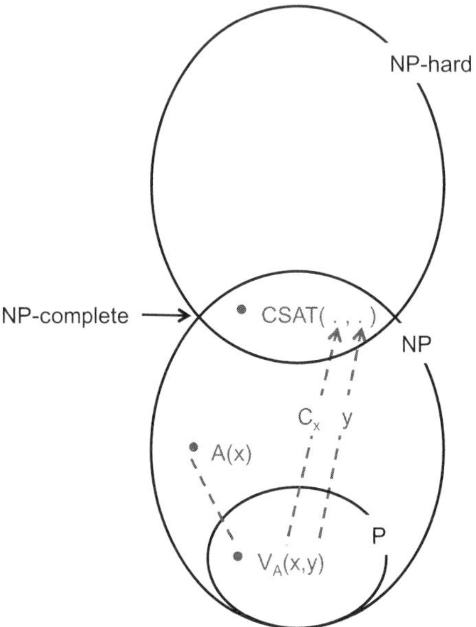

Figure 6.7
A problem to which any problem in NP can be reduced is called NP-hard. The circuit satisfiability problem (CSAT) is an example of an NP-hard problem that is also in NP. CSAT answers "Is there is an input that causes the given circuit to output a 1?" Any problem A in NP can be reduced to CSAT by constructing a circuit that simulates the verifier for fixed input x and variable input y [$C_x(y)$]. If CSAT says "y verifies circuit $C_x(y)$," then $y= A(x)$ is also verified. CSAT was the first example of an NP-complete problem.

y values unspecified. When $C_x(y)$ is satisfiable, there is a y such that $C_x(y) = 1$, which can only be if $A(x) = y$. Thus, CSAT's answer to this circuit is the value of y making $A(x) = y$ (see figure 6.7).

Because CSAT is in NP and any other problem in NP reduces to it, CSAT is NP-complete.

Shortly after Cook showed that CSAT is NP-complete, Richard Karp (1972) produced a list of twenty-one other problems that are also NP-complete. A few years later, Garey and Johnson (1979) cataloged 3000 common problems in science, engineering, business, and more; all are NP-complete. This finding is profound. If someone should find a fast algorithm for any of these 3000 problems, that algorithm would translate into fast algorithms for the remaining NP-complete problems and all the problems in NP. A huge number of real problems that are currently thought to be intractable would become tractable. Here is a partial list of NP-complete problems:

- Circuit SAT (considered above). Is there an input that makes the circuit's output 1?
- SAT (Boolean satisfiability). Is there a set of values that makes a given Boolean formula true?
- Knapsack problem. Is there a solution to a knapsack of value at least *V*?
- Subset sum. Given a set of numbers, is there a nonempty subset that sums to *K*?
- Unscrambling words. What dictionary word(s) are obtained by unscrambling a random sequence of letters?
- Hamiltonian path. Is there a path visiting all nodes of a graph exactly once?
- Traveling salesman. What is the shortest tour of a set of cities on a map?
- Cliques. In a social network, find sets of nodes that all know each other.
- Deadlocks. Find a set of nodes in a network each stopped, waiting for a signal to arrive from another node in the set.
- Graph or network questions:
  - Coloring. What is the smallest number of colors such that no two adjacent nodes of a graph have the same color?
  - Node cover. Find a minimum set of nodes (vertices) in a network that collectively touch every edge of the graph.
  - Subgraph isomorphism. Does a given graph contain a subgraph isomorphic to another given graph?
  - Independent set. Find a set of nodes (vertices) in a network none of which is adjacent to any other in the set.
  - Dominating set. Find a smallest subset of nodes (vertices) in a network so that every node outside the set is adjacent to a node in the set.

Many of these are stated as graph problems because graphs are such a convenient representation for the many networks we encounter every day.

Despite many great minds trying to find fast algorithms for these problems, no one has done so. This is taken as strong empirical evidence that there is no fast solution to any NP-complete problem, and hence that P ≠ NP.

Fortnow (2009, 2013) speculated about how the world would change if a fast algorithm were found for any NP-complete problem. Such a find would prove P = NP. He predicted that would precipitate an economic revolution as many hard problems became tractable. Others are not so sure because the tremendous progress with heuristics has come up with many acceptably good approximations for real-life instances of these problems, and the optimal solutions would not be such a giant step forward.

Noncomputable Problems

In the 1930s the mathematicians looking at computing all realized that there had to be functions that were not computable. The reason is that there are not enough programs to go around for all the functions. The technical way of saying this is that the set of all possible programs is denumerable, whereas the set of all possible functions is nondenumerable: the function space is a higher order of infinity than the programs space. Figure 6.8 sketches why this is so.

This would be of no interest if the noncomputable functions did not impact our daily lives. In fact, they do. There are many things we would like to know that cannot be computed. Turing's example (1937) was the halting problem: Can we inspect a program and its input and decide whether the program halts for that input or not? It is usually not obvious whether a program halts because the conditions that terminate loops may not be known ahead of time. Programs that do not halt loop forever. Whatever method we might design to decide halting cannot rely on simulation because the program we are asking about might enter an infinite loop and our simulator would fail to decide anything. We would dearly love to have a test that tells us, prior to execution, whether a program contains an infinite loop. However, there is no such test.

Turing's proof that the halting problem is a noncomputable well-defined function is an exercise in logic. He supposes to the contrary that a program H exists that evaluates to $H(P,x) = 1$ if program $P(x)$ halts and to 0 if $P(x)$ does not halt. We have to assume that suitable binary codes have been devised to represent programs (such as P) and their inputs (such as x). If the program H exists, we can use it as a subroutine in the program G shown in figure 6.9. A paradox arises if we present G with a copy of its own program. No matter what we assume G does in the case that its input is a copy of its own program, we get a contradiction. Therefore our assumption that H can exist as a software module is invalid.

This contradiction is monstrous! Many people find this proof mindboggling, and react as though it is a parlor trick.

The famous statement "This sentence is false" presents a similar kind of paradox. It seems to be a legitimate statement, and yet it contradicts itself the moment you assume it is true or false. Or, consider Bertrand Russell's question: "If the only barber in town shaves only those who do not shave

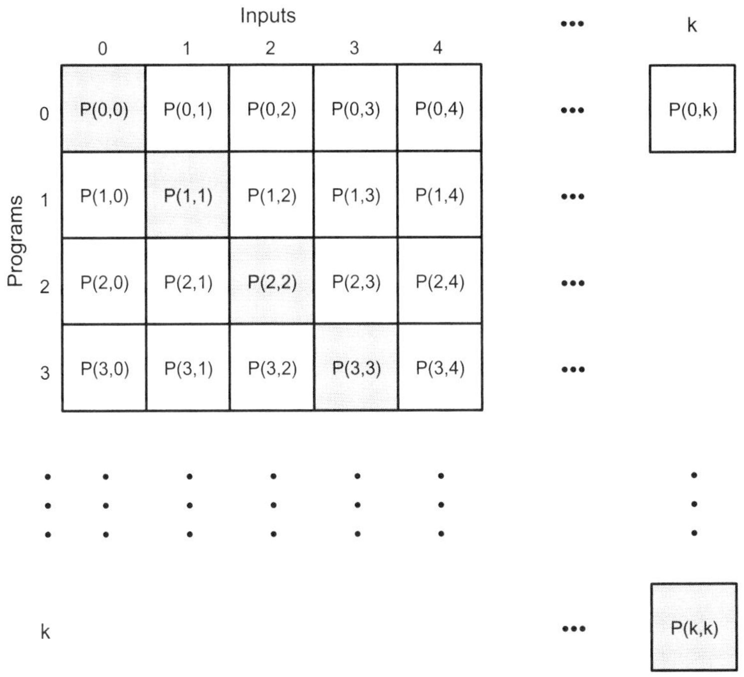

Inputs

Programs	0	1	2	3	4	•••	k
0	P(0,0)	P(0,1)	P(0,2)	P(0,3)	P(0,4)	•••	P(0,k)
1	P(1,0)	P(1,1)	P(1,2)	P(1,3)	P(1,4)	•••	
2	P(2,0)	P(2,1)	P(2,2)	P(2,3)	P(2,4)	•••	
3	P(3,0)	P(3,1)	P(3,2)	P(3,3)	P(3,4)	•••	
⋮	⋮	⋮	⋮	⋮	⋮		⋮
k						•••	P(k,k)

Figure 6.8

A diagonalization argument shows why there are too few programs for all the possible functions. We can enumerate all the possible inputs to programs along the top simply by noticing that every integer is a possible binary string that could be input to a program. We can enumerate all the possible programs down the side by a more elaborate procedure: we generate each possible number and test its binary string through a compiler to see if it represents a valid program; if so, we add it to the programs list. Then *P(i,j)* represents the output of program *i* when its input is *j*. Because every program and every input appears somewhere in the array, all programs and inputs are accounted for. However, if we change all the diagonal elements—for example, replacing *P(k,k)* with *P(k,k)* + 1—the sequence of diagonal values defines a new program. But that program cannot be listed in the array, for if it were listed, it would conflict in at least one output with every other program already there. This form of argument was used by the mathematician Georg Cantor to prove that there are more real numbers than rational numbers. It is sometimes called a "Cantor diagonalization."

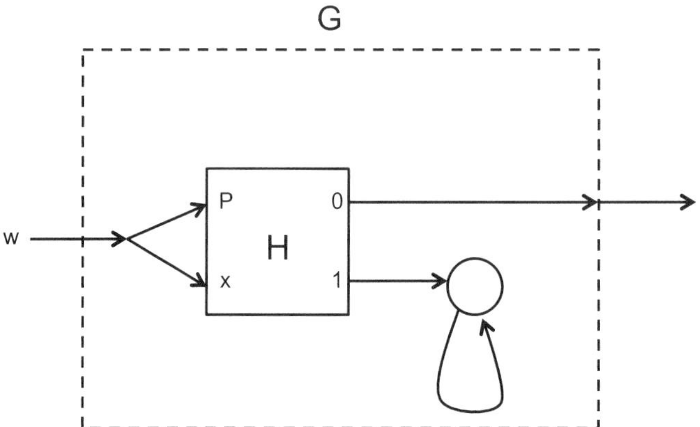

Figure 6.9
If the halting problem were solvable, there would be a computable function H that tells whether $P(x)$ halts (1) or not (0). Because it is computable, we can write a software module H containing the method. Then we can build a larger software module G by including H as a subprocedure. G asks whether $H(w,w)$ halts. If the answer is "yes" (1), G enters an infinite loop. If the answer is "no" (0), G simply returns the 0 output of H. A contradiction arises if the input $w = G$; that is, it is a copy of G's program. If we assume $G(G)$ halts, then $H(G,G) = 1$, which forces G into an infinite loop. If we assume $G(G)$ does not halt, then $H(G,G) = 0$, in which case G halts. Both assumptions—$G(G)$ halts and $G(G)$ does not halt—lead to contradictions. Therefore our assumption that H is computable must be incorrect.

themselves, who shaves the barber?" A contradiction arises as soon as you assume the barber does shave himself (or not).

The root of the paradox is self-reference. Whenever we can construct a sentence that asserts a property about itself, a paradox is possible. This is what the program G is doing. When it is asked to make a statement about itself, it is paradoxical and makes no sense.

In the case of the halting problem the paradox means we cannot build a halting-tester program. The moment we try, we hit a contradiction. The rules of logic will not let us do it.

There is no way out of the contradiction. A common attempt to avoid the contradiction is to add a test to the beginning of the G program to notice whether the input is G's own program; if so, G returns 0 immediately. The problem with this is that there are many (in fact, infinitely many) programs that implement any given function. A trivial example is the addition function $A(x) = x + 1$; it could be implemented as $x + M - N$ for any integers M and N such that $M = N + 1$. So even if G can refuse to operate if its input is G, there will be some other input G' that computes the same function and will trigger the contradiction because $G(G')$ is a paradox.

There are numerous other noncomputable problems of practical interest. In each case we discover that a proposed solution would also decide the halting problem, which contradicts the undecidability of the halting problem. Examples:

- Busy beaver problem. $BB(x)$ is the maximum number of moves any program consisting of x instructions can generate and still halt. [If we could compute BB we could solve the halting problem by simulating a program of x instructions for $BB(x)$ steps—if it has not halted by then, it will not halt.]
- Totality problem. Does $A(x)$ halt for every possible input x? [If so, we construct $B(x)$ that ignores x and computes $F(y)$ for any chosen function F with chosen input y. Then B halts on all inputs if and only if $F(y)$ halts.]
- Equivalence problem. Do programs A and B compute the same function? In other words, is $A(x) = B(x)$ for all inputs x? [Construct $B(x)$ to run $A(x)$ and output 1 if and when $A(x)$ halts. Construct $C(x)$ that ignores x and simply outputs 1. An algorithm that decides whether B and C are equivalent answers the totality problem for $A(x)$.]
- Line of code problem. Does any particular (given) line of code in a program ever get executed? [Modify the program so that that line is executed if and only if $A(x)$ halts.]
- Correspondence problem. Given two codes, A and B, is there a message sequence $x_1, x_2, x_3, \ldots x_K$ such that $A(x_1)A(x_2) \ldots A(x_K) = B(x_1)B(x_2) \ldots B(x_K)$? The same message sequence produces the same encoding in the two codes. For example let $A = (a, ab, bba)$ and $B = (baa, aa, bb)$; the message sequence 3231 gives *bbaabbbaa* in both codes. [We can devise codes that represent single-instruction executions of a program so that $A(i)$ is the machine configuration just before instruction i is executed, and $B(i)$ just after. We can get the A and B sequences to match if and only if the program halts. In other words this system is powerful enough to enable us to encode the execution of a program. If a solution to the Correspondence Problem exists, it tells us the encoded program halts.]

There are many more examples of practical things we would like to know about programs, all of which are undecidable. We know that these are not computable because we have shown that, if we could decide any of these questions, we could use that method to decide halting problems.

Any by-inspection method that purports to answer almost any interesting question about code could also decide the halting question. Alan Turing used this observation to conclude that the actions that mathematicians perform while proving theorems are inherently computational, and thus, even "by inspection" methods are computational; and a computational method answering a question about another computational method can usually be fooled into asking that question of itself. That always generates a contradiction.

Conclusions

We have covered a lot of ground in this chapter. Let us summarize the key points.

All computational methods take time and consume energy. We estimate time (or energy) by counting the number of instructions executed.

We use the order notation $O(f(n))$ to say that for large n, the instruction count of a computation grows proportion to $f(n)$. The notation ignores constants and focuses only on long-term growth. For example, a computation whose time is $An + B$ is $O(n)$ regardless of A and B; for large n, its growth is proportional to n.

All problems (functions) can be rated by the difficulty of their best known algorithms. For example, sorting is $O(n \log n)$ because the best algorithm takes time proportion to $n \log n$. There are worse sorting algorithms, $O(n^2)$ for example.

Many problems are formulated as decision problems with yes (1) or no (0) answers. For example, does program $A(x)$ halt? Is there a path through all the cities of length less than k? Other problems are stated as optimizations. For example, find the best knapsack or shortest tour. For consistency we recast optimization problems into associated decision problems. The optimization version of a problem is always at least as difficult as the decision version.

We group into the class P all the problems whose decision procedures require polynomial time. We group into the class NP all problems for which a solution can be verified in polynomial time. Even if the only known solution method of an NP problem A is exponential, its verifier is polynomial. The verifier could be used to find a solution to A, but to do so it would have to search through all the values of input and might actually be slower than A. The question of whether P = NP is considered one of the most important open questions in mathematics and computer science.

Reduction is a process of transforming a problem for one method A into a problem for another method B, such that the solution from B is also the solution to A. "A reduces to B" means that B is powerful enough to answer all A inputs.

A problem is NP-complete if all problems in NP reduce to it. The circuit satisfiability problem CSAT is an NP-complete problem. Every NP-complete problem can be reduced to any other. A polynomial-time algorithm for any one could be transformed to a polynomial-time algorithm for any other. There are over 3000 known NP-complete problems from all parts of science, engineering, economics, and social sciences. That means that the best algorithms we know for any of these problem are exponential or worse. It also gives empirical evidence for believing that $P \neq NP$ because thousands of people have been unsuccessful at finding a fast method for any of those problems.

There is also a large class of undecidable problems such as the halting problem. These problems are undecidable because they ultimately allow a program that can answer a question about any program to ask that question of itself, producing a paradox. It is logically impossible to answer these questions.

We are left with a dilemma. Many of the problems we would like a computer to solve for us are so complex that they will never return an answer within a reasonable time. Other problems are logically impossible to compute. As a result we rely heavily on heuristics (approximation methods) that are fast but do not decide or optimize accurately for every input. We rely on experimental methods to characterize when heuristics work or do not work. The limitations imposed by computational complexity force us to be experimental in understanding computations.

7 Memory

In the Internet, retrieval is worse than looking for a needle in a haystack; it's looking for a specific needle in a needle stack.

—Hubert Dreyfus

Cache randomly accessed disk pages that are reused every five minutes.

—Jim Gray and Franco Putzolu

"Can I find it?" is one of the most common questions in computing. The information we seek is stored somewhere in "memory," a simple word that belies the complexity and vastness of storage systems. It is important not only to find information quickly in memory but also to move it rapidly to where it is needed.

The structure of a storage system has a major effect on performance. As an example of the difficulties, consider a weather forecast scenario. The algorithm designers divided the forecast region into 10,000 small atmospheric cubes and assigned each one to its own 1-GHz processor on a supercomputer. They ask whether the system can realize the 10 THz combined processing rate of this bank of processors. If it could, they reckon, tomorrow's forecast would be available in 3 hours. But suppose their algorithm, running on each processor, pauses every million instructions (1 millisecond) to retrieve a chunk of raw weather data from a hard disk, which has access time of 10 milliseconds. The total time to complete 1 million instructions is the processor time plus the disk time, or 11 milliseconds. The effective speed is eleven times slower than the rated speed. Tomorrow's forecast would actually take 33 hours to compute. The supercomputer is useless because its memory system cannot get data to processors fast enough.

Storage has been a major concern for information systems even before general-purpose processors were invented. For instance, IBM was a business machines company long before it became a computer company in the

1950s. They built sophisticated machines for selecting and tallying data on punched cards. Companies used IBM machines to maintain payrolls, track customers, and manage inventories. IBM's introduction of disk storage in 1956 promised a revolution in business processing because warehouses of file cabinets could fit into a single disk store, where a CPU running sophisticated algorithms could retrieve and analyze data.

Computer engineers have always recognized that storage limitations are a strong throttle on a computer's actual speed. While programmers coped with small memories and engineers built larger memories, performance analysts worked out methods to forecast the speeds of computations when memory is limited.

The history of computing shows a long struggle to build memory systems that could keep up with processors and to find ways to mitigate the costs of retrieving data from local and remote disk storage devices. The engineers discovered three broad classes of principles for organizing storage so that high-speed processing is a realistic goal. The principles of *naming* are concerned with creating bit strings or alphanumeric strings that identify digital objects. The principles of *mapping* are concerned with translating a name to a connection between a processing site and the storage locations containing the digital object. The principles of *positioning* are concerned with optimizing performance by judiciously moving data from distant storage to nearby storage. One of the earliest scientific theories within computing—*locality theory*—was developed to deal with optimization of information movement in storage systems.

Memory Systems

In chapter 3 on Information we noted that information can be represented by any physical quantity capable of retaining a state that can be observed by a sensor. A large number of technologies can serve as memory systems. Table 7.1 is a taxonomy of the basic properties of memory systems. We discuss these properties in this chapter and identify the principles that bring order to potentially very complex memory systems.

Memory systems are most often seen as repositories. We store data in them and retrieve (recall) the same data later. The RAM on a desktop computer is a repository of bytes holding programs controlling the central processing unit (CPU) and data on which these programs operate. A hard disk or cloud server is a repository of files. But not all memories look like repositories. A neural net model of the brain stores patterns that are combinations of current sensory data and all previously recorded sensory data;

Table 7.1
Basic Memory Properties

Aspect	Property	Definition	Examples
Physics	States	Any physical state that can be altered and observed	Magnetic field, magnetized patch, electron spin, pockmark on a disk, direction of current in a loop, sound wave in acoustic delay line, phosphor on cathode-ray tube, neural loop
	Volatile	State disappears on power loss, very fast access.	Random Access Memory (RAM), CPU registers, CPU cache
	Persistent	State persists until changed or erased, much slower access	Hard disk, tape, compact optical disk
Storage and Recollection	Exact	Retrieved data exactly the same as previously stored data	RAM, hard disk, Internet cloud server
	Associative	Retrieved data related to stored data but not necessarily the same	Sparse distributed memory (Kanerva), associative memory, neural networks
	Verifiability	Test whether data previously stored is still present	Cloud servers, file system checking software
Access Time	Random	Access time for all locations is equal	RAM, Internet packet round-trip time (approximate)
	Positional	Access time depends on position of data in medium	Juke box, cathode ray tube, hard disk, compact disk, DVD
	Sequential	Access time depends on position in a sequence	Token ring, acoustic delay line
	Mixed positional-sequential	Access time depends on positioning something and then accessing sequence	Hard disk: position the arm; then read or write from spinning disk
Access Control	Verify at object	Object manager verifies requesting subject has permission to perform requested operation	Access control list in file or database system, access control field in directory entries
	Verify at subject	Subject manager grants permissions for specific operations on objects	Access bits in virtual memory mapping tables and capability lists, capability addressing of objects

on retrieval, the memory returns a pattern that shares characteristics with prior patterns but may not be the same as any one (see Kanerva 2003).

Memory hierarchies are permanent features of computing systems. The fastest devices are at the top because they are the only ones that can keep up with a CPU. The slower devices are lower and are used for permanent storage and backup. Data are moved upward as needed by the CPU and downward when no longer needed. However, speed at the top comes at the price of volatility—very fast memories lose their data when the power goes off. Slower devices, such as hard disks, retain their data indefinitely until they are explicitly erased. As a consequence of the hierarchy, performance optimization is not simply a matter of finding algorithms with lowest CPU instruction counts; it depends greatly on the arrangements of data in the hierarchy.

These tradeoffs are reflected in the prices of memory. In 2014, RAM with access time about 15 nanoseconds sold for about $5 a gigabyte. Hard disks with access time around 5 milliseconds sold for about $0.10 a gigabyte. These two technologies have an access time differential of over 3×10^6. What a difference from 1960, when magnetic-core RAMs and disk storage systems each cost about $0.30 a byte for up to 5 megabytes, and the access time differential was about 10^4.

Very large, fast, and persistent memories may come to be. They will depend on new technologies such as electron spins or organic states. Even so, the trade-off between speed and cost will continue to motivate a hierarchy of memory devices.

Basic Model for Memory Use

We use the subject-object model to describe the generic mechanisms of memory access. A subject is any entity that can request access to a stored digital object. A digital object is a container of a set of bits representing something. The most common example of a subject is a computational process (program in execution) acting on behalf of a particular user. For example, if user "pjd" started process "372," the memory system would allow process 372 to read memory location 433 only if subject "(pjd,372)" has read access to object "memory location 433."

This model—subjects requesting operations from objects—reveals three essential aspects of memory systems:

1. *Naming* every object, by giving the bit or symbol pattern used to designate the object and distinguish it from all others.

2. *Mapping* the name to the memory locations containing the object, thereby establishing an information flow path between the subject and the object.
3. *Authenticating* that the owner of the object has given permission for subject to complete the requested access.

Once those three steps are completed, the requested operation is performed, and information flows along the subject-object path.

Naming

Given the large number of memory technologies in use, it should be no surprise that there are numerous ways to access data. A principal reason for the variety of access methods is that data are structured to facilitate their use in specific environments. For example, a programmer sorts data to enable frequent binary searches. A company organizes its employee records with a standard record structure so that it can find all records matching search criteria specified by a manager. A library organizes its books and documents by the Dewey Decimal System so that patrons can quickly locate books in the stacks. Many fields such as medicine, biology, and accounting have developed taxonomies that facilitate identifying and classifying new objects. A data organization that works well for one purpose may fail miserably for another purpose. The unstructured Internet has disappointed many people because, despite the hype about access to all the world's information, it is a poor information retrieval system.

Yet amid all this diversity there are only six main modes of naming data. Most people use all six every day. Table 7.2 is a taxonomy.

In the first three modes the name is a fixed-length binary string—an address, address pair, or handle. *Addresses* name locations in linear address spaces; a common address size is 32 bits. Address pairs select one of many address spaces and name a location within it. *Handles* are all-time unique identifiers for objects such as files and directories; they are usually much longer than addresses, for example, 128 bits. Handles are longer because they must be unique in the whole Internet. A common way for a local operating system to generate a handle is to combine a local clock time stamp with a unique machine identifier such as the media access control (MAC) address used in local networks. Handles generated this way must be at least as long as the size of the local clock (for example, 64 bits) plus the size of a MAC address (48 bits). Because a machine cannot create two objects simultaneously, this method guarantees that no other machine

Table 7.2
Access Modes

Mode	Purpose	Mapping	Primary Uses	Examples
Fixed address (n bits)	Select a location in a linear address space spanning 2^n locations. Typically $n = 32$ or 64.	Memory hardware maps addresses to physical locations.	Locations of variables and statement labels are in machine code output from compiler. They are recognized by the hardware.	RAM, virtual memory, machine code. Internet Protocol (IP) addresses.
Fixed address pair (n bits each)	Select a location in a segmented address space spanning 2^{2n} locations. Typically $n = 32$ or 64.	Memory is divided into segments, each a linear address space. An address (s,x) selects location x of segment s.	Some compilers assign individual objects to their own segments. Some operating systems treat all files as a segmented address space.	File system, where each file is a linear sequence of bytes. Objects in Java programs.
Fixed handle (n-bit handles)	A unique n-bit identifier is assigned to every object in a system. n = 128 is typical. Handle space is sparse: very few handle strings map to anything.	Operating system maps a handle to an object descriptor, which gives details about the object in memory.	Operating systems assign unique handles to every object, including new versions. Identifiers are recognized by subsystems that manage particular kinds of objects, for example file handles are recognized by the file system.	Unix/Linux files are given unique "*i*-nodes" on creation. All publishers assign digital object identifiers (DOI) permanently distinguishing each publication from every other.

Table 7.2
(continued)

Mode	Purpose	Mapping	Primary Uses	Examples
Symbolic sequence	User objects are arranged in trees with symbolic node names. A pathname is the unique sequence of symbolic names from root to object in the tree.	Operating system represents trees as hierarchies of directories, each a list of distinct names and their associated handles.	Operating systems map pathnames to handles. Internet domain name system (DNS) maps hostnames to IP addresses. HTTP protocol maps URLs to files on specific hosts.	Users choose the names appearing in directories. Internet domain names are hierarchical. Internet URLs are pathnames.
Query statement	Formula that selects and composes matching records of a database.	Database management system selects all records matching criteria in query.	Locate records that match the query expression. Make lists, combinations, and statistical summaries.	Commercial database systems such as Oracle with MySQL interface language.
Text string	Text string that could be contained in a document.	Search system finds sets of documents that contain the text string, or something semantically "close" to it.	Find relevant documents in large collections.	Information retrieval systems used by libraries. World Wide Web search engines such as Google, Bing, Yahoo.

can generate the same handle. Because the number of objects in existence is many magnitudes smaller than the size of handle space—on order of 2^{20} objects compared with 2^{128} handles—most potential handles are never used.

In the fourth mode the name is a symbolic string that means something to users. Internet host names, file pathnames, and web URLs are examples. This mode is layered on top of the others (see figure 7.1).

The last two access modes map a symbolic expression chosen by the user to a *set* of data objects. The expression selects items from a large collection, such as employee records in a business database or documents from a library. The query mode uses a formal logic language to specify a set of criteria that match some records but not others. The text mode simply looks for documents containing a given text string. Both modes involve a lot of searching. Depending on the size of the database, for example, a query can take a few seconds to a few minutes. Google has shown that generating a list of matches for a search string can be done in less than half a second once the contents of all web pages have been processed into an index that enables a quick decision about whether a given word is in a document. It is normal to have tens of thousands or millions of "hits" in a web search. It is quite remarkable that the Google presentation algorithm orders the hit list in such a way that many users find useful information among the first ten hits (MacCormick 2012). Even so, many users find that web searching can be like looking for a specific needle in a needle stack (Dreyfus 2001) (see figure 7.2).

All six access modes provide *location independence*: users can perform operations on digital objects without knowing their locations. Location independence has been a boon since its first use in virtual memory systems of the 1960s. In virtual memories every virtual address always retrieves the proper values, no matter where the addressed data are located in the memory hierarchy. The Networked File System (NFS), introduced by Sun Microsystems (1984), lets users access files anywhere in the network simply by giving their pathnames in a global directory tree. Today's cloud data warehouses are crash-tolerant distributed systems that spread copies of data over thousands of servers without changing the name of the data. A web URL maps to a file on a host without regard to the location of the host or the internal structure of its file system. The Internet protocol routes packets to the designated server without regard to its location. The Domain Name System (DNS) converts host names to current IP addresses without regard to the geographical locations of hosts. Whenever physical location is not meaningful, systems that hide location will be simpler and more reliable to

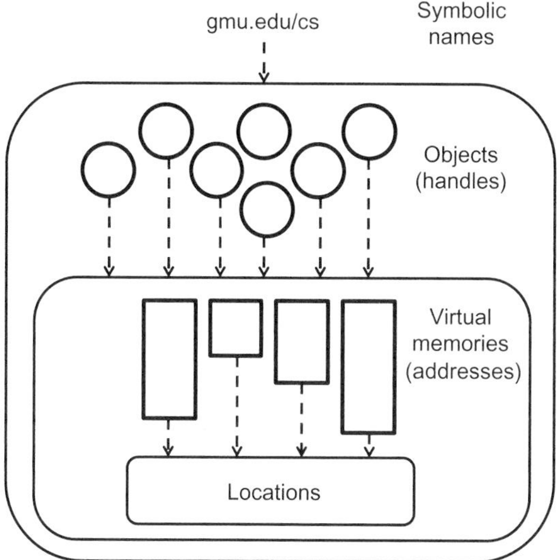

Figure 7.1

Names are designators of individual digital objects. Four kinds of names are layered on top of each other, with names at one level being mapped to names at the next lower level (*dashed arrows*). The top level comprises all the symbolic names generated by users, for example, web URLs. The next lower level comprises all the handles generated by the operating systems on the machines that create objects. To enable universal sharing of any object in the Internet, handles must be all-time unique. The next lower level comprises address spaces in virtual memories used locally by CPUs as they execute processes. The bottom level comprises locations in physical memories, such as pages of RAM or records of disks. In this example the symbolic name "gmu.edu/cs" refers to a file "cs" on the host "gmu.edu"; the name might be presented as part of a request to read a web page. The Internet Domain Name Service (DNS) converts the host name to its Internet Protocol (IP) address, and the operating system at that IP address converts "cs" to the handle of a file. The file system on that machine maps the handle to a file in the virtual memory of a process, which responds to the web page read request. The virtual memory maps the addresses of the file to the locations containing the file. The ability to change the mappings dynamically confers important advantages. For example, virtual memory components, such as pages, can be relocated without changing addresses. Files can be relocated without changing handles. New versions of digital objects can receive new handles without changing URLs.

	Name	Salary	Sex	Seniority
1	Alice	50,000	F	10
2	Bob	45,000	M	1
3	Charlotte	60,000	F	3
4	David	42,000	M	2
5	Elizabeth	55,000	F	6
6	Fred	51,000	M	15
7	Georgia	59,000	F	12

Figure 7.2
A database can be visualized as a table with many records, each having a standard set of field names. A query is a logic formula that selects the records matching criteria in the query. For example, "salary > 50000 & sex=F" matches records 3, 5, and 7. And "sex=M & seniority > 10" matches only record 6. And "sex=M & salary > 55000" matches no records. The query access method is a way of finding information by content or characteristic rather than by name. A typical query returns many items. Database systems rely on four principles to avoid data loss and inconsistences: (1) Records are replicated on multiple servers. (2) Transactions are "atomic," meaning that their entire effect is committed to the database in a single step. (3) Transaction states are temporarily recorded so that they can be rolled back in case of error. (4) Databases are stored as multiple tables that can be composed together quickly to answer a query.

use. But location independence is not always useful: many mobile device apps rely on "geolocation" services.

Internet search is the hardest of the six modes. The set of objects matching a given set of search terms is likely to be enormous—there can be thousands or millions of matching documents. URLs give virtually no clues to the content of documents. Even though Google's page-ranking algorithm does a remarkable job at presenting useful documents, users often find that the highest-ranked documents are still not useful. Moreover, a substantial amount of information is in a "deep web" of Internet-connected database systems protected by passwords and query interfaces. Search engines cannot index them. No one knows how large the "deep web" is, but most estimates put it at over 90 percent the total information on the Internet. Hence, the idea that "all the world's information is on the Internet" is misleading: most of the information is not searchable, and the searchable can still give a bad case of information overload.

Mapping

Mapping is the process of translating a name to a location. With all the different possible access modes and memory technologies, mapping technologies can become pretty complex. Fortunately, they all rest on a few simple principles.

The basic idea of a map is to implement a dynamic function F such that $F(x)$ is the current location of the object named x. The map F is stored as a table. Whenever a program requests to read (or write) object x, the operating system reads (or writes) location $F(x)$. When the operating system relocates object x, it updates the table to show the new location. Separating names from locations enables location independence—the same program can be executed no matter what configuration its objects occupy in the memory.

Virtual Memory

The mapping principle has been a cornerstone of virtual memory systems since their beginnings in the early 1960s (Kilburn et al. 1962). Virtual memory was invented to automate data movement between secondary memory (the disk) and primary memory (the RAM). Automating the moves relieved programmers of a considerable burden, thus doubling or tripling their productivity (Sayre 1969). Virtual memory systems had to solve two problems:

1. Making individual program address spaces separate and location independent.
2. Minimizing the number of very time-consuming data moves between the disk and the RAM.

Location independence is important because, with the constant movement of data in the memory, the exact locations of individual data items cannot be predicted in advance and should not matter to the program's execution. A simple version of the mapping principle, based on paging the address space, solves this problem. A program's address space is divided into equal-size blocks called pages and the RAM into similar fixed-size blocks called frames. Any page can be loaded into any frame. The execution of a RAM access is as follows: (1) a linear address from the program decomposes into page and line numbers, (2) the map converts page number to frame number, and (3) the frame number and line number recompose into a linear offset into RAM. We have learned how to do this very efficiently.[1]

Virtual memory provides a powerful means to partition RAM among multiple programs when multiprogramming (Denning 1970) (see figure 7.3).

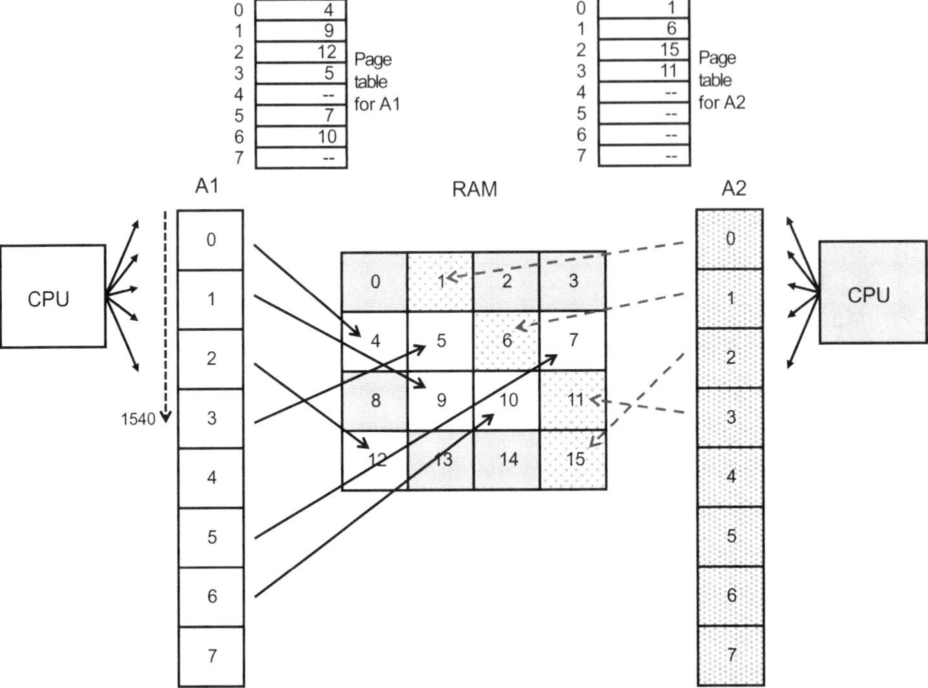

Figure 7.3
In this example two CPUs refer to objects in their separate address spaces, A1 and A2. The address spaces are divided into eight 512-byte pages, and the RAM into sixteen 512-byte frames (page holders). The CPUs use 12-bit addresses, 3 for the page number and 9 for the line number ($512 = 2^9$). The RAM uses 13-bit addresses, 4 for the frame numbers and 9 for the line number. The arrows show which pages are loaded in RAM; for example, the left CPU's page 3 is in frame 2 and the right CPU's page 3 is in frame 11. The associations indicated by the arrows are stored in page tables associated with each CPU. The page tables are stored in a private area of RAM outside every address space. The left CPU is asking for linear address 1540, which is on page 3 line 4. Using the page table, the memory mapping unit (MMU, not shown) changes that to frame 2, line 4, which is a linear offset of 1028 into RAM. Six pages of RAM are not assigned to either address space (gray). If a CPU calls for a page not in RAM, a "page fault interrupt" asks the operating system to bring the page into an empty frame and update the page table.

A CPU can access only the pages listed in its page table. Pages belonging to other address spaces are invisible; there is no way the CPU can generate their RAM frame addresses. This near-perfect isolation of address spaces is a very potent method of information protection. Many systems use virtual memory to get this benefit even when they have enough RAM to fully load every process's address space.

Minimizing data moves is the trickier problem. A complete copy of the program's address space resides in a file on the disk. At any given time only a subset of the program's pages are in RAM. The page table identifies them by marking them as "present" in RAM; in figure 7.3, for example, not-present pages are shown as blanks. If the memory mapping unit encounters a not-present page, it obviously cannot complete the translation. Instead it triggers a page fault interrupt, which invokes an operating system page-fault-handler routine to do the following: (1) move a copy of the missing page from disk to an empty frame of RAM, (2) update the page table to show the page as now present in that frame, and (3) return control to the interrupted program, which retries the address translation.

The operating system employs a replacement policy to determine which pages are in RAM. When an empty frame is needed, that policy selects a page in RAM not expected to be reused soon, synchronizes it with the disk copy, marks it as not present, and adds its frame to the free-frames list. The performance of the system is very sensitive to the replacement policy because every replaced page is a future page fault. Policies that exploit the principle of locality (discussed later in this chapter) minimize the number of replacements and allow soonest completion time. Programmers who are aware of the locality principle can arrange their data references to accentuate locality, thereby exacting even better performance from the virtual memory system (Sayre 1969).

Sharing

Unfortunately, virtual memory's ability to shield address spaces from each other stands in the way of another common objective of memory systems: allowing users to share data. Some operating systems have attempted to augment virtual memory to allow sharing, but with limited success.

One method is to provide an operating system interface that provides shared memory blocks outside address spaces. A group of processes can share memory as follows. The leader of the group requests the operating system to allocate a block of shared memory; the leader then distributes a copy of the block's pointer to the others in the group. Group members can then read and write the shared block by further calls on the operating system. When the group is done, the leader partner notifies the operating system to release the shared block. This scheme has numerous problems. It is clumsy and error prone. Synchronization of the partners to avoid race conditions in the shared memory is difficult. No one will release the shared memory if the leader crashes. The shared memory is available only to processes on the same machine sharing the same operating system.

A variation on this scheme avoids the operating system interface by loading the shared data into a frame, choosing an unused page in each address space, and mapping each chosen page to the one frame. This makes the shared frame a member of the partner process address spaces. Although it eliminates the need to call the operating system to read and write the shared page, it brings another major drawback. The page tables of all the partners must be updated if any change is made to the location of the shared page. That update can take a while if there are many partners or some of their computations are suspended.

A much better way is to define a new kind of name space for all shared objects. The handle space does this job. Capability systems embody this principle.

Capabilities

Capability addressing is a general method for sharing objects globally. Capability addressing was invented in 1966 by Jack Dennis and Earl Van Horn and has been refined over the years.[2] A capability is a large bit pattern containing a handle, an access code, and a checksum (see figure 7.4). When a subject asks the operating system to create a new object, the operating system generates a new capability with the creator as the owner. The owner can hand out copies of the capability, downgrade their rights, and even stipulate that a copy cannot be further copied.

Each process has its own capability list of all the handles it has for objects. A mapping structure based on hashing efficiently represents the associations between capabilities and objects (Fabry 1974) (see figure 7.5). Capability lists enumerate all the objects, not just pages, to which a CPU has access. Details such as whether a particular object is implemented with pages are left to the subsystems that manage that type of object.

A crucial assumption in capability addressing is that the holder of a capability has the rights specified in it. Object managers simply accept capabilities and do not check access control lists to determine if callers have permission. Theoretically, a hacker who gets inside the kernel could modify capabilities or make illegal copies. But the probability of such compromises is low enough to make the systems viable.

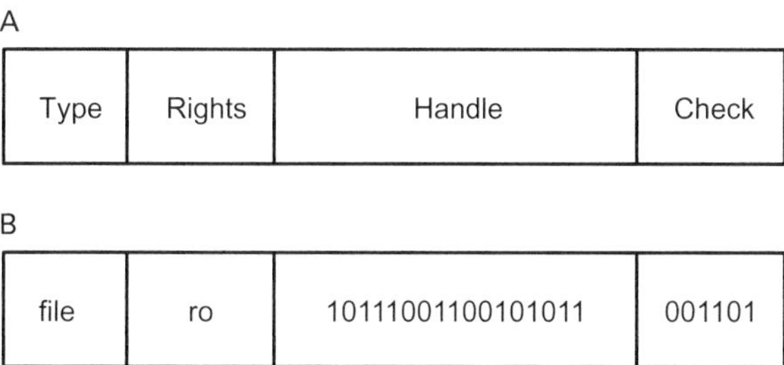

Figure 7.4
A capability (A) is a long bit pattern organized as four fields. The *type* specifies the kind of object to which the capability points, for example, a file, a database record, or an Internet connection. The *rights* field is a series of bits specifying which operations on the operation of the given type are allowed by this capability; for example, rights for a file might be four bits corresponding to the file operations open, close, read, and write. The *handle* field contains a handle. The *check* is a cryptographic checksum that can verify that the contents of the capability have not been changed since they were created. The example (B) is a file capability allowing reading and opening ("ro") of the file pointed to by the handle. The file system (object manager for files) maps handles to file locations using a hash table as in figure 7.5. The file system will accept only file capabilities; it will reject all others.

Capability systems are very effective at "confinement," which means that every computational process can be granted rights to just the objects it needs to do its job, and no others. Capability systems are highly fault tolerant because errors are confined to small protection domains and cannot propagate through the system. Capability addressing is a key principle in implementing object-oriented systems (Wulf et al. 1974, Miller 2003) such as Java, Smalltalk, and Python. It extends easily into distributed environments such as Amoeba (Tanenbaum and Mullender 1981) or Tahoe-LAFS,[3] because capabilities can be passed as parameters in messages between clients and servers in the network. The cryptographic checksums included in capabilities make them unforgeable, which means servers can trust them and accept them as proofs that their clients' accesses are authorized.

A form of the capability-addressing principle was independently discovered and implemented for digital objects in the Internet. The motivation was to overcome a limitation of the standard web URL. It is all too common that an object's owner changes the content, moves the object to a different host, or deletes the object. Customers can be unpleasantly surprised at unexpected changes of content or apparent disappearance of a critical object. In the first case the content may not be what the customers of the

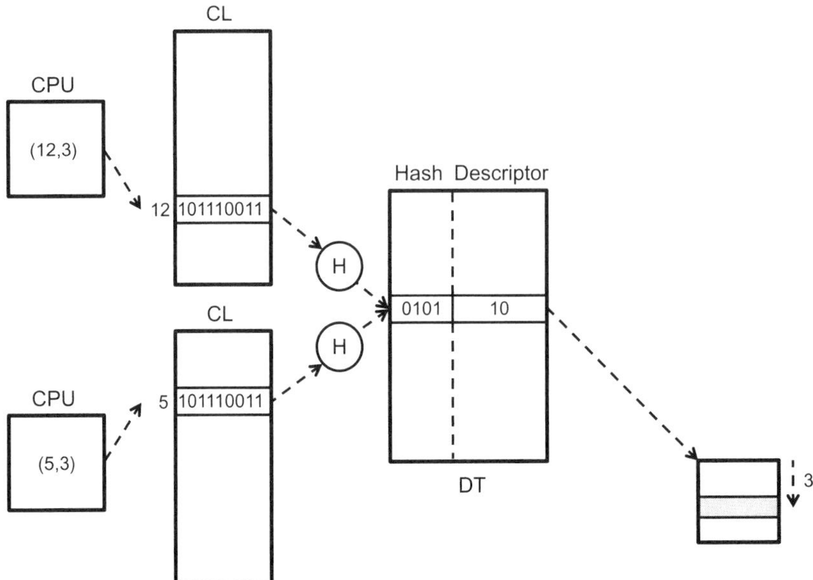

Figure 7.5
A two-level mapping structure enables sharing digital objects. The descriptor table (DT) is the only table listing the location of every object. The capabilities containing the unique handles of digital objects are stored in a process's capability list (CL). A hash function *H* maps the handle into a short hash code that quickly locates the object descriptor, which points to the memory locations containing the object. In this example the top process lists the shared object as capability 12 and the bottom CPU lists it as 5. Both CPUs are asking for line 3 in the object. The hash function converts the handles into a 4-bit hash and uses the hash to index the DT. The DT entry contains a descriptor pointing to location 10, the base address of the object. If the operating system relocates the shared object for any reason, it simply updates the descriptor to show the new base address, and all the sharing partner processes will be directed to the new location.

shared object expected; in the second and third cases there is no way to notify customers that the object has a new URL or is gone. These limitations are unacceptable for publishers, who want citations to their works to work every time and in perpetuity. To fix these problems without requiring any changes in the operating systems of network nodes, Robert Kahn and Robert Wilensky (1995) overlaid the capability-addressing principle on to the Internet. They developed a service, called handle.net, that enables users to register handles and their associated URLs; users share objects by making the handles available (see figure 7.6). The handle system provides a means to get to any registered object, even if years go by and the object has been moved to new servers and new URLs. The Library of Congress

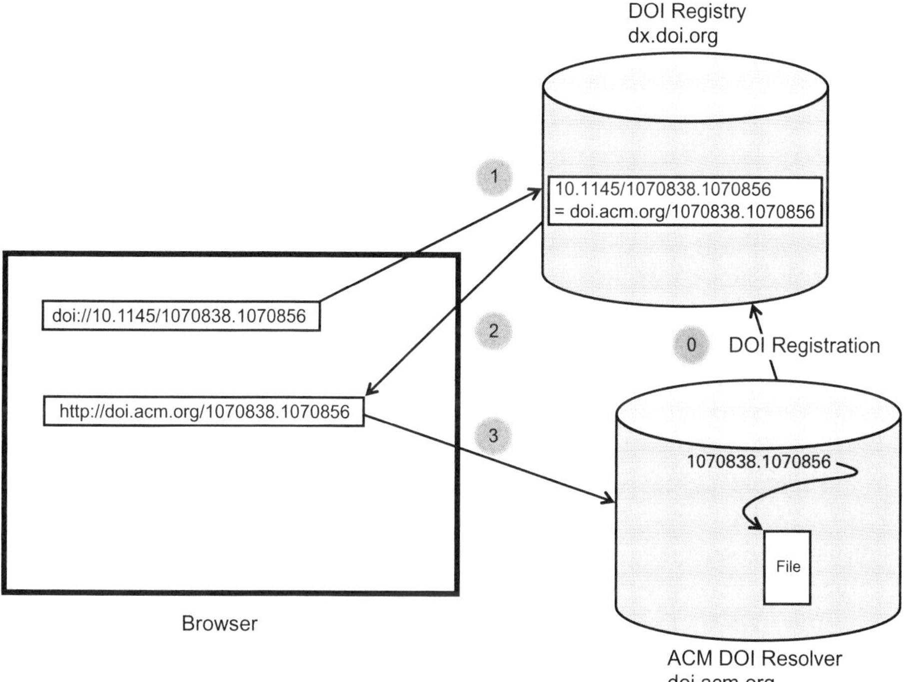

Figure 7.6
The digital object identifier (DOI) system brings the features of handle systems to the Internet. This example uses the digital library of ACM, a professional society. The access protocol consists of four steps. To initialize, ACM generates a DOI for a newly published object. The DOI consists of ACM's unique number (10.1145) followed by a unique string chosen by ACM. Thereafter, a user can take the DOI from a citation and ask the registry to resolve it (step 1). The registry returns the URL of the object in the ACM Digital Library (step 2). The ACM Digital Library Resolver directs the access to the specified object (step 3).

created its digital object identifier (DOI) system to enable all publishers to generate handles for their publications and register them with the Library. The Library depends on publishers to maintain their content; if a publisher goes out of business and does not transfer its content to new servers, then its content becomes inaccessible because its DOIs will not map to anywhere (Denning and Kahn 2010).

Authentication

Since the earliest days, the protection of information has been a primary concern of operating systems designers (Dennis and Van Horn 1966, Wilkes 1968a, Denning 1971, Lampson 1974, Saltzer and Schroeder 1975). As part of mapping a name to an object, the operating system verifies that the requesting subject has permission to perform the requested operation. The verification procedure is called access control.

Normally the owner of an object (its creator) declares who can access it and in what ways. A permission is a statement of the form "subject *s* may perform function *f* on object *x*" and can be abbreviated (*s*,*f*,*x*). A subject is usually a combination of a user and a process owned by that user; for example, *s* = (Ann,317) means process 317 is acting for Ann. A permission such as, "Any process belonging to Ann may read file 'abc'" is abbreviated ((Ann,*),read,abc) where the asterisk matches any process number. The allowable functions depend on the type of object; for example, read applies only to files or memory pages, and suspend only to processes. Every object manager is responsible to block accesses that would violate permissions; for example, the file system would block Ann's attempt to write "abc" when the only permission was ((Ann,*),read,abc).

An access control list (ACL) is a common way to represent permissions. The owner of an object *x* creates the ACL[*x*], whose entries are of the form (*s*,*f*). Thus, the file system allows Ann to read file "abc" only if ACL[abc] contains the entry ((Ann,*),read). Directory systems and database systems attach ACLs to directory entries and records.

The Unix system compresses ACLs to nine bits. It assumes only three types of user: the owner, a member of a group defined by the owner, or the general public. It defines three permission bits for each type of user: read (r), write (w), and execute (x). The resulting nine-bit code is stored in the object's directory entry rather than in a separate ACL file. For example, Ann's declaration that she cannot execute her file "abc," her group can only read it, and the general public can read and execute it, would be stored as the access code (rw-r--r-x) in the directory entry for file "abc."

Another common way to represent permissions is with access codes in capability lists, such as page tables and object lists. When it creates a subject *s*, the operating system creates its capability list CL[*s*], pointing to all objects accessible to *s*. Thus, Ann's read permission for file "abc" would be stored as (read,abc) in CL[Ann]. ACLs and CLs are often used together: capability lists are initialized with permissions from ACLs when files are loaded into address space.

Some military and government systems label each user with a clearance and digital objects with security tags such as unclassified, secret, or top secret. The relations between clearances and tags define additional constraints on access. Users may neither read from objects tagged higher than their clearances nor write into objects tagged lower than their clearances. These systems control access according to the allowable information flows subjects can generate while reading and writing objects (Bell and LaPadula 1976, Denning 1976).

To make permissions management and other operations easier, most systems include an account "root" (or "superuser" or "administrator") that has all permissions for all objects in the system. Only a small number of trusted administrators may log in to that account. The existence of a root account is a major security vulnerability for most systems. An attraction of capability-based addressing is that it eliminates the need for a superuser (Wilkes 1968a).

Positioning in the Hierarchy

Positioning refers to placing data in the different levels of a memory hierarchy or nodes of a network in order to guarantee good performance of the system. Performance is very sensitive to positioning. Recall the example at the beginning of this chapter, a hypothetical supercomputer that ran at 1/11 its rated CPU speed because the memory system could not provide new sensor data fast enough.

Cost analysis is a principle underlying every approach to the positioning problem. If the cost of keeping a block of data in RAM for the times between block reuse is less than the cost of retrieving the block from secondary disk, we keep the block in RAM. This can be stated as a formula as follows. Let R be the mean time interval between reuses of the data block, B the block size, U be the unit cost per time unit of a byte of RAM, and D the cost of retrieving a block from the disk. When $UBR < D$ or, equivalently, when

$$R < D/UB$$

it is cheaper to retain the block for the entire reuse interval. Using costs and block sizes from the Tandem computer systems in 1985, Gray and Putzolu put the threshold for R at 5 minutes. In other words, keep a data block in RAM if its reuse time is less than 5 minutes; otherwise keep it on the disk. Twenty years later the same rule applied for larger block sizes between hard disk and RAM and for smaller block sizes between flash memory and RAM (Graefe 2007).

This idea can be restated as principle of optimality. Because the parameters D, U, and B are fixed for a system, we can lump them into a decision threshold $T = D/UB$. Then just after using a block,

1. If the time until next reuse exceeds T, immediately remove the block from RAM.
2. Otherwise, keep the block until the next reuse.

There is no point is keeping a block in RAM for part of the interval until reuse, for that would only add a RAM cost for the part of the interval but would not eliminate the retrieval from the disk.

This rule is applied after each *use*. Thus, if the next reuse of a block is within the threshold window, the same rule is applied just after that use even though the block is already loaded. Because this rule is applied separately to each block just after it is used, the total amount of used RAM can vary. If more blocks are used in time T, the RAM allocation will increase; if fewer are used, it will decrease. In 1976 Prieve and Fabry defined the policy VMIN for variable-space minimization using exactly this decision rule and showed that it is optimal. No other policy can generate fewer block-loads for a given average RAM allocation.[4]

This principle is not easy to apply in practice because the number of data blocks can be very large and their reuse times are random variables. Moreover, the decision in the present moment about whether to hold a block until next reuse is uncertain because we cannot see the future. To be able to make useful predictions of reuse times, we plainly need a predictive model of how computations refer to and reuse their code and data.

The search for predictive models of memory use began in the 1960s after virtual memory was introduced. Virtual memory relies heavily on its page replacement policy—the rule to decide which RAM-resident page should be displaced when the CPU encounters a missing-page fault. Replacement policies were expressions of different predictive models. The performance of virtual memory was quite sensitive to choice of predictive model.

In 1966 Les Belady of IBM conducted a highly influential study of replacement policy performance in fixed-size RAMs. He concluded that the least recently used (LRU) policy, which selects the resident page that has not been used for the longest time, is consistently better than the others. As a benchmark, he defined the policy MIN, meaning minimal page faults, which selects the resident page that will not be reused for the longest time into the future; MIN generates fewer page faults than any other fixed-partition policy (Aho et al. 1971). Unfortunately, MIN is not implementable without exact knowledge of future memory references or at least a very good predictive model of the future. There was quite a gap between the performance of LRU and MIN. The search was on to find policies close to MIN.

Researchers used reference maps to help them see exactly how executing programs used memory. A reference map is a time series of samples from address space, showing which pages were used in each sampling interval. These maps consistently revealed striking patterns of clustered references that lasted for long intervals. They were distinctive, like a voiceprint, for each program (see figure 7.7). The used area of a reference map represents the space-time footprint that maximizes system throughput (see figure 7.8).

The tendency for programs to cluster references to subsets of address space for extended periods is called the *principle of locality*.[5] As seen in figure 7.7, we can describe a computation's memory demand as a sequence

$(L_1,P_1), (L_2,P_2), \ldots, (L_k,P_k), \ldots$

where each L_k is a locality set, that is, a subset of objects of the address space, and each P_k is a phase, that is, the time duration of the locality set. If we knew the locality sets and phase times, we could solve the positioning problem simply by keeping each locality set resident in RAM for the duration of its phase. We will see shortly that this is very close to optimal.

The working set is a measuring instrument to track the changing locality behavior of a program (Denning 1968a). The working set identifies the pages of address space that have been used in a recent past virtual-time window of size T.[6] We want a small window, conducted in the virtual time of the program, that is just long enough to sample all the pages of the current locality set. Many studies, such as the one depicted in figure 7.7, have shown that a good sampling window is typically a small fraction of the phase lengths. With such a window, the working set becomes an excellent predictor of the immediate-future locality set and gives system performance close to optimal (see figure 7.9).

When the locality principle is applied to multiprogramming, it says that the ideal RAM allocation for each program is its current working set and that no program should be started unless its working set can fit in the

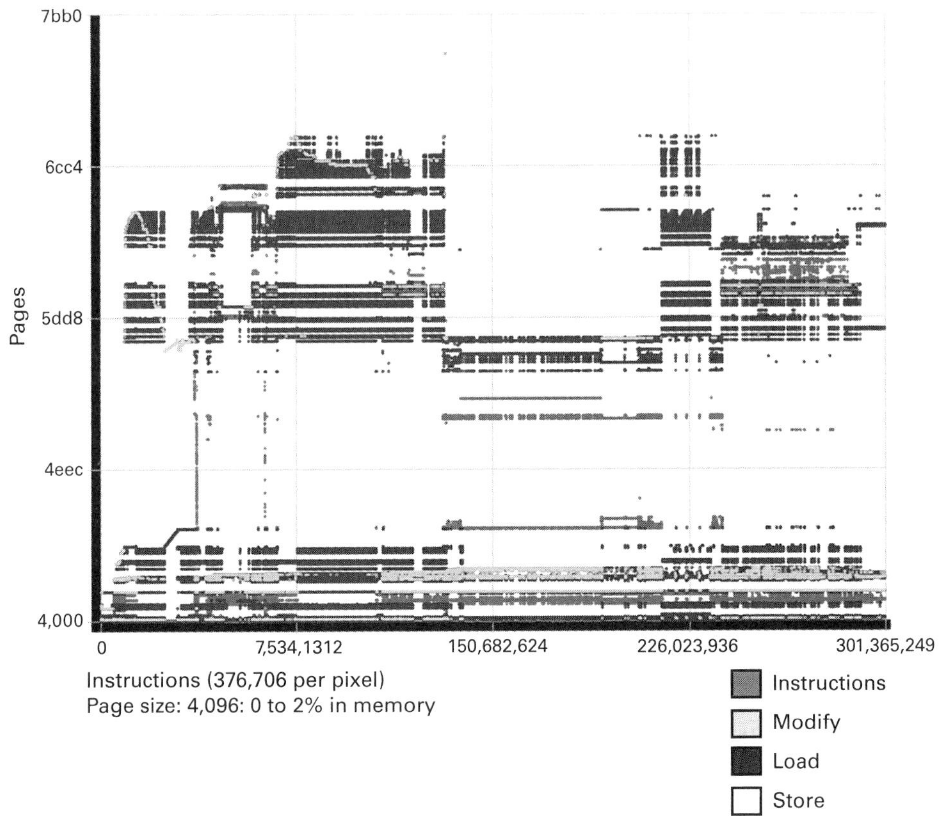

Figure 7.7

This is a page reference map of the Firefox web browser in a Linux system. The horizontal axis represents virtual time, measured in memory references (about 380K references per pixel), and the vertical represents virtual addresses of pages. A darkened pixel indicates that the page was referenced during the associated window of 380K references. The map reveals the locality sets of the program and shows dramatically that locality sets are stable over extended periods (phases), punctuated by shifts to other locality sets. In this picture the locality set seen in a sample interval typically persists for 30–60 samples. For over 97 percent of the time, the pages seen in a sample interval are a near perfect predictor for the pages used in the next sample interval. These striking diagrams show that each program has its own unique locality behavior. There is no randomness in the way programs use their code and data. (Source: Adrian McMenamin (2011), experiments conducted in 2010)

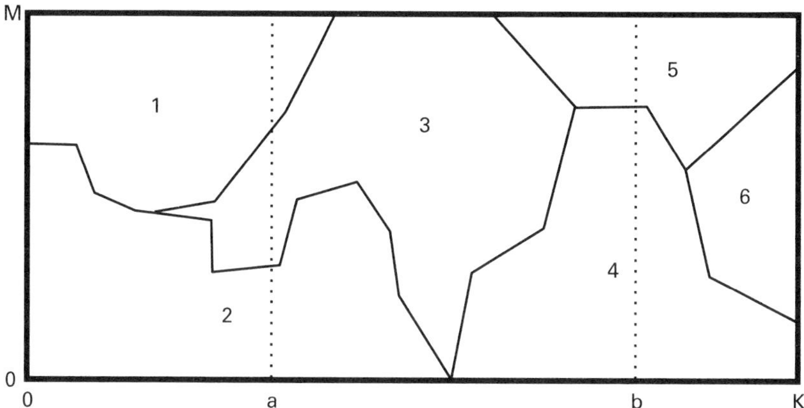

Figure 7.8
Performance analysts measure memory usage with space-time, which are the numbers of page-seconds accumulated over time by a program in memory. Here we see a memory of size *M* observed for *K* seconds. The six areas represent the space-times of six programs that used the memory. At time *a*, programs 1, 2, and 3 were resident; at time *b*, programs 4 and 5. Memory space-time is related to system throughput by the remarkable law $M = XY$, where *X* is the throughput in programs completed per second, and *Y* is the average space-time of a program (Buzen 1976). In this case the throughput is $X = 6/T$ because six programs were completed, and the mean space-time per program is one-sixth of the total available space-time *MK*. Ideally, if each program were as small as the space-time of its reference map, the maximum number of programs would consume the available *MK*, maximizing throughput.

unused part of RAM. Virtual memory systems managed under this principle cannot thrash.[7]

When the locality principle is applied to a CPU cache, it says to replace cache items according to the LRU rule because the least recently used pages tend to belong to past locality sets that are no longer relevant. The cache therefore protects the pages most likely to be used in the immediate future, mimicking MIN.

When the locality principle is applied to the Internet, it says to place copies of web pages on "edge caches" close to clusters of users, for example, in a local network. A cluster has its own locality behavior, and the edge cache positions the locality pages close to where they are processed. In the Internet long queues of backlogged requests can otherwise clog popular sites, causing long delays; the caching breaks up the long queues of the centralized server. Akamai Technologies has been particularly successful at this: their edge caches serve 30 percent of Internet traffic. Their algorithms

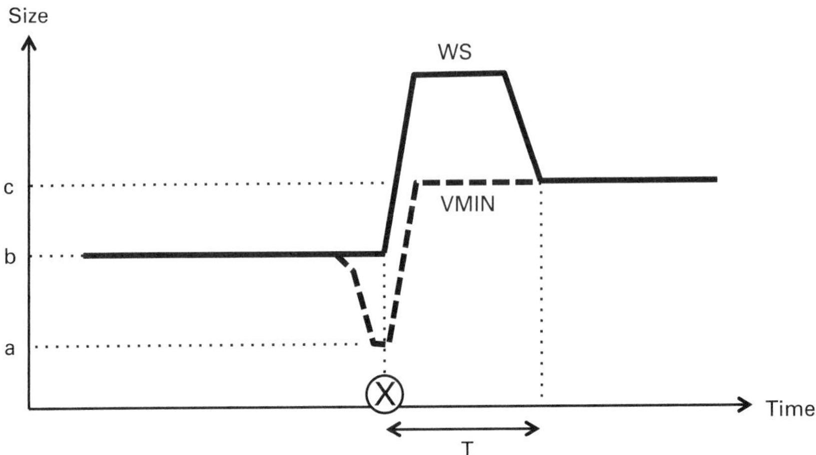

Figure 7.9

When memory allocation varies to track locality sets, Belady's MIN is not optimal; VMIN is (Prieve and Fabry 1976). For a given *T*, VMIN looks ahead to the next reference of a page; if that page is used sooner than *T*, VMIN retains it in RAM for the entire interval until reuse; otherwise VMIN removes it immediately, to be reclaimed later by a page fault. The parameter *T* trades off between the cost of retaining a page and the cost of recalling it later. When *T* is less than phase lengths, VMIN and WS (working set) both see and retain the locality set. The only differences between them occur at phase transitions. The diagram shows a transition from a smaller locality set (size *b*) to a larger one (size *c*) with an overlap (size *a*). When the transition begins (circled "x"), WS accumulates the new locality pages in addition to the old ones; within time *T* into the new phase, WS settles to see only the new locality pages. VMIN anticipates the transition by removing pages immediately after their last uses in the old phase. The discrepancy between WS and VMIN for *T* time units after the transition is $b - a$ pages until close to the end of the *T* window, and then the decay of WS to meet VMIN mirrors the VMIN decay *T* time units before. Therefore, if the old phase is of duration *P*, the relative discrepancy in space-time is at most $(b - a)T/bP$, which is less than T/P. Thus, if *T* is 3 percent of a phase length, as in much of figure 7.7, WS is within 3 percent of optimal.

measure where the demand comes from and calculate the best positions for caches. In the Internet, as in the individual computer, locality is predictable, and locality models can significantly improve performance.

Why Locality Is Fundamental

There is plenty of empirical evidence that locality is a fundamental property of all computations. A large number of programs have been observed through reference maps, which always show the locality-phase behavior and confirm that working sets with windows small compared to most phase lengths will accurately observe the locality sets. Moreover, the universal success of CPU caches and edge caches in the Internet is an even stronger confirmation of locality.

Might locality behavior be an artifact of compiler optimizations? For example, might the compiler's strategies for clustering blocks of code and data that reference each other account for the behavior? Madison and Batson (1976) showed that locality behavior is already present in the source code of programs. The locality behavior therefore seems to come from the way humans go about problem solving. For example, the common strategy of divide and conquer guarantees that algorithms will cluster references into small subsets of code and data for extended periods. Algorithms that use linear arrays, strings, or vectors generate locality behavior by localizing references inside those objects for the durations of loops. Good compiler optimizations preserve locality, and the memory system will operate efficiently; conversely, poor optimizations obscure locality, and the memory system will be inefficient.

Locality goes even deeper than this. In 2010 Yuri Gurevich published a report seeking to answer the question, "What is an algorithm?" He formulated an algorithm as the control of an agent that performed operations on data. Among the requirements of allowable operations for the agent is a bounded-domain principle: an operation can only alter a finite, bounded region of the data structure. In other words, to qualify as an algorithm, a computational method must necessarily obey a locality principle.

Conclusions

Storage is as fundamental to computing as processing. The memory systems in which code and data are stored are hierarchical, with high-speed devices of relatively low capacity coexisting with slow-speed devices of high capacity. The high-speed devices enable high-speed computation, while the low-speed devices enable reliable long-term storage and very large data sets. Huge networks of these memory systems are interconnected in the Internet.

The usability of storage systems depends on the resolution of four large issues: naming, mapping, authenticating, and positioning. *Naming* means to assign alphanumeric or bit strings to identify objects. *Mapping* means to associate a name with a memory location containing the object. *Authentication* means to verify that the requesting subject has permission to perform the requested operation on the object. *Positioning* means to place data at locations within a memory hierarchy, or within the Internet, for optimal performance.

There are six primary access modes for storage—addresses, address pairs, handles, pathnames, queries, and text searches. Each serves a particular purpose, and all are present in most computing systems or the Internet. The systems that implement each of these modes can be quite complex.

Positioning is based on the principle that a data object should stay at a position in the memory system if it is cheaper to keep it there between reuses than to retrieve it later on demand from another position. In many systems, typified by virtual memory, the positioning decisions are determined by the ratio of those costs. The principle of locality—computations cluster references into small subsets of address space for extended periods—was extended into a well-validated theory for predicting which objects are most likely to be used in the immediate future. Predicted localities should be positioned close to their processing sites. Locality theory has supported the design and performance optimization of memory systems.

Over the years critics predicted that virtual addressing methods would disappear because RAM technology would eventually be so good that most programs would never have to page at all. A simpler operating system with no paging could give everyone all the RAM they need. This outcome is quite unlikely. Virtual addressing methods are here to stay because they solve important problems of sharing, naming, authenticating, and preventing programs from interfering. They are essential even if their data-positioning policies are never switched on. Moreover, because so many of the computations we wish to run deal with "big data"—meaning data that exceed our current storage systems—there will never be enough RAM.

8 Parallelism

We have arranged the whole system as a society of sequential processes whose harmonious cooperation is regulated by explicit mutual synchronization statements.
—Edsger W. Dijkstra

Ubiquitous commercial multicore chips are forcing computational thinking to go parallel.
—Walter Tichy

E pluribus unum.
—Original motto of the United States

In visualizing computations we are used to thinking of single processes controlling a single CPU carrying out an instruction sequence. Many of our definitions of algorithms emphasize step-by-step behavior—one thing at a time.

But in real life we do many things at once, and we interact with many other people who are doing likewise. We can see this in the conduct of our daily affairs and in mobile and desktop operating systems. The information processes we collectively generate in the Internet may have some sequential components, but they are mostly many agents operating concurrently. The modern computational world cannot be adequately described in terms of sequential processes. It is a cacophony of many independent, autonomous agents trying to achieve individual and shared goals.

How do we describe and manage such computations?

We do this under the heading *parallel computation,* a term that ordinarily refers to computations performed cooperatively by multiple, concurrent agents. The term implicitly suggests that "serial computation" is a special case and may be the basic building block of parallel systems. However, there are many computations where, even at the fine level of detail, it is hard to discern sequential components.

Designers of parallel computing deal with two broad classes of phenomena:

1. *Cooperative parallelism* Many processes (autonomous computational agents) synchronize together to accomplish a common goal. For example, a supercomputer with 10,000 processors starts a computation with 10,000 processes, one running on each processor, in order to complete a weather prediction 10,000 times faster than a single processor could do it.
2. *Competitive parallelism* Many processes with little or no mutual synchronization simply use the finite resources of a network to accomplish their individual goals. Queues form at some resources where demand is high. Resources with long queues act as bottlenecks that limit the speed at which individual processes get responses from the system. For example, the cell phone network can get overwhelmed in emergencies, and subscribers will experience long waits before they can place calls.

The two classes are not independent. For example, some supercomputer operating systems allow many processes to compete for fewer processors. Google avoids bottlenecks at its servers under a load of 1 billion queries a day by dividing each query into thousands of subqueries dispatched to thousands of processors, which cooperate to answer each query in under 0.5 second.

We discuss cooperative parallelism in this chapter and competitive parallelism in the next chapter on queueing.

Early Directions of Parallel Computing

In the 1940s the main focus of computer engineers was on machines with serial processors, executing one instruction at a time in sequence. They saw this as the best path to reliable machines. Parallel machines and parallel algorithms were too much to take on for such a young technology.

Even so, parallelism was never far from most computer engineers' minds. The electronic circuits implementing the CPU contained many parallel pathways for signals to follow. Engineers knew that *race conditions* were a major problem for reliability. A race condition exists when more than one input signal flows along parallel paths and the value of the output depends on the speeds of the paths. For example, an output that the designers intended to stay constant at "1" could fluctuate briefly to "0" if the faster signal got to the output before the slower signal. That

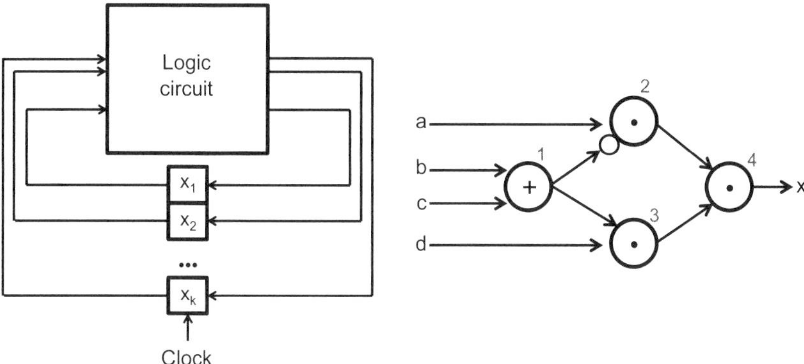

Figure 8.1
Logic circuits in a CPU are connected to one-bit flipflops (x_1, x_2, ..., x_k) that represent the circuit's most recent state (*left*). The arrival of a clock pulse causes the flipflops to be set to the current values of the circuit's output. The new flipflop values propagate to the circuit's input, leading to a new set of outputs. However, while the new signals move through the circuit, the output can change spuriously. To avoid the danger of spurious outputs being read into the flipflops, the clock tick interval is set longer than the circuit-settling time. The example logic circuit (*right*) has an OR gate (*1*) connected two AND gates (*2, 3*), which are in turn connected to another AND gate (*4*). The input to gate 2 from gate 1 is negated, meaning that signal from gate 1 is reversed. If this circuit is in either state *abcd* = 1001 or 1011, the output is $x = 0$. However, when the *c* input changes from 0 to 1, a slower propagation via gate 2 relative to gate 3 will cause a momentary change to $x = 1$ for the time difference between the two gates.

fluctuation could cause the malfunction of the downstream circuits intended to receive that output. Maurice Karnaugh (1953) demonstrated a technique to design logic circuits so that fluctuations caused by racing signals could not happen. Unfortunately, Karnaugh's method did not scale well to very large circuits.

Hardware engineers incorporate a clock to maintain stability of large circuits. They built machines as logic circuits with one-bit flipflops in feedback cycles (see figure 8.1). At a clock tick pulse, the logic circuit's outputs are written into the flipflops. The duration between clock ticks was longer than the slowest path through the logic circuits. Fluctuations caused by internal races in the logic circuits were no longer observable to the users of the circuits.

Unfortunately, clocked circuits do not scale up well. In the time between ticks of a 3-GHz clock, light travels about 4 inches. That is ample time for a signal to traverse a typical 3-cm chip. However, for a circuit the size of a 1-foot circuit board, we would need to slow the clock to 1 GHz or less.

Many circuit designers sought to mitigate these signaling problems by building modular circuits, applying the clock only to the modules, and using asynchronous (unclocked) signaling between modules. For example, CPU and disk controller cabinets could have their own internal clocks and use a ready-acknowledge protocol to exchange requests and data. In a ready-acknowledge protocol the sender places the data to be transmitted in a buffer and sends a ready signal to the receiver; after the receiver has acquired the data, it sends an acknowledgment signal back to the sender. This protocol works for any length cycle between the sender and receiver. Ivan Sutherland (2012), one of the earliest proponents of asynchronous circuits, argued in 2012 that the case for removing the clock is stronger than ever if we wish to continue scaling circuit sizes upward and lowering energy consumption.

Many designers looked to parallelism rather than clocks for a more aggressive way to speed up computations. If a problem to be solved could be broken into many small, independent tasks, each could run on a different processor. Then N processors could complete the whole job in $1/N$ of the time a single processor would take. Massively parallel supercomputers have driven this principle to huge values of N, some upward of a million processors (see figure 8.2).

Unfortunately, few problems decompose into completely independent pieces. Consider, for example, a highly simplified algorithm for weather forecasting on a two-dimensional grid representing the entire country. In the computation each cell records its own pressure, wind direction, and wind velocity. Each cell interacts with four neighbors—call them north, east, south, and west—by allowing the four neighboring values to affect it, producing new local values of pressure, direction, and velocity. Consider just the pressure calculation. Let t denote a time step in the computation and $P(t)$ the pressure in a cell at time step t. The new value of pressure in a cell might be computed as the average of the neighboring pressures at the previous time step as[1]

$$P(t) = [P_{north}(t-1) + P_{east}(t-1) + P_{south}(t-1) + P_{west}(t-1)] / 4$$

The allowable clock time between time steps would be the time for the network to deliver the four neighbor values plus the time for the cell to sum them, divide by 4, and store the result. Because all the communication is local, this can be scaled up to a large number of cells at the same clock time step.

Figure 8.2
The Blue Gene/P supercomputer at Argonne National Lab runs over 250,000 processors, grouped in 72 cabinets connected by a high-speed optical network. It is typical of modern "cluster" machines, which achieve very high computational rates through massive parallelism. Another common supercomputer configuration is the "grid," in which thousands of computers in the Internet are mobilized when otherwise idle to work on pieces of a large computation. The world speed record in 2013, 18×10^{15} floating point operations per second (18 petaflops), was held by the Cray Titan supercomputer at Oak Ridge National Laboratory. Michael Flynn (1972) characterized this architecture as MIMD (multiple instruction multiple data) and predicted it would achieve the fastest speeds.

With a separate processor for each cell, the entire grid of N processors would compute the entire pressure profile for all time steps $t = 1, 2, 3, \ldots$ and could speed up the computation by a factor of N. By letting time evolve into the future, the grid can predict future pressures.

What about normal programs coded for single-processor machines? Could they be speeded up by N with N processors? Would it be possible, without having to reeducate programmers, to build parallelizing compilers that could translate normal programs for multiprocessor machines? In the 1960s Gene Amdahl, a computer architect for IBM, asked how much a parallelizing compiler could actually accomplish. He stated a formula, known now as Amdahl's law, for calculating the speed-up. If a fraction P of a program is parallelizable and can achieve a speed-up of N, the parallelized program will take $(1 - P) + P/N$ as long to complete. For example, if 10 percent of the program is parallelizable and 10 processors are available, the program will complete in 91 percent of the time it would take on a single processor. Amdahl calculated that many common programs contained too many serial dependencies to benefit much from a parallel processor.

Nobody complained because Moore's law kept doubling the processing speeds of chips every 18 months or so. However, around 2000, chip makers began encountering the difficulties cited earlier in scaling up clocked chips. They turned to parallel processing to enable them to maintain the speed doublings promised by Moore's law. Instead of making a chip twice as fast by cutting feature sizes and doubling the clock speed, they put two parallel CPUs, called "cores," on the same chip and kept the old clock speed. Within a decade 16-core chips were routinely available. But there was a catch: applications programmers had to learn how to write parallel programs for these new chips. What principles can they use to do this well?

Since the 1960s operating system designers have accumulated knowledge of building effective parallel systems. Operating systems implement individual programs' concurrent processes and assign CPUs to them by cycling through processes waiting in a "ready list." Operating systems are very good at running many user processes in parallel on a limited set of resources.

Many intuitions about serial algorithm design and debugging break down spectacularly for parallel programming. Parallel programming brings with it the serious possibility of race conditions and timing-dependent intermittent bugs plus a host of synchronization problems when processes exchange signals or get tangled by deadlocks. Computational thinking has had to move from serial to parallel computations.

Models of Parallel Systems

Although there was not much place for parallel programming in the commercial world of the 1950s through the 1970s, researchers studied the subject actively and amassed an extensive theory of parallelism. They learned how to build reliable asynchronous circuits, exchange signals and messages, eliminate race conditions, avoid deadlocks, and prevent timing-dependent bugs. They designed programming languages that explicitly represented the parallelism naturally present in a problem, so that most of the code output from a compiler would benefit significantly from a machine with many processors. Unfortunately, most of the theory went fallow in the 1980s and 1990s because the industry had little interest in parallel computing. That started to change around 2000 with multicore chips. The old principles came back into vogue for all programmers. These principles have been embodied into several basic models.

Cooperating Sequential Processes

This model is commonly used to organize operating systems. A parallel system consists of a set of sequential processes operating concurrently at unknown speeds. A process, also called a thread, is the sequence of CPU states generated while executing a program in a single address space. A process can spawn new processes ("children"). Processes coordinate by exchanging signals and messages.

A computation consists of one or more processes operating in a shared address space. Computations can be terminating or nonterminating. A terminating computation is one in which all the processes terminate; its output is the values left in the shared memory. A nonterminating computation is one in which at least some of the processes execute in repeating cycles; its outputs are sequences of values emitted from designated processes in the set.

Communication between processes (whether in the same or different computations) is accomplished with explicit signals; no data are exchanged through hidden channels. Implicit communications, such as leaving data in a shared memory area, are common sources of errors. Programmers must identify coordination requirements and deal with them explicitly using synchronization protocols. Coordination requirements typically include the following:

1. *Race conditions* The value in a memory cell depends on the order in which concurrent processes write values to that cell.
2. *Mutual exclusion* Different processes cannot concurrently execute critical sections of code.
3. *Serialization* A code segment is executed as a unit and is never interleaved with concurrent code segments that could race with it.
4. *Synchronization* A process cannot continue past a designated point until it receives a signal from another process.
5. *Rendezvous* A group of processes waits at a designated point until all members of the group have reached the same point; then they all proceed.
6. *Message passing* Processes send messages to each other.
7. *Deadlock prevention or avoidance* Processes never get into a circular wait in which each is stopped waiting on a signal from another process in the set.
8. *Arbitration* When two signals are near simultaneous, select one to be first and the other second, without losing either one.

Functional Systems

A parallel system consists of a partially ordered set of tasks sharing a memory. Each task implements a function that maps values in its input memory cells to values in its output cells. A task executes in an interval from its "initiation" to its "completion." After initiation (also called "firing") it can read its inputs and write its outputs according to its internal function. When done, a task signals completion to the next tasks explicitly marked as its successors in the partial order. A task cannot initiate until all its predecessors in the partial order have sent it their completion signals. There are many variations on this theme including Petri Nets, Parallel Program Schemata, and Dataflow Graphs. Programming languages such as APL and VAL were developed to represent parallel computations in this model.

Event-Driven Systems

Event-driven systems are collections of processes in which signals notify processes when certain defined events occur. For example, a network manager process waits for two kinds of events: packets arrive from the Internet, whereupon they must be delivered to their proper recipient user processes; requests arrive from user processes, whereupon their packets are transmitted into the Internet. Another example is a real-time control process, such as a patient-monitoring system in a hospital, which must respond within specified deadlines to sensor notifications. These systems extend the model of cooperating sequential processes by allowing a waiting process to be awakened by any one of a set of signals rather than just for a specific signal and by allowing processes to time share mutually excluded regions. Programming languages recognizing this model have been in wide use since the 1970s; they include monitors (Brinch Hansen 1973, Hoare) and object-oriented languages such as Modula, Smalltalk, CLU, and Occam.[2]

MapReduce Systems

MapReduce systems were originally developed to deal with parallel processing of queries and retrievals from very large databases (Dean and Ghemawat 2004). They have been very successful for "big data," meaning the analysis of very large data sets for trends and patterns. The key idea is that programmers must divide their problem into many thousands of small, parallel pieces that can be implemented on servers scattered around the Internet and whose solutions can be quickly combined into a solution to the original, larger problem. The idea was developed at Google to enable massively parallel searching of their web databases, portions of which reside on servers around the world, so that they could respond to every search query in under 0.5 second. Hadoop is an open-source language for implementing MapReduce.

Because of space limitations, we do not discuss event systems and MapReduce systems further. The models of cooperating sequential processes and function systems are sufficient to reveal the essential principles of coordination in large parallel systems.

Cooperating Sequential Processes

This model begins with the process abstraction. The designers of the first time-sharing systems invented the abstraction to deal with some difficult problems in reliably switching the CPU among many programs.[3] Edsger Dijkstra (1965, 1968a, 1968b) proposed that an operating system be implemented as a set of cooperating sequential processes. This idea was widely accepted. Tony Hoare (1978) codified it with a model called CSP (cooperating sequential processes), which yielded the language Occam for programming such systems. Occam was used in some supercomputers in the 1980s.[4]

Implementing the process abstraction involves a complex lot of low-level operating system actions. Dijkstra hid all that complexity behind a very simple user interface. The interface gives operations to create and delete processes, suspend and resume processes, and exchange signals between processes (see figure 8.3).

Parallel processes brought the problem of race conditions to software. Most programmers were not used to dealing with race conditions because their programs were sequential, ran on hardware that had no circuit-level race conditions, and did not interact with other programs. Figure 8.4 illustrates the problem for Alice and Bob accessing a shared bank account simultaneously from different ATMs. Various different outcomes can result if the codes run by the ATMs can be interleaved in time. The implementation violates Alice and Bob's mental picture of their transactions running without mutual interference. They expect their transactions to be *serialized*, which means that the two processes always go one before the other, but never simultaneously. Serialization is a solution to race conditions.

Machine designers tried to solve this problem with a lock, which is a location in memory that holds the value 1 (locked) or the value 0 (unlocked). A lock is assigned to protect a particular set of shared data. A process sets the lock when using the shared data and unlocks when done. Any process wanting to use the data tests the lock and proceeds only if the lock is not

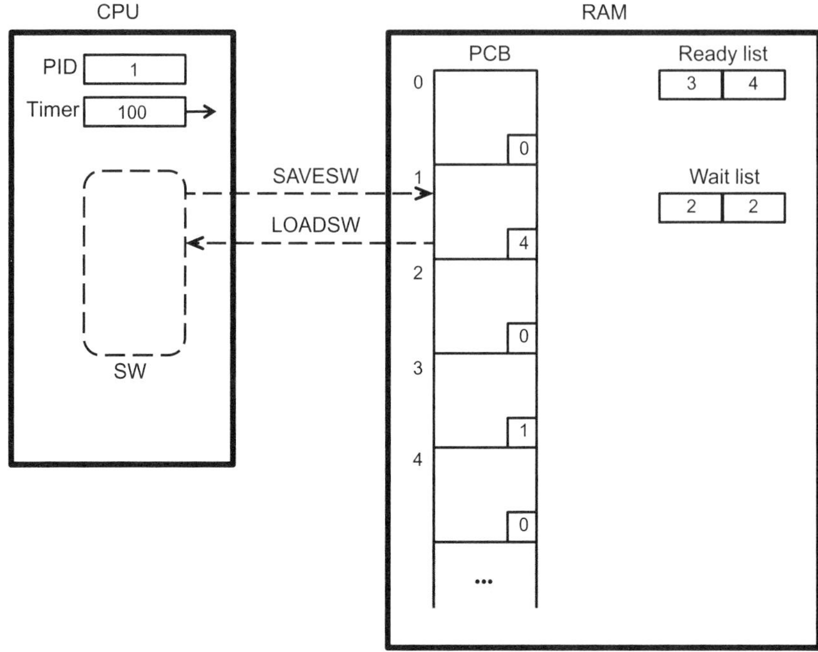

Figure 8.3

The mechanism for multiplexing a CPU among a set of processes is founded on the automatic saving and loading of process statewords. The *stateword* (SW) is the set of values in all the CPU registers that belong to the process—for example, the program counter, stack pointer, and arithmetic registers. The operating system maintains a list of *process control blocks* (PCBs), each containing a snapshot of a stateword. The register PID (process identifier) holds the number of the process currently running on the CPU; here process 1 is running. The instruction SAVESW copies the stateword of process PID into its PCB. When PID contains process number *i*, the instruction LOADSW copies the saved stateword from PCB[*i*] back into the CPU so that process *i* can continue from where was last interrupted. A TIMER register, initialized to the time slice value (here 100 milliseconds) by LOADSW, counts down and triggers a time-out interrupt when it reaches 0. The time-out interrupt handler executes SAVESW, loads PID with the next process number at the head of the ready list, and executes SAVESW. The *ready list* is a queue of processes ready to be run. Here, its head is process 3, and its tail is process 4. The small boxes in the PCBs tell which process is next in the list; thus, the full ready list is (3, 1, 4). There is also a wait list of processes that cannot run because they are waiting for certain events, such as disk transfer completions; for example, here process 2 is waiting. When the event occurs, process 2 is transferred from the head of the wait list to the tail of the ready list. Process 0, called the *idle process*, is automatically at the end of the ready and wait lists and will run whenever no other process is ready. Having a process 0 ready to run whenever no user process is ready protects the system from crashing when the ready list is empty.

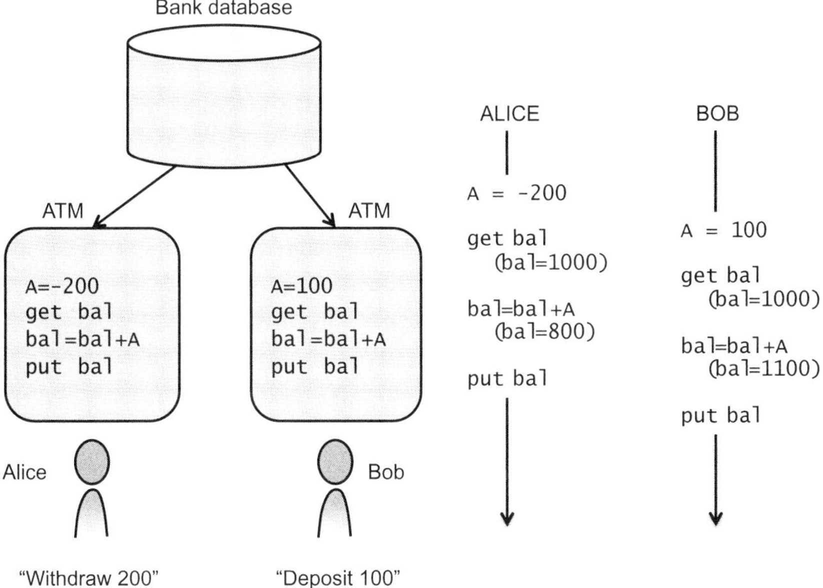

Figure 8.4
Race conditions can arise during parallel execution of software codes. The left picture shows Alice and Bob at ATMs attempting transactions on the same account from separate ATMs at the same time. Each ATM contains a simple program that gets the account balance from the bank database, adds or subtracts the transaction amount, and puts the result back into the bank database. Alice and Bob both assume their transactions as indivisible actions that would leave the account balance at 900 no matter who goes first or second. However, as shown on the right in two parallel timelines, the two ATMs can malfunction if they start the transactions at about the same time and interleave their individual instructions. For example Alice does "get balance," then Bob does "get balance," then Alice subtracts 200 from her local copy of the balance, then Bob adds 100 to his local copy of the balance, then Alice does "put balance," and finally Bob does "put balance." After this sequence, the final value in the account will be 1100, which is incorrect. A slight shift of timing, so that Alice does "put balance" after Bob, leaves 800 in the account, which is also incorrect.

set. Figure 8.5 shows how this would work. A hardware assist, in the form of a test-and-set instruction, is needed to avoid a fatal race condition while testing the lock.

The locking solution of figure 8.5 comes with a price—a costly problem called *busy waiting*. Busy waiting means that the CPU loops, testing the lock and waiting for it to be unlocked. Busy waiting can devastate a time-sharing system by wasting large amounts of CPU time. It would be much better to suspend the process the moment it waits for a lock and resume it when the lock is released.

Edsger Dijkstra (1968a, 1968b) solved this problem with the invention of the *semaphore*, a lock that contains a queue of processes waiting for it to be unlocked. Any process attempting to pass the locked lock is taken off the CPU's ready list immediately and placed in the semaphore queue. The operations *wait* and *signal* lock and unlock, respectively, and manage the queues (see figure 8.6).

Semaphores yield elegant solutions to many other synchronization problems among parallel processes. Every synchronization involves three aspects:

1. One or more sender processes
2. One or more receiver processes
3. Coordination between senders and receivers such that no receiver can pass a designated point until every sender has reached a corresponding designated point

A sender process uses a semaphore to signal that it has reached the designated point. A receiver process uses the same semaphore to stop and wait at the designated point until the signal comes. The semaphore is the simplest possible channel and queueing mechanism for such signals.

One common synchronization pattern is to have processes borrowing units of a resource from a shared pool and returning them later. Pages of memory are examples. At a page fault, the virtual memory manager withdraws an unused page from the free-pages pool and assigns it to the faulting process; later, the page is returned to the pool by the replacement algorithm. A semaphore synchronizes the use of the pool: its counter records the number of items remaining in the pool, the wait operation grants permission to withdraw an item, and the signal operation notifies when an item is returned to the pool.

Another common synchronization problem solved with semaphores is the transmission of a stream of items from a "producer" process to a "consumer" process via a buffer. The buffer is a limited storage area that holds

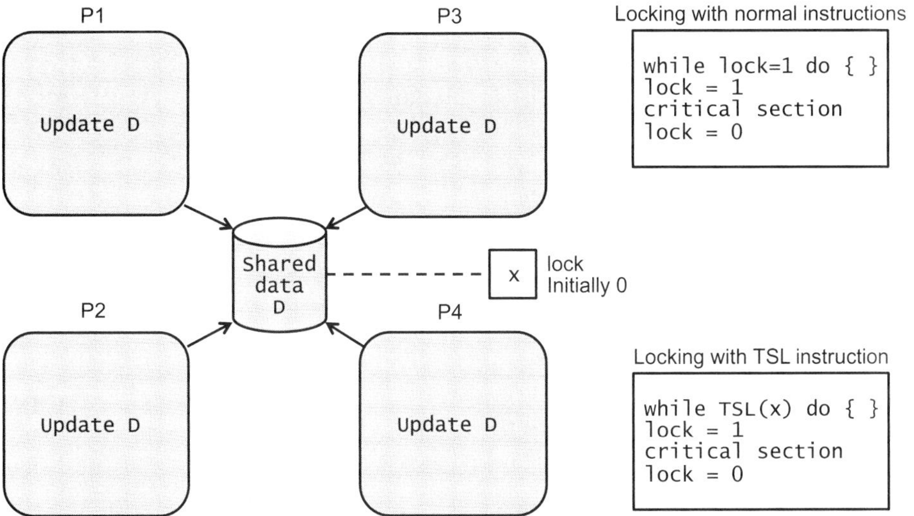

Figure 8.5

The instructions of any process seeking to update data must be executed as a unit to avoid the race malfunction. Above, four processes access a shared data object *D* using "update *D*," which could be any series of instructions that read and write *D*. If the four processes begin their updates together, the final value of *D* will depend on which goes last and may be different from the value that would be in *D* if they went in any serial order. A segment of code, such as "update *D*," which must be executed as a unit, is called a *critical section*. Critical section races can be avoided by locking the shared data when any process is updating it. A lock is a variable (here *x*) stored in RAM and associated with the shared data *D*. The value $x = 0$ means that *D* is unlocked and any process can access it. The value $x = 1$ means that *D* is locked by one process and no other may access it. This lock protocol is summarized at the upper right. Unfortunately, the protocol itself contains a bug, called "race on the lock": if two processes read lock=0 at the same time but before either sets lock=1, both can enter the critical section at the same time. To prevent this problem, most CPUs implement a hardware instruction test-and-set lock, abbreviated "TSL *x*"; executing TSL returns the value of *x* and sets $x = 1$. TSL is implemented in one memory cycle so that it cannot be interrupted by any other TSL.

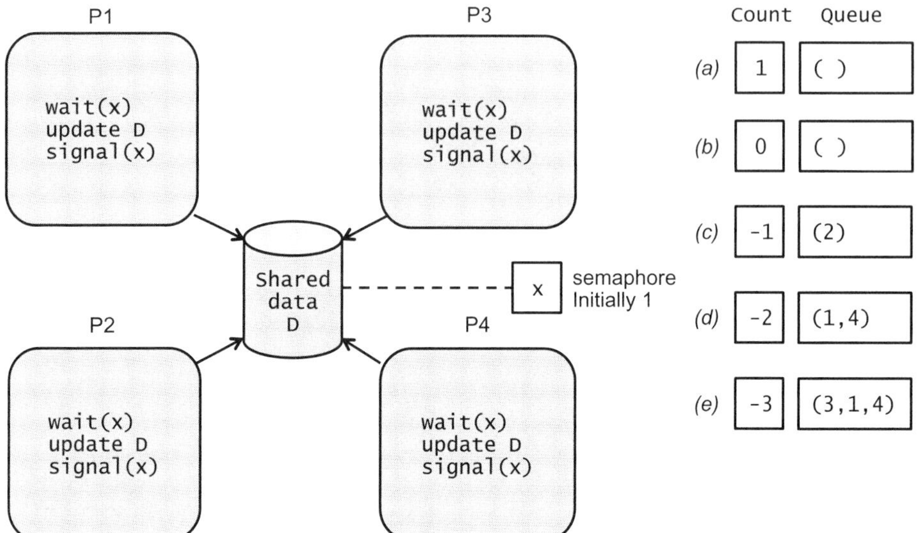

Figure 8.6

Edsger Dijkstra invented the semaphore as a way of locking a critical section without the busy waiting inherent in the TSL solution (figure 8.5). A semaphore passes a signal from one process to another and delays the recipient until a signal is available. It consists of a counter and a queue. The counter is the number of signals that can be picked up without waiting. The wait(x) operation on semaphore x subtracts 1 from the counter and, if the result is negative, puts the caller to sleep in the queue. Notice that the magnitude of a negative counter is the length of the queue. The signal(x) operation adds 1 to the counter and if the result is not positive wakes up the first process in the queue. At the right are examples of possible configurations of the semaphore. Configuration *a* is the initial configuration with a count of 1 and empty queue; the first process to request the critical section will pass without waiting. Configuration *b* means that some process is in the critical section and no one is waiting. Configuration *c* means that one process (here process 2) is waiting. Configuration *d* means that two processes are waiting and the queue is (1, 4); the next signal operation will release process 1. Configuration *d* means that three processes are waiting and the queue is (3, 1, 4); the next signal releases process 3.

items while they are "in transit." The problem is to prevent buffer overflow and buffer underflow. Overflow means that the producer has filled the buffer and overwrites previous items before the consumer removes them. Underflow means that the consumer has read the whole buffer and rereads old items. Overflow can cause the loss of items, underflow the duplication of items. The protocol for this synchronization uses two semaphores:

1. The "empty" semaphore has its count initialized to *N*, the buffer size. Its count represents the number of unused buffer slots.
2. The "full" semaphore has its count initialized to 0. Its count represents the number of used buffer slots.

To insert an item into the buffer, the producer waits on the empty semaphore, places the item in the next unused slot, and signals via the full semaphore. To remove an item from the buffer, the consumer waits on the full semaphore, takes the item from the next used slot, and signals via the empty semaphore.

Although they are capable of solving a host of synchronization problems among parallel processes, semaphores introduce new problems. The most challenging is the *deadlock*. A deadlock is a circular wait condition among a set of processes holding and requesting shared resources. Assume that each resource has a lock indicating that it is in use. In a deadlock a set of processes are all stopped, each holding a lock and waiting for another process in the set to release a lock. The only way out of a deadlock is to kill the processes in the set, release all their locks, and start over.

An example of deadlock can be seen in the prior ATM problem. Consider the ATM account transfer transaction. It subtracts an amount from the "from" account and adds the same amount to the "to" account. We can avoid the race condition by programming the ATMs to lock both accounts before doing the transfer. Once the accounts are locked there is no danger that another transaction can access the two records while the first transaction is using them. Consider what happens in two ATMs if Alice and Bob are attempting transfers at the same time (see table 8.1). Both semaphores *A* and *B* have initial counts 1.

Suppose they both start at the same time and execute their first instructions, leaving both semaphore counts at 0. Now they are doomed because ATM1 will be put to sleep on semaphore *B* and ATM2 on semaphore *A*. Neither can proceed.

There are numerous approaches to dealing with deadlocks. We mention the three most important.[5] The first is to let deadlocks happen, then extricate the system by killing the processes involved. Detection algorithms

Table 8.1
Setup for a Deadlock

ATM 1: "Transfer 100 from A to B"	ATM 2: "Transfer 200 from B to A"
wait(A)	wait(B)
wait(B)	wait(A)
A = A - 100	B = B - 200
B = B + 100	A = A + 200
signal(A)	signal(B)
signal(B)	signal(A)

simply make a graph showing which processes have locks or are requesting locks and look for a cycle in the graph. The cycle is the circular wait. This approach is often unsatisfactory not only because it can be expensive to kill deadlocked processes but also because the method cannot detect imminent inevitable deadlocks. For example, the ATMs above are not deadlocked immediately after their first wait operations, but the inevitable deadlock will not be detectable until both have stopped at their second wait operations.

A second approach seeks to prevent deadlocks by *up-front acquisition* of locks. Before performing the critical code, a process enters a loop in which it acquires all the needed locks before proceeding; if the process finds that a needed lock is already locked, it releases *all* the locks it already holds and starts over. This protocol prevents deadlock at the cost of possible *livelock*—two or more processes can loop endlessly in synchrony, preventing each other from acquiring all the locks needed.

A third approach seeks to prevent deadlocks by enforcing lock acquisition in a fixed priority order. The locks are numbered or assigned alphanumeric names. A process is allowed to request a new lock only if its number or name is higher than any lock it already holds. With this constraint it is impossible to get a circular wait among processes.[6] When this approach is applied to the earlier ATM example, the transfer program would sort the incoming account names into ascending alphabetic order and perform the wait operations in that order.[7]

Functional Systems

The cooperating sequential process model implicitly assumes each process runs on a CPU whose instruction rate and circuits are controlled by a clock. Concurrency occurs between processes, not within processes.

Clocked systems do not scale well. The clock tick interval must exceed the time for signals to propagate through longest path on a chip. Larger chips mean slower clocks. Faster clocks on denser chips create a heat dissipation problem.

Ready-acknowledge signaling can be used to build self-timed circuits, that is, circuits without a clock. When component *A* has a request for component *B*, for example to transfer data or to start an operation, *A* sends *B* a ready signal. The ready signal activates *B*. When *B* has completed its action on the request, *B* sends an acknowledge signal back to *A*. This cycle allows the next *A-B* interaction to begin and can be repeated indefinitely. Self-timed circuits use far less energy because component state changes occur only when data are transferred or transformed.

The simplest (and earliest) model of a self-timed system is a network of tasks with access to a shared memory. Each task implements a simple function. Some of the tasks have precedence constraints, meaning that they cannot begin until their predecessors have finished. Tasks with no precedence constraint between them are *concurrent*. A task can *fire* at any time after all its predecessors have completed. When a task fires, it reads values from a designated input set of memory cells, performs its function, and writes values into a designated output set of memory cells. A firing sequence of the network is a list of the tasks in the order performed, consistent with the precedence constraints. Networks with a few precedence constraints and many concurrent tasks have many firing sequences (see figure 8.7).

In a network without race conditions, we would expect that there is exactly one output from the network for every input to the network. Each network output value would depend uniquely on the initial values in memory—and not on the firing sequence. The task system of figure 8.7 does not implement a function.

A task network whose overall behavior is a function, independent of its firing sequence, is called *determinate*. Figure 8.7 illustrates a nondeterminate system. Even though individual tasks implement functions, there is no guarantee that a system of tasks as a whole implements a function.

Determinacy is critically important for many large computations such as weather predictions, oil explorations, or aircraft wing designs. The small tasks making up the computation are mostly concurrent, enabling them to run in parallel and give high performance. If the results of the computation depend on the exact firing order of the tasks, the results cannot be guaranteed to be correct. How would we know which executions were correct? We do not want airplanes to fall from the sky because of unpredictable firing

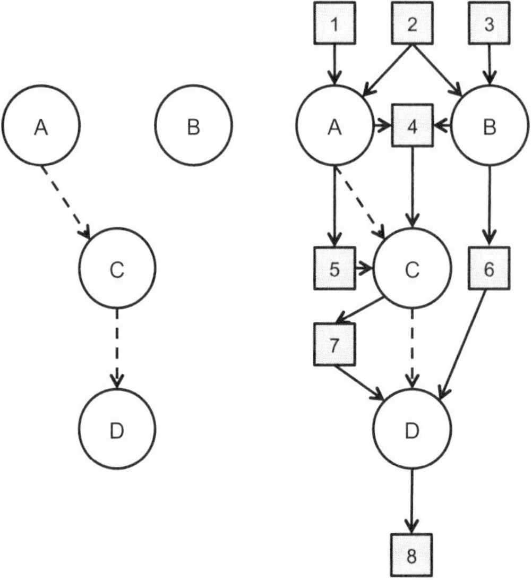

Figure 8.7
Task graphs connect functions implemented by task nodes (*circles*) into networks. The left figure shows four tasks, *A*, *B*, *C*, and *D*, with two precedence constraints indicated by *dashed arrows*. Tasks can fire, and perform their functions, in any order consistent with the constraints. Possible firing sequences are *BACD*, *ABCD*, *ACBD*, and *ACDB*. The right figure shows that each task takes input from some memory cells (*gray boxes*) and writes output into others. For example, *A* receives input from cells 1 and 2 and writes its results into cells 4 and 5; *C* receives input from cells 4 and 5 and writes its result into cell 7. Different firing sequences produce different final results at cell 8. Assuming the initial values in memory cells are the same as the cell numbers, and all cells perform additions, firing sequence *BACD* produces 11, *ABCD* produces 13, *ACBD* produces 11, and *ACDB* produces 12. These differences result from two types of race conditions. (1) In an output-output race, two concurrent tasks write into the same memory cell; for example, the value in cell 4 depends on the firing order of *A* and *B*. (2) In an input-output race, one concurrent task writes into a memory cell read by the other; for example, cell 6 is in an input-output race between *B* and *D*, affecting the value in cell 8, and cell 4 is in an input-output race between *B* and *C*, affecting the value in cell 7. To prevent races, no task can write into any cell that any concurrent task reads or writes.

orders of tasks inside the supercomputers that designed the wings or in the avionic systems that control the wings in flight.

Nondeterminacy is also a serious problem for debugging. Debugging is difficult or impossible if the bug cannot be isolated and reproduced. Bugs that depend on the firing orders of parallel tasks look like random, intermittent failures. They cannot be reproduced. When they are detected, it is very hard to locate the specific defect in the task system that produces the failure. Designers of early task systems called these timing-dependent problems "lurking bugs."

Fortunately, a very simple constraint will guarantee that a task network is free of lurking bugs and that every execution with the same input will produce the same output: *no task can write into any memory cell that any concurrent task reads or writes*. This is called the *determinacy theorem* for parallel systems.[8]

We close this section with a comment on how task systems might be implemented on a self-timed computer with no clock. A dataflow architecture doing this was designed by Jack Dennis and David Misunas (1975) of MIT. Although dataflow architectures have not been commercialized, they are a proof of concept for large-scale self-timed machines. Because they can be scaled much larger than current-generation supercomputers and would use less energy, they may yet one day be commercially attractive.

A basic dataflow machine consists of three parts: an execution unit, a data memory, and an interconnection network. The execution unit contains components much like those of a traditional CPU, such as adders and multipliers. The data memory contains a representation of the task system graph like that in figure 8.7 but much larger. Two special types of task, selectors and iterators, control the activations of entire subgraphs. The interconnection network is a highly parallel network that transmits packets representing fired tasks to the execution unit, where they are carried out; and it returns packets containing results. Although the time to execute a task is slower than on a conventional CPU because of the round-trip cycle of the packets from the data memory, the overall throughput is potentially very high because of massive parallelism.

A standard representation for any task is a data item with fields for inputs and outputs and an operation code for the task function. For example:

(in1, p1, in2, p2, OP, out1, out2)

where

- in1 and in2 are slots for data values that will be inserted by the completions of other tasks

- p1 and p2 are bits indicating whether the values are present or not
- OP is the name of the operation
- out1 and out2 are the addresses of task inputs that will receive the output results of OP

The cycle of execution is:

- An operation is enabled when both p1 and p2 are 1
- The data memory creates a packet containing a copy of the data values, operation code, and result addresses of an enabled operation and sends the packet to the execution unit
- The execution unit routes the packet to the function unit for the type of operator
- The function unit performs the operation on the values provided in the packet
- The function unit creates output packets addressed to the recipients using the addresses provided in the packet
- The output packets flow back to the data memory, which copies their values into the inputs of the tasks addressed and sets the p-bits to 1

With this arrangement, actions are triggered by the arrivals of packets into the data memory and the execution unit.

Designing the hardware for dataflow is not the real bottleneck—modern architectures already contain pipelining, multicore chips, and graphics processors, all of which rely on dataflow methods. The real bottlenecks are algorithm design and language design.

In 1976, John Rice of Purdue University published a study of the performance of numerical computations, such as solving for the vector field of airflows around a flying wing. Since 1940 the hardware speeds had improved by a factor of 1 million (10^6), and the algorithms themselves had improved by another factor of 1 million, for a total improvement factor of 10^{12}. In other words half the improvement came from algorithm design.

Algorithm design is as important today as it was in 1976. A crucial difference is that the improvements reported by John Rice were created by experts in numerical computation and encapsulated into standard mathematical libraries of numerical functions. Everyday programmers simply used the libraries and did not have to think about the internal structure of the algorithms.

Today, with multicore computers, programmers everywhere must design ever more parallel algorithms. However, most programmers have not been trained to "think parallel." Multithreading has been a clumsy add-on for many programming languages. Only a few languages offer parallel functions as part of their base design. To get most programs more parallelizable, programmers will need to learn to think parallelism from the outset, train their minds to deal with all the parallelism present in the world, and use these new languages to express their designs.

Conclusions

It seems almost odd that computers that execute one step at time dominate a world so rich in concurrent activity. Parallel systems are a much better fit. Because they can mobilize massive number of processors, they offer significant potential speedup over serial computation.

This benefit comes with a cost. Parallelism brings new challenges for programmers, most notably race conditions, synchronization, and deadlock. Debugging is significantly more difficult. How can we restrict a system to only the "correct" executions, especially when the number of possible execution sequences grows exponentially or worse with the size of the system? To do this we have developed an arsenal of protocols for using semaphores, sharing memory among concurrent tasks, and waiting for contested resources.

The model of parallel processing as a collection of cooperating sequential processes has been in use for many years because it offers straightforward extensions of the traditional sequential process model. This model has proved to be difficult to scale to very large computations. An important alternative is the function system model, in many simple tasks "fire when ready" and collectively implement a solution to a problem. These systems rely on self-timed circuits that operate without clocks. A simple structural rule—that no task can write into memory read or be written to by any other concurrent task—is sufficient to guarantee that a task system of any size is determinate.

9 Queueing

Unpredictable behavior of deterministic systems arises from lack of certainty about the workloads that drive these systems.

—Jeffrey P. Buzen

The original idea of a network was sharing computers, applications, software, and data among many people.

—Leonard Kleinrock

A major airline has set up a computerized reservation system and has authorized 1000 agents around the world to use it from their workstations to sell seats on their aircraft. A data center in an undisclosed, secure location contains all the records of flights, routes, and reservations. On average, each agent issues a job against this database once every 60 seconds. Every job makes an average of 10 requests on the directory disk in the data center to locate other disks containing the actual data. The directory disk takes an average of 5 milliseconds to service each request, and it is busy 80 percent of the time.

How many jobs per hour are serviced worldwide on this system? What is the average response time experienced by an agent in Paris? What would happen to the response time if a new method of storing the directory reduced accesses to five per transaction? What would happen to the response time if the number of agents doubled?

These are typical questions relating to the capacity of a network of computers to respond to the demands of competing, autonomous processes—what we called "competitive parallelism" in the previous chapter. We are asked to predict how the network will behave under different loads. Algorithms analysis, discussed in chapter 6 on Computation, is woefully inadequate to answer these questions. Algorithm analysis focuses on the CPU time needed to solve a problem but not on other delays for needed services such as Internet connections, input and output, and storage access. Moreover, the delays for these services depend not only on the mechanics of the servers but also on the queues that build up as other processes compete for the same servers. Algorithm analysis can answer questions about running time of a standalone process, but it cannot answer questions about the performance of a system of processes competing for resources.

We turn instead to queueing analysis for answers to such questions (Denning 1991a, 1991b). Most people would expect that the answers to the four questions above depend on detailed knowledge of the system structure—the locations and types of the agents' workstations, the communication bandwidth between each workstation and the data center, the number and types of disks in the center, access patterns for the disks, local processors and random-access memory within the center, the type of operating system, the types of transactions, and more. It may come as a surprise, therefore, that the first two questions—concerning throughput and response time—can be answered precisely using only the information given. For the changes of configuration proposed in the third and fourth questions, reasonable estimates of system behavior can be made from the available information and a few plausible assumptions.

Queueing Theory Meets Computer Science

Queueing theory is a branch of mathematics started in the early 1900s to predict delays in waiting lines. It began with the research of A. K. Erlang (1909), a Copenhagen telephone engineer, who set out to predict the loss probability for an automated telephone exchange. When he investigated the demands callers would place on a telephone system—specifically, the times between arrivals (attempts to make calls) and the service times (the lengths of calls)—he found that the arrival and service times were exponentially distributed. That is, the probability that an interarrival time would exceed t seconds is $e^{-\lambda t}$, where $1/\lambda$ was the average time between arrivals. He similarly found that the probability a call length would exceed t seconds is $e^{-\mu t}$, where $1/\mu$ was the average duration of a call. The assumptions of exponential arrivals and services greatly simplified Erlang's mathematics and enabled a highly accurate model for telephone exchanges. The letters λ and μ became fixtures for arrival and service rates in queueing theory.

A few years later Erlang (1917) published a model that predicted the loss probability for a telephone exchange. The model was motivated by the practical concern for the cost and complexity of telephone switching. A center that could accept 100 percent of all possible phone calls would be prohibitively expensive even in a small town. Erlang showed that a much smaller, affordable center could serve if townspeople would accept a small chance that the system could not accept a call when they wanted to place it.

Erlang's method used the Markov chain invented by the Russian mathematician Andrey Markov in 1906. A Markov chain is a random process that follows a sequence of states such that the probably of next state depends only on the current state but not any previous states. When the distributions of times between state changes are exponential, Markov chains allow relatively easy calculation of the equilibrium state distribution, which is the long-term probability of finding the system in a given state. Erlang used a Markov chain to describe the state of a telephone exchange as the number of calls simultaneously in progress, and with that was able to calculate the probability of loss of a call.

The method of using Markov chains with exponential arrivals and services to find equilibrium state distributions of queueing systems was very powerful. It led to successful analysis of queueing problems in many fields such as transportation, crowd control, inventory control, telephone calling, manufacturing, hospital management, and toll booth management.

Computer designers began to apply queueing theory in computing systems in the 1960s for capacity planning of networks and time-sharing systems. Capacity planning is concerned with calculating how much of a resource is needed to keep queues from growing too large and to keep response time within acceptable limits. In his PhD thesis Leonard Kleinrock (1964) presented models for predicting delays of message traffic in communication networks. Network packets experience queueing delays as they move from router to router en route to their destinations. Kleinrock's models (1975, 1976) were used to optimize the routing structure of the ARPANET.

Capacity planning for a computer system is much harder. Instead of routers, computational servers such as CPUs, file servers, and input-output servers are at the nodes of the network. J. R. Jackson (1957) presented the first model for an open computer network in which all servers had exponential service times. An open network accepts every arrival, and the number in it varies. Ten years later W. J. Gordon and G. F. Newell (1967) solved the same problem for a closed network. A closed network contains a fixed number of jobs. Closed networks are common, for example, a system where all the users stay inside the system perimeter, a network protocol that limits the number of packets on the network, or a system where an external scheduler adds a new job to a system the moment another job leaves. The mathematical structure of Jackson-Gordon-Newell networks very nicely fit many computer systems. Unfortunately, the only known algorithms for computing their formulas were exponentially hard, making the solution of all but toy systems impossibly difficult. For this reason the Jackson-Gordon-Newell models had little practical value.

That changed in 1973. In that year Jeffrey Buzen (1973) discovered a hidden structure within the Gordon-Newell solution and demonstrated an algorithm that would solve the network in quadratic time rather than exponential time. Buzen's algorithm enabled a new generation of analysts wielding portable calculators to solve throughput and response time problems for systems in many fields. It also enabled a flood of experimental studies comparing predictions of closed network models with real systems, often finding amazing agreement—throughputs within 5 percent of measured values and response times within 25 percent.

Two years later Forest Baskett, Mani Chandy, Richard Muntz, and Fernando Palacios (1975) published a theorem, known now as the BCMP theorem, that generalized the Jackson-Gordon-Newell networks to arbitrary routing and service distributions and multiple job classes, provided that all the servers use one of four basic scheduling disciplines in their queues. The four scheduling disciplines are FIFO, processor sharing, pure delay, and preemptive resume last-come-first served. Buzen's algorithm generalized along with the model, allowing fast computational solutions of almost any network likely to be encountered in practice. Martin Reiser and Steve Lavenberg (1980) soon discovered a new algorithm that directly computed means of throughput, response time, and queue lengths. Buzen's algorithm did not compute these means directly. Their "Mean Value Algorithm" became the standard for computing queueing models.

The success of the models exposed a paradox. Computing systems did not fit key assumptions of traditional stochastic models, notably equilibrium and exponential service distributions. Yet the models predicted their throughputs and response times well. For example, computing systems do not exhibit equilibria—their performance varies with the workloads, which change at different times of day and days of the week. Performance analysts discovered that the much weaker assumption of flow balance, which means that the number of arrivals equals the number of completions, led to the same mathematical equations as for stochastic equilibrium (Buzen 1976, Denning and Buzen 1977, 1978). Flow balance is closely approximated in many computer systems during many time intervals.

Another anomalous aspect of computer networks is that service distributions are often conspicuously not exponential. Performance analysts discovered that a much weaker assumption of server independence, in which the output rate of a server in a network depends only on its local queue lengths but not on the queues of any other servers, gave the same mathematical equations as the stochastic models (Buzen 1976, Denning and Buzen 1977, 1978). Server independence is approximated in many computing systems during many time intervals.

The conclusion was that the traditional assumptions of queueing theory can be replaced by the simpler assumptions of flow balance and server independence and still yield the same formulas as traditional queueing network models. The simpler assumptions are close to what is observed in many computing systems. This is why queueing theory works so well for computing systems.[1]

Calculation and Prediction with Models

Queueing models are a way of deriving formulas that express the values of performance *metrics* (such as throughput, response time, or congestion) in terms of workload *parameters* (such as the mean service times and number of visits jobs require at each server of a network). By suppressing many details of the system, the models offer the means to calculate performance metrics much faster than a direct measurement. Analysts validate the model by comparing its calculations with the values of metrics measured in the working system. Validated models can often bypass direct measurement (see figure 9.1).

By far the most common use of models is *capacity planning*, where designers use models to evaluate whether a future system can meet throughput and response time targets. For example, they can calculate the largest load the system can tolerate within its throughput and response time targets or how much capacity needs to be added at a bottleneck to achieve its targets. They can also evaluate whether proposed structural changes will be effective, for example, whether a proposed control system will prevent thrashing.

Servers, Jobs, Networks, and Laws

A computer network is a set of interconnected servers. Servers can be workstations, disks, processors, databases, printers, displays, and any other devices that carry out computational tasks. Each server receives and queues up messages from other servers specifying tasks; a typical message might ask a server to run a computationally intensive program, to perform an input-output transaction, or to access a database. A job is a specified sequence of

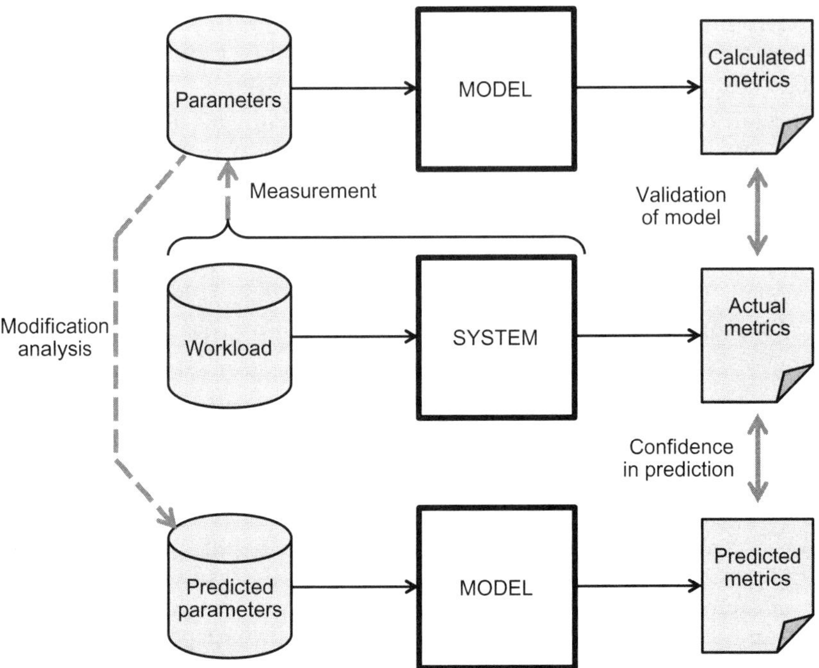

Figure 9.1
Performance prediction of systems is enabled by validated models. A system and its workload can be measured to obtain actual values of metrics such as throughput and response time (*middle*). A model is an algorithm whose inputs are measured parameters of the workload and system and whose outputs are calculated values of the metrics (*top*). In validation the model is repeatedly compared against various systems to build confidence that the model calculates metrics well. A validated model can be used for prediction. To predict the values of metrics at a future time, the analyst modifies the parameters by asking what will change and how it will change. The model is then used to calculate the predicted metrics (*bottom*). Because the model is validated, errors in the prediction most likely result from errors in the modification analysis.

tasks submitted to the network; when a server completes a particular task, it deletes the request from its queue and sends a message to another server, requesting that it perform the next task in the same job. Thus, a job flows through the network, visiting servers one at a time.

Our goal is to predict performance metrics (such as throughput and response time) for such a computer network given the parameters of the workload (the jobs) and the system (the interconnected servers).

Measurements of servers are always made during a definite observation period that lasts T seconds. Let us examine how we might measure parameters and find equations relating them to the metrics during the observation period.

By counting outgoing messages and measuring the time that a server's queue is nonempty, it is easy to measure the output rate X, the mean service time S, and the utilization U of a server. These three empirical quantities satisfy the relation $U = SX$, known as the *utilization law* (figure 9.2).

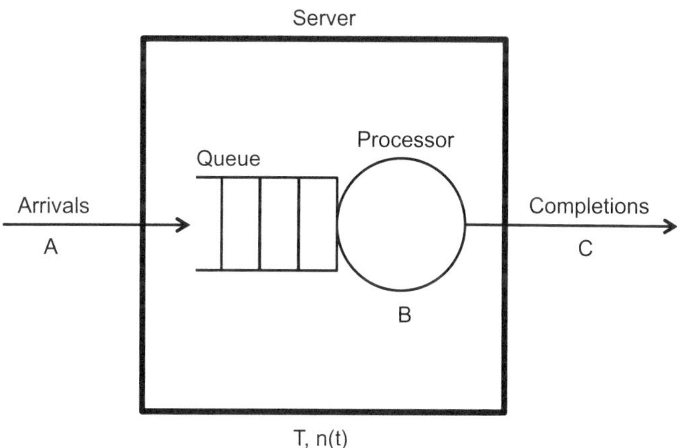

Figure 9.2
A single server system consists of a processor and a queue (storage area) to hold jobs waiting for service. In an observation period of T seconds, A jobs arrive and join the queue, and C jobs complete service and leave the queue. The state of the system $n(t)$ is the number of jobs in the system, in or waiting for service, at time t. The state increases at arrivals and decreases at completions. The system is busy at those times t when $n(t) > 0$, and idle when $n(t) = 0$. The timer B records the total busy time of the processor. The utilization of the server is $U = B/T$, the completion rate is $X = C/T$, and the mean service time per completed job is $S = B/C$. Because $B/T = (C/T)(B/C)$, we have the *utilization law*: $U = SX$. Because U cannot be greater than 1, X cannot be greater than $1/S$, meaning that the completion rate cannot be faster than one job every mean service time.

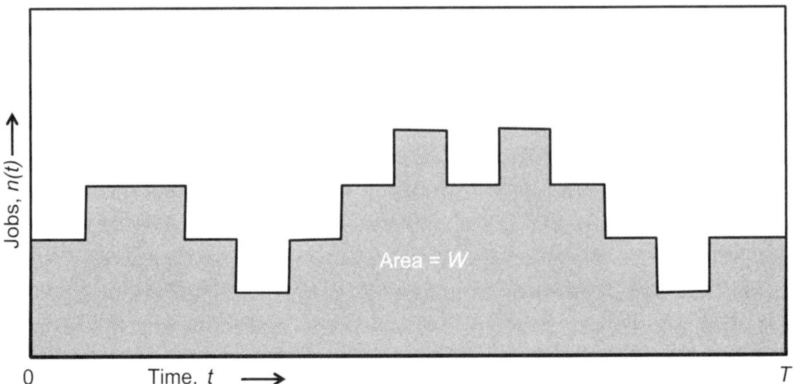

Figure 9.3
Average queueing and response time of a server can be calculated from the area W under the graph of $n(t)$ during the observation period. W is the number of job-seconds accumulated by all jobs in the system. For example, a job that waits 10 seconds in queue and then receives 2 seconds of service accrues 12 job-seconds. W is the counterpart of "square-foot months" used by real estate agents to compute rent, or "person-months" used by project managers to compute labor costs. The mean number of jobs at the server is $Q = W/T$, the average height of the graph. The mean response time is $R = W/C$, which apportions W among all the jobs completed. Because $W/T = (C/T)(W/C)$, we have *Little's law*: $Q = RX$. The mean service time S and mean response time R are not the same; R includes queueing delay as well as service time.

Similarly, by measuring the "job time" accumulated by queued tasks, it is easy to determine the mean queue length Q and the mean response time R: these quantities satisfy the relation $Q = RX$, known as *Little's law* (1961) (figure 9.3).[2]

Little's law is a most remarkable formula. It applies in any situation where there is a black box that holds items, a response time inside the box, and a flow through the box. Consider a simple example. A restaurant owner has a fine wine collection and sells an average of twenty bottles of fine wine per day each year. She wants to age every bottle for ten years before serving it to her customers. How large a wine cellar does she need? It is obvious that she must be able to withdraw 7300 = 365 × 20 bottles a year, and thus 10 years' worth of aging wine will demand a cellar of 73,000 bottles. Her calculation actually uses Little's law:

$$73{,}000 = Q = RX = (10 \text{ years})\ (7300 \text{ bottles/year})$$

The tasks making up a job can be regarded as a sequence of visits by the job to the servers of the network. The average number of visits per job to a

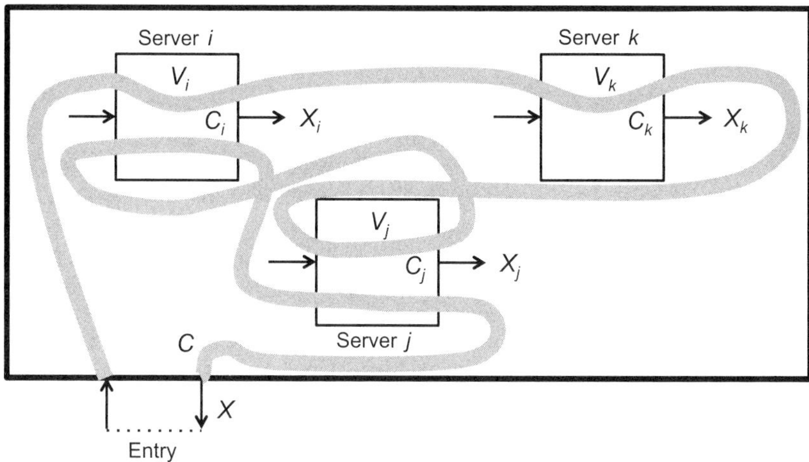

Figure 9.4
Flows of jobs through a network of servers can be represented with visit ratios. The entry is a designated point where jobs enter and exit the system. The system is open if the number jobs within it can change and closed if the number of jobs is fixed (dotted path across entry). The gray path shows how a job might visit the servers; in this case it visits server k once and servers i and j twice. For an observation period of length T, the completion counts C_i, C_j, and C_k are measured at those servers, and the completion count C at is measured at the system exit. The average number of tasks per job for server i is $V_i = C_i/C$; V_i is called the *visit ratio* because each task is regarded as a "visit" by the job to that server. The identity $C_i/T = (C_i/C)(C/T)$ reduces to the *forced-flow law*: $X_i = V_iX$. This law says that the task flow at one point in the system determines the task flows everywhere.

particular server i is called the visit ratio, V_i, for that server; the server's output rate X_i and the system's output rate X satisfy the relation $X_i = V_iX$, which is known as the *forced-flow law* (figure 9.4). This remarkable law shows that knowledge of the visit ratios and the output rate of any one server is sufficient to determine the output rates of every other server and of the system itself. This law holds regardless of the interconnections among the servers; any two networks with the same visit ratios will have the same flows.

It simplifies an analysis to assume that the input and output flows of a server are identical, a condition of flow balance. Balanced flows are called throughputs. The basic quantities and laws described above do not depend on or imply flow balance. Nonetheless, flow balance is a realistic assumption for practical systems. Because there is a limit N to the number of jobs that can be in the system at once, the largest possible difference between

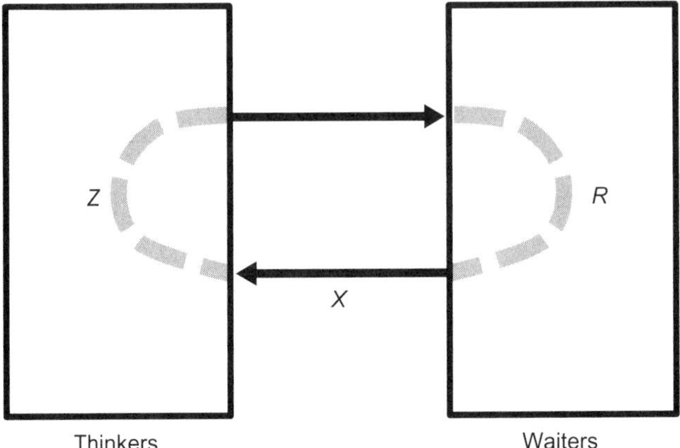

Figure 9.5
Users of a computer system alternate between periods of "thinking" and periods of "waiting" for a response from the system. The total number of users—thinkers and waiters—is fixed at N, a closed system. The average response time per transaction is R, and the average thinking time is Z. Applied to the thinkers box, Little's law says that the mean queue there is $Q_1 = ZX$. Applied to the waiters box, Little's law says that the mean queue there is $Q_2 = RX$. Because Q_1 and Q_2 sum to the fixed value N, we have $N = (R + Z)X$. Solving for R, we obtain the *response-time formula*: $R = N/X - Z$. This formulation assumes flow balance.

initial and final states of the observation period is N; as long as the number of completions at every server is large compared to N, the error introduced by assuming flow balance will be negligible.

When a network of servers receives all of its requests from a finite population of N users who each delay an average of Z seconds until submitting a new transaction, the response time for a request in the network satisfies the *response-time law* $R = N/X - Z$ (figure 9.5), which is exact for flow balance.

These formulas are sufficient to answer the throughput and response-time questions posed at the start of this chapter for the airline reservation network. We can represent the information given earlier as $V_i = 10$, $S_i =$ 0.005 second, and $U_i = 0.8$ for the directory disk. Combining the forced-flow law and the utilization law, we have for total system throughput:

$X = U_i/V_iS_i = 0.8/(10 \times 0.005) = 16$ jobs per second,

which comes to 57,600 jobs per hour. The response time experienced by any one of the 1000 agents is:

$R = M/X - Z = 1000/16 - 60 = 2.5$ seconds

We do not need to measure throughput and response time directly because we can calculate them exactly from simple measurements. If these calculations were compared to the actual system during the same observation period, as in figure 9.1, they would be exact. However, they might not be exact for a future period because the future parameters might not be the same as the present parameters.

We have just completed the most difficult part of queueing networks—learning six basic raw measures of a server, five metrics, and four laws. Tables 9.1, 9.2, and 9.3 summarize.

Bottlenecks

The last two questions on the list for the airline reservation system ask for estimates of response time in a future observation period having different conditions—for example, the directory-disk visit ratio is reduced, or the number of agents is increased. Because operational laws deal only with relations among quantities observed in the *same* observation period, they

Table 9.1
Basic Raw Measures of a Server

Notation	Description
T	Observation period
A	Number of arrivals
B	Total busy time of server
C	Number of completions
$n(t)$	Number in the system at time t, receiving or waiting for service. Also called queue length
W	Area under the graph for function $n(t)$ for the observation period

Table 9.2
Basic Performance Metrics of a Server

Notation	Definition	Description
X	C/T	Completion rate (jobs/second)
U	B/T	Utilization of server (fraction of time busy)
S	B/C	Mean service time (seconds)
Q	W/T	Mean queue length (jobs)
R	W/C	Mean response time per job (seconds)
V_i	C_i/C	Visit ratio for server i

Table 9.3
Operational Laws

Law	Formula
Utilization law	$U = SX$
Little's law	$Q = RX$
Forced flow law	$X_i = V_i X$
Response time law	$R = N/X - Z$

are not sufficient for making predictions. We must introduce additional, forecasting assumptions that extrapolate measured parameter values from the past observation period into the future observation period; the laws can then be used to calculate the response time expected in that future period (refer again to figure 9.1).

One common type of forecasting assumption is that, unless otherwise specified, the demands placed on the various servers, V_i, will be the same in the future period as they were in the base observation period. Similarly, unless otherwise specified, the mean service times, S_i, which depend primarily on mechanical and electrical properties of devices, will be the same. The utilizations, throughputs, and response times will change when any of these parameters changes.

Consider the question about what happens if the directory disk visit ratio drops from 10 to 5 with a new disk-indexing algorithm. What happens next depends on whether or not the directory disk is the bottleneck of the system. If it is not, some other server would be the system bottleneck, most of the jobs would be queued there, and its utilization would be near 100 percent. Under these conditions, reducing the demand for the directory disk will have only a negligible effect on the utilization and throughput of the bottleneck disk; the forced-flow law tells us that the overall throughput and response time of the network will therefore be unchanged.

If the directory disk is the bottleneck, we could speculate, based on the forced flow law, that halving the demand on it will double system throughput. But this speculation leads to a nonsensical answer: for the numbers given above, the formula yields a calculated response time of –28.75 seconds. The obvious absurdity of a negative response time—signifying that answers are received before questions are asked—indicates that the directory disk cannot be the bottleneck after demand on it is reduced by half, even if it had been the bottleneck originally. All we can say with the given information and the given forecasting assumptions is that halving the demand for the directory disk will reduce the response time from 2.5 seconds to some small nonzero and nonnegative value. If the 2.5-second response time is already acceptable, this proposed change in directory search strategy would not be cost effective.

Consider the question about what happens to response time if the number of agents is doubled. Again, we are limited by the lack of knowledge of the other servers. If the directory disk is the bottleneck, then doubling the number of agents is likely to increase its utilization to 100 percent, giving a saturation value of throughput:

$X = 1/V_iS_i, = 1/(10 \times 0.005) = 20$ transactions per second

With the response-time formula, these values yield:

$R = N/X - Z = 2000/20 - 60 = 40$ seconds

If the directory disk is not the bottleneck, some other server will have a smaller saturation throughput, forcing response time to be longer than 40 seconds. Thus, doubling the number of agents will produce a response time that is likely to be considered unacceptably high.

This example illustrates that bottleneck analysis is a recurrent theme in forecasts of throughput and response time (see figure 9.6). Suppose the visit ratios and mean service times are known for all the servers and do not vary with N. Each server generates a potential bottleneck that would limit the system throughput to $1/V_iS_i$ and would give a lower bound to the response time of $NV_iS_i - Z$. Obviously the server with the largest value of V_iS_i gives the least of the upper bounds on the throughput and is the real bottleneck. The products V_iS_i are all we need to identify the bottlenecks of a network.

Bottleneck analysis is a simple but powerful method for calculating the limiting asymptotes of throughput and response time. The bottleneck is always the server with the largest total demand (V_iS_i). The lower bounds $R(1)$ and $NV_1S_1 - Z$ can be close approximations for both small and large N. The biggest error between these asymptotes and the actual $R(N)$ occurs when the asymptote line crosses the horizontal axis, at $N = Z/V_1S_1$. To get more precision in that vicinity of load, we must turn to the computational algorithms described in the next sections.

Balance Equations

Balance equations are an essential tool for a more precise analysis of a queueing system. Queueing theorists from Erlang (1917) onwards have used them. We will illustrate the method for a single server system. Refer to figure 9.7 during the following discussion.

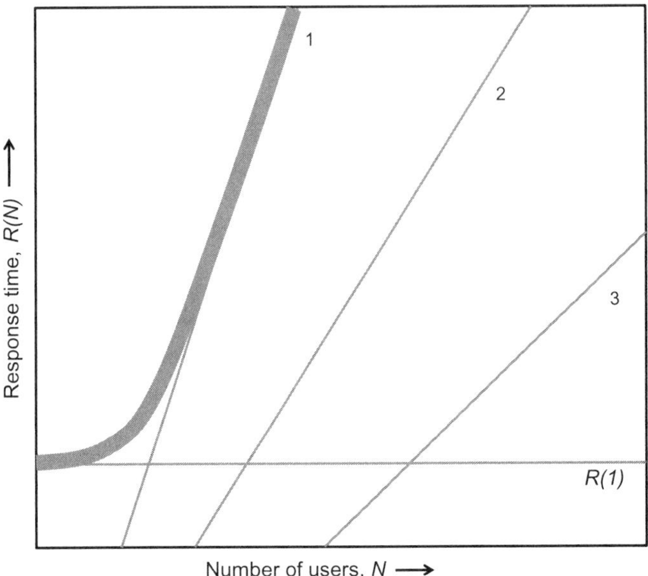

Figure 9.6
Bottleneck analysis shows how the response time changes as a function of N. When $N = 1$, the single user's jobs encounter no queueing delays from other transactions, whence $R(1) = V_1S_1 + \ldots + V_KS_K$, where K is the number of servers. Combining the utilization and forced-flow laws, $X = X_i/V_i = U_i/V_iS_i < 1/V_iS_i$ because $U_i < 1$. Thus, $R(N) > NV_iS_i - Z$ for all i. Each of the lines defined by these relations (such as 1, 2, and 3) is a potential asymptote for $R(N)$ with large N. The actual asymptote is determined by the largest of the potential asymptotes. Assume that the servers are numbered so that V_1S_1 is the largest, V_2S_2 the second largest, and so on. Then server 1 is the bottleneck, and $R(N) > NV_1S_1 - Z$. The bottleneck analysis assumes that the products V_iS_i do not vary with N.

The first step is to define the states of the system. For a single server the state is $n(t)$, the number of jobs at the server. For most real systems there is an upper limit N to the number of jobs that can be accommodated by the server. The states are therefore 0, 1, 2,…, N.

The second step is to define the allowable transitions between the states. For example, an arrival when the system is in state 3 will take it to state 4, whereas two simultaneous arrivals will take it to state 5. For most real systems, arrivals and completions are necessarily distinct events. So we model simultaneous arrivals as a series of arrivals very close in time. Thus, the only moves we can observe are "go up by 1" on an arrival and "go down by 1" on a completion, subject to the constraint that we cannot go up from state N or down from state 0.

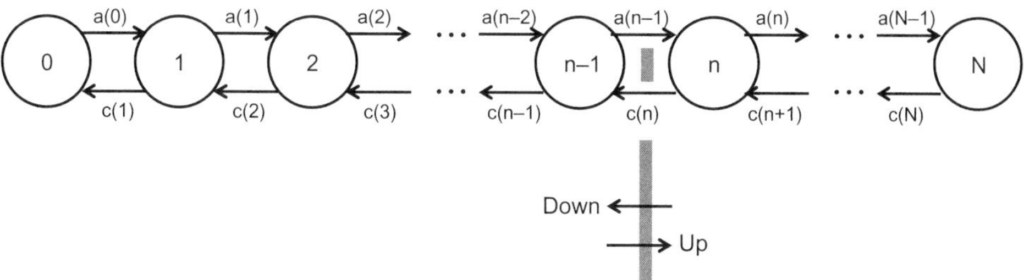

Figure 9.7
A state space analysis for a single server system leads to a balance equation. Here is the state space for a single server with capacity *N* jobs. The quantity $a(n)$ is the number of arrivals that occur when the system is in state n, and $c(n)$ is the number of completions when the system is in state n. Balance means that the initial and final states are the same, which implies that the number of up transitions from state $n - 1$ is the same as the number of down transitions into state $n - 1$; in other words $a(n - 1)=c(n)$.

The third step is to invoke flow balance and write a balance equation. Flow balance means that the final state of the system for an observation period is the same as the initial state; that is, $n(0) = n(T)$. In this case the number of transitions up from any state $n - 1$ is the same as the number of transitions down into state $n - 1$:

$$a(n-1) = c(n)$$

This is algebraically the same as

$$\frac{a(n-1)}{T(n-1)}\frac{T(n-1)}{T} = \frac{c(n)}{T(n)}\frac{T(n)}{T}$$

The first term of the left-hand side is the definition of $\lambda(n - 1)$, the arrival rate when the system is in state $n - 1$. The first term of the right-hand side is the definition of $\mu(n)$, the completion rate when the system is in state n. The second terms of both the left-hand and right-hand sides are just instances of $p(n)$, the proportion of time the system is in state n. Thus, we have the balance equation

$$\lambda(n-1)p(n-1) = \mu(n)p(n)$$

or

$$p(n) = p(n-1)\frac{\lambda(n-1)}{\mu(n)}$$

When combined with the condition that the $p(n)$ sum to 1, this balance equation can be solved very easily on a spreadsheet.[3] This equation shows that the arrival and completion rates completely determine proportions of time the system is at any particular state in a flow-balanced system.

Once we have the solution for the $p(n)$, we can see that the utilization of the server is simply $U = 1 - p(0)$. We can calculate the completion rate as the weighted average of completion rates from each state n

$$X = \sum_{n=1}^{N} \mu(n) p(n)$$

We can calculate the mean queue length as the expected value of the probability of being in state n

$$Q = \sum_{n=1}^{N} n p(n)$$

The response time comes from Little's law as $R = Q/X$.

These calculations are mathematically identical to those in standard queueing theory but rest on different assumptions. In standard queueing theory the $p(n)$ are the long-term equilibrium probabilities of observing the system in state n. Here the $p(n)$ are the fractions of time the system is observed in state n; they are exact if the system is flow balanced and good approximations if the system has many arrivals or completions compared to N. This is why the equilibrium formulas from standard queueing theory work so well in real computer systems.

Let us illustrate this method with three examples of computer system configurations.

An ATM

A bank ATM looks like a single server that can build up a queue of length no larger than N, the size of the waiting area. The number of potential customers is so large that the aggregate arrival rate is steady, no matter how long the queue. In this case the arrival rate is $\lambda(n) = \lambda$, and the service rate is μ because only one customer is served at a time. The balance equation is

$$p(n) = p(n-1)\frac{\lambda}{\mu}$$

Figure 9.8 illustrates an analysis when this balance equation is programmed into a spreadsheet.

A Telephone Exchange

This is the problem studied by A. K. Erlang in 1917. The state n of a telephone exchange is the number of calls in progress. Equipment limitations

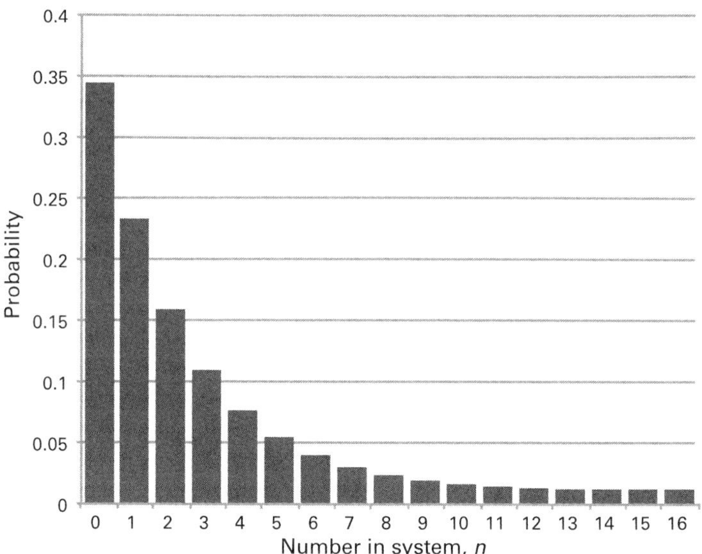

Figure 9.8
A spreadsheet graphed $p(n)$ for the ATM problem with maximum queue $N = 16$ and various values of the ratio $r = \lambda/\mu$. This graph shows the distribution $p(n)$ when $r = 2/3$. Because $\lambda < \mu$, it is strongly biased toward small queues: the queue is 2 or fewer 70 percent of the time and idle 33 percent of the time. When the values of the arrival and completion rates are interchanged ($r = 1.5$), a mirror-image graph (not pictured) shows the system spending 70 percent of its time with fourteen or more customers in queue and no idle time. When arrival and completion rates are the same ($r = 1$), all the bars are equal height; all sixteen queue lengths are equally likely, and the system is idle 6 percent of the time.

impose a limit of N calls at once. A customer attempting to place a call when the state is N will be turned away. Because the customer population is large, the arrival rate is a steady λ for all states. The average duration of a call is $1/\mu$. In state n the n calls are happening in parallel, so the combined completion rate is $n\mu$. This gives the balance equation

$$p(n) = p(n-1)\frac{\lambda}{n\mu}$$

Erlang's design problem was to choose N, the exchange capacity, so that the chance of a customer being turned away is acceptably low. For example, the acceptable loss rate might be set at 0.001, meaning that we want to find N such that $p(N) < 0.001$. Figure 9.9 illustrates an analysis when this balance equation is programmed into a spreadsheet.

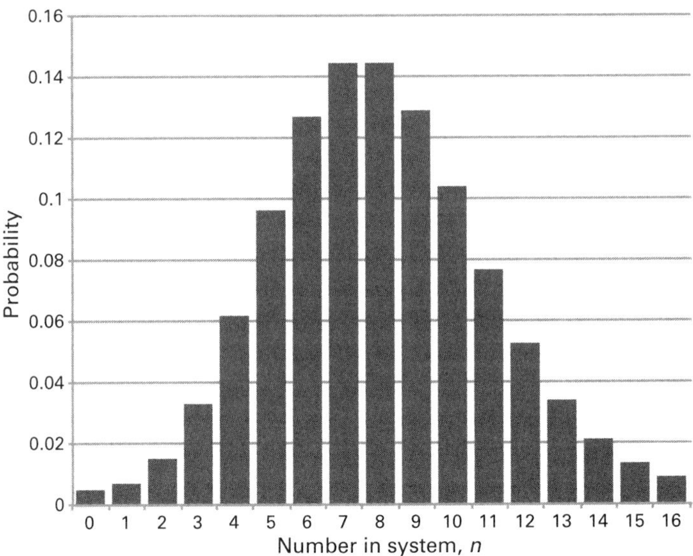

Figure 9.9

A spreadsheet graphed the $p(n)$ for the telephone exchange problem with call maximum $N = 16$ and ratio $r = \lambda/\mu = 1$. This graph shows that the exchange has a strong preference for states where the exchange is half full. This exchange is seldom empty and has a small loss probability $p(16) = 0.005$.

A Time-Sharing System

Allan Scherr (1965) at MIT built a performance model of the compatible time-sharing system (CTSS) that predicted its throughput and response time with surprising accuracy. He used a model from queueing theory called machine repairman, which works as follows. In a shop a repairman services N machines that break down individually at rate λ and require an average time $1/\mu$ to fix. The state of the system is the number of machines broken down and queued for repair. This model translates to a time-sharing system in which N is the user population, the repairman becomes the CPU with mean service time $1/\mu$, and the machines become the users with individual think times $1/\lambda$. In this case the arrival rate to the CPU in state n is $\lambda(n) = (N - n)\lambda$ because $N - n$ users are thinking when n are waiting at the CPU. The completion rate from state n is $\mu(n) = \mu$ because only one job is served at a time. The balance equation is

$$p(n) = p(n-1)\frac{(N-n+1)\lambda}{\mu}$$

Scherr validated the model by inserting probes into the kernel of the CTSS operating system to capture event records of jobs starting and finishing, samples of the CPU queue lengths, and samples of response times. He was then able to compare his data with calculations from the model and validate that the model gave good predictions of throughput and response time of CTSS.

Scherr's result was a surprise to many people, who could not believe that such a simple model could account so well for the throughput and response time of a complex time-sharing system.

Computing with Models

As a final step in the modeling process, we would like to extend the model for any queueing network. As before, we need to define the system states and their balance equations. The states of a network of K servers are more complicated than for a single server. The state is represented as a vector whose components tell the number of jobs at each of the K servers. Figure 9.10 shows a model for the airline reservations system and a list of its ten possible states when $N = 2$.

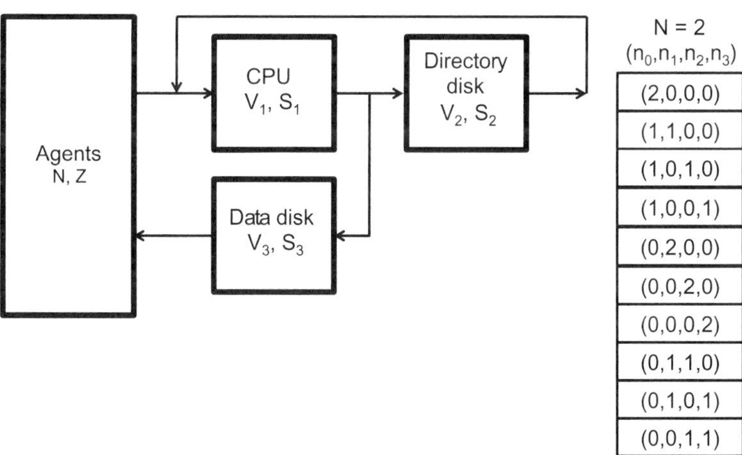

Figure 9.10
This model represents the airline reservation system as four servers: Agents, CPU, Directory, Data. When $N = 2$, this system has ten possible states, listed at the right. The sum of components of each state must equal $N = 2$. For example, state (2, 0, 0, 0) means that both users are thinking and all the servers are idle. State (0, 1, 0, 1) means that one user's job is running on the CPU and the other user's job is running on the Data Disk.

Table 9.4
Mean Value Equations

Equations	Justifications
(1) $R_i(N) = S_i(1+Q_i(N-1))$, all i	When a job arrives at server i, it sees a queue that is approximately the same as an outside observer would see when there is one less job in the system. Its response time is one service time for each job in the queue just after its arrival.
(2) $R(N) = \sum_{i=1}^{K} V_i R_i(N)$	Each visit to server i accumulates one local response time.
(3) $X(N) = \dfrac{N}{R(N)+Z}$	Little's law applied to the total time to loop through a think-wait cycle.
(4) $Q_i(N) = X(N)V_i R_i(N)$, all i	Little's law applied at each server.

A balance equation for each state expresses that the number of transitions into the state equals the number out over the observation period. Unfortunately, the number of states grows exponentially with the number of users N and the number of servers K. The model of figure 9.10 has 10 states when $N = 2$, 286 states when $N = 10$, and 176,851 states when $N = 100$. For a network with thousands of users and servers, the number of balance equations is so large that a computational solution is intractable.[4]

Jeff Buzen (1973) discovered a way to calculate the basic metrics from this model in $O(NK)$ steps. His discovery was a major breakthrough for performance analysts. A few years later Martin Reiser and Steve Lavenberg (1980) found a slightly better algorithm. Their method is called *mean value analysis* (MVA) because it directly computes the means of the response times, throughputs, and queue lengths. It is summarized in table 9.4.

The equations give the server response times $R_i(N)$, system response time $R(N)$, system throughput $X(N)$, and server queue lengths $Q_i(N)$. The equations ingeniously build the quantities for load N from the previously computed queue lengths at load $N-1$. The mean value algorithm evaluates the four equations in a cycle for $N = 1, 2, 3, \ldots$ until the desired value of N is attained.

On inspection you should be able to see immediately that equation 2 in table 9.4 is simply an operational law for system response time in terms of server response times. Equation 3 is the response time law. Equation 4 is Little's law $Q_i = R_i X_i$ combined with the forced-flow law $X_i = V_i X$. What about equation 1?

Equation 1, which is not a law, is an approximation based on the following simple idea. When a job arrives at a server, it joins a queue of some size k, increasing it to $k + 1$. Each job in the queue, including itself, requires an average service time of S seconds. Therefore, the response time is $R = S(k + 1)$. What value should be used for k?

Reiser and Lavenberg got their answer from a theorem called the *arrival theorem*. It says that the queue length at a server when a job arrives is the same as an outside observer would see with one less job (itself) in the system. In other words jobs arriving at servers act as outside observers. Thus, the expected value of k is $Q(N - 1)$.

For large N this algorithm can be wasteful. If you want to find the throughput and response time for $N = 1000$ in our airline example, you have to compute and then discard all the values for $N = 1, 2, \ldots, 999$. Yan Bard (1979), in consultation with Paul Schweitzer, found a shortcut. They employed an approximation for the mean queue length:

$$Q_i(N-1) = Q_i(N)\frac{N-1}{N}$$

This approximation simply scales the queue length at N to the queue length at $N - 1$ in proportion to the loads. When this is substituted in the first equation, the resulting equations express the mean values only for load N. That leads to the simplified equations of table 9.5. We can solve them by using the equations to generate a series of guesses for the mean value quantities, starting with the (incorrect) guess that the queue lengths are N/K. After a relatively small number of iterations, this procedure converges rapidly to values very close to those computed by the full-fledged mean value equations. It is easily implemented on a spreadsheet.

We applied the simplified model to figure 9.10 after choosing the two missing parameters and used it to answer the two prediction questions posed at the beginning of this chapter (see figure 9.11).

Table 9.5
Simplified Mean Value Equations

Equations	Justifications
(1) $R_i = S_i\left(1 + Q_i\frac{N-1}{N}\right)$, all i	Equation 1 of table 9.4 with the approximation for $Q_i(N - 1)$ substituted
(2) $R = \sum_{i=1}^{K} V_i R_i$	Same as equation 2 of table 9.4
(3) $X = \frac{N}{R+Z}$	Same as equation 3 of table 9.4
(4) $Q_i = XV_iR_i$, all i	Same as equation 4 of table 9.4

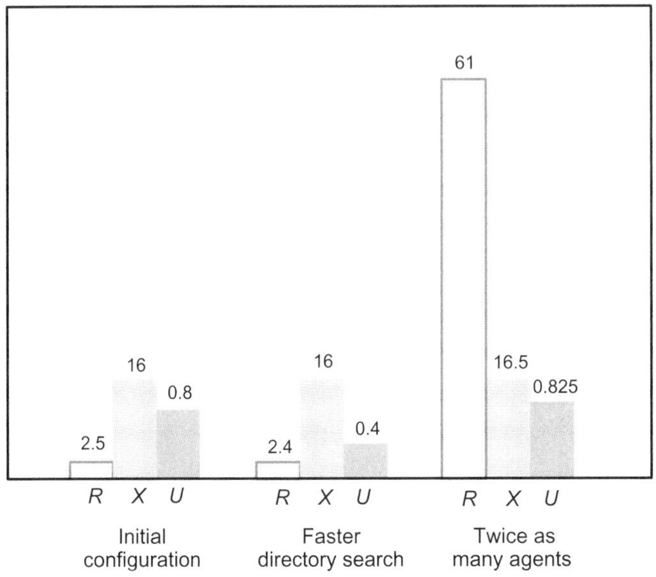

Figure 9.11
These graphs show the model results for the two prediction questions about the airline reservation system modeled in figure 9.10. We chose the two missing parameters, S_1 and S_3, as follows. We chose the total CPU time to be 50 milliseconds and solved $S_1V_1 = 50$ milliseconds, giving $S_1 = 4.5$ milliseconds. We chose S_3 as 60 milliseconds. The total demands for the three servers are $V_1S_1 = V_2S_2 = 50$ milliseconds, and $V_3S_3 = 60$ milliseconds, making the data disk the bottleneck. With these values, the equations of table 9.5 yielded the results shown at the left. Consider the two prediction questions. The first prediction question is: What happens if a new Directory Disk structure reduces visits there to five, everything else being the same? The model gave the results shown in the middle: the Directory Disk utilization is cut in half with little effect on throughput and response time. The reason is that speeding up the Directory Disk did not change the fact that the Data Disk is the bottleneck. The second prediction question is: What happens if agents are doubled to 2000? This change, shown at the right, has little effect on the throughput because the CPU and Directory Disk are already near saturation, but it has a significant negative effect on the response time.

Conclusions

One of the most difficult questions about computations is: How long does it take? This question is difficult on networks of servers where jobs compete and queues form. Although jobs and the network are deterministic, the response times are random. The uncertainty is caused by randomness in the arrivals of jobs and in the lengths of their service times at servers in the network. Queueing theory has proved to be a remarkably accurate way to overcome the uncertainty and predict throughput, response time, and congestion in networks of computers (Buzen 2011).

Computer scientists began using queueing theory in the 1960s. They made two major contributions that advanced the theory and its application. They discovered very fast algorithms for computing performance metrics from queueing models whose formulas had appeared to require exponentially hard computations. With these algorithms, the models could be evaluated rapidly. That enabled an explosion of experimental studies that demonstrated simple models were likely to predict throughput to within 5 percent of measured values and response times to within 25 percent. And when they could not explain why the agreement was so good even when the system did not fit key model assumptions, computer scientists found simpler assumptions that applied to many real systems and led to the same equations.

A key principle of queueing analysis is to develop balance equations for flows in and out of each state of the system. The solutions of the balance equations are the proportions of time each state is occupied. The proportions of time are then used in formulas for throughput and response time.

One of the most remarkable theorems contributed by computer scientists was that the queue length seen by a job arriving at a server is the same that any outside observer would see when the system load is one less. In other words the arriving jobs act as outside observers for a system without them in it. This theorem led to the mean value equations, which give a very fast algorithm for computing mean throughput, response time, and queue lengths of any network of computers.

10 Design

Simplicity is inherently complex.

—Peter G. Neumann

Descriptions of software entities that abstract away their complexity often abstract away their essence. Good judgment comes from experience, and experience comes from bad judgment.

—Frederick Brooks

I vividly remember the day when I realized I would be spending a substantial part of the rest of my life trying to find the mistakes in my programs.

—Maurice Wilkes

We are searching for some kind of harmony between two intangibles: a form which we have not yet designed and a context which we cannot properly describe.

—Christopher Alexander

In late summer 1944 a remarkable group of designers came together to discuss the structure of a general purpose, stored program, digital computing machine. They were J. Presper Eckert and John Mauchly, the chief engineers of the ENIAC project, John von Neumann, a well-known mathematician, and Arthur Burks and Herman Goldstine, also mathematicians. They had vigorous and lively discussions about what had been learned from prior projects to design computing machines. They rapidly distilled the best of older ideas and added new ideas to create a package of principles that became the basis for the design of most stored-program electronic computers since then (Goldstine 1993, Wilkes 1995). From detailed analyses they knew that the stored-program principles would lead to a computer that was much faster and more efficient than any that had gone before. They built a machine, EDVAC, and got it working in 1951. Maurice Wilkes at the

University of Cambridge, UK, adopted the principles and built a machine, EDSAC, in his laboratory; it went into operation in 1949. The stored-program machine has been a remarkably durable design (see figure 10.1).

As they gained experience with programming, the designers on these projects made refinements to make the machines more efficient and less error-prone. They invented index registers, which allowed the computer to access tabular data, known now as array data, by adding an index to the memory address contained in the instruction. They designed instructions for subroutine call and return. They designed interrupt systems, which enabled the processor to jump to subroutines in response to external signals. And they designed virtual memory to automate the error-prone process of manually encoding data moves up from secondary memory to main primary memory.

These machines gave birth to a new profession, programming, and eventually to a software industry.[1] The first scientific programmers designed numerical methods, and the first business programmers designed methods of processing large data sets. They all realized early on that programming is difficult and inherently error-prone. System designers looked for ways to make programming easier and more reliable. One of their great advances in this direction was the invention of higher-level programming languages: Fortran (1957), Lisp (1958), Algol (1958), and Cobol (1959). These languages allowed programmers to formulate concise, succinct expressions for complex algorithms. Compilers automatically translated their programs into machine code. Debugging tools helped programmers find and correct mistakes in their programs. Libraries of well-tested and verified common programs came into wide use; examples were mathematical software and system utilities.

Despite the attention to tools, methods, and libraries, it was widely acknowledged that most software was unreliable and untrustworthy. In 1968 a group of leading software experts came together at a famous NATO workshop on software systems. They declared the entire software industry to be in a state of perpetual crisis because the size and complexity of needed systems always seemed to exceed our tools and skills for building them. They called for a new field of "software engineering" to bring rigorous engineering methods to software development. Many universities responded by creating new curricula in software engineering methods. Throughout the software industry, many developers produced new tools and methods to help reduce errors and make software predictably reliable.

Eighteen years later Fred Brooks, a software expert and former manager of the IBM 360 operating system project, wrote "No Silver Bullet," a famous

Figure 10.1

Maurice Wilkes and William Renwick stand by the EDSAC at University of Cambridge circa 1949. EDSAC was the first working stored-program computer implementing a package of six ideas developed by Eckert, Mauchly, von Neumann, Burks, and Goldstine in 1944. The six ideas were: (1) Everything was electronic; there were no moving parts except for input and output. (2) Inside the computer numbers were represented in binary, greatly increasing tolerance against transient or noisy signals in the circuits. (3) The instruction set was the user interface to the machine; users controlled these machines by writing programs in it. (4) Instructions are executed sequentially. (5) A single main memory made no distinction between instruction codes and data. (EDSAC used mercury delay lines for its main memory.) (6) Instructions could be modified during execution. Machines based on these principles have come to be known as "von Neumann architectures" because the first published version was von Neumann's notes from the group meetings (von Neumann 1945). (Photo source: Cambridge Computer Laboratory Relics Project, with permission) assessment of the progress of software engineering (Brooks 1986). He said that despite tremendous advances in tools, our ability to create dependable, reliable, usable, safe, and secure software systems had not materially improved. He said that the hard part of software design was getting an intellectual grasp of the problem to be solved by software. That will never be easy. Success depends largely on the cultivation of people who have the requisite skills.

This is a profound conclusion. In large measure the success of a design depends on the engineer's skill, not on formal mathematical analysis or derivations from first principles. It also depends on knowledge of history in the designer's field, which informs the designer on what works and what does not work.

It should be obvious by now that designers play a central role in computing. Through their skill at shaping software and hardware, they create computations that produce intended meanings and support intended practices. The hardware and software are just tools in their hands. This chapter is about how designers get organized so that they can produce the results they intend despite the complexity.

Among the greatest challenges in computer science are the design and construction of large computing systems that their users judge to be dependable, reliable, usable, safe, and secure, or DRUSS for short. The best methods have been encoded into structures of languages and operating systems that allow everyone to benefit. This chapter is about not only design principles and skills for computing but also the structures that designers use to attain the DRUSS objectives.

What Is Design?

Design is familiar in many fields including fashion, products, architecture, engineering, science, and software development. Design is a process in which we create and shape artifacts that solve problems. In software, for example, design means crafting software that does jobs users want done. Software designers intentionally support practices, worlds, and identities of the software's users. Designers have accumulated much practical wisdom that is expressed with design principles such as separation of concerns, modularity, abstraction, layering, wholeness, utility, resiliency, beauty, and timelessness. Design principles in computing guide us to ways of building machines whose behaviors are useful and meaningful in their user communities (Norman 2013, Winograd 1996).

It would be wrong to conclude that the skill of design can be captured by design principles and patterns. Design is a subtle and deep skill with many aspects that can only be learned from doing under the guidance of good mentors. Generally speaking the job of a designer is to listen to a community deeply to understand their concerns, issues, and interests and then to propose a combination of existing components and technologies that address those concerns, issues, and interests. Designers watch how people react to the proposals and then make new and better proposals. There are many cycles of evaluation and learning in the designer's work. Moreover, design is heavily historical because designers must work with existing components and concerns, which are constantly changing.

Design had been a concern in many fields long before software designers appeared. Architects seek buildings and bridges that are functional, safe, esthetic, and enduring.[2] Clothing designers seek new ways to make clothing fashionable and functional. Industrial designers seek consumer products satisfying the Rams principles—innovative, useful, esthetic, understandable, unobtrusive, honest, long lasting, thorough, environmental, and simple.[3] Engineers seek to build complex engineering systems that are dependable, reliable, and safe. The term "design thinking" has been used to describe a mindset that approaches problem solving in these ways (Denning 2013).

Software systems designers have had to meet two sets of standards: the traditional engineering standards of design, expressed by the DRUSS objectives, and the standards of industrial design, expressed by the Rams principles. Different schools of design have emerged within computing corresponding to different emphases on these aspects.

Seasoned designers constantly run experiments with prototypes to learn how well their artifacts work and how users might react to them. Maurice Wilkes (1913–2010) stressed this point in his 1967 ACM Turing Lecture, saying that a great strength in the early days was the willingness of research groups to construct experimental computers without necessarily intending them to be prototypes for commercial production. Their experiments produced a body of knowledge about what would work and what would not work (Wilkes 1968b). In his 1995 memoir he strongly criticized the more recent trend to ignore the historical development and try to design from scratch. Without the knowledge of what worked and what did not, designers have tended to repeat the same mistakes (Wilkes 1995, p. 90). We can see this today: the designers of personal computer operating systems and software tried to avoid the mistakes of the previous, mainframe era by ignoring them ("keep it simple") and wound up repeating the mistakes a generation later and then struggling to believe that solutions had been found many years before. Like Fred Brooks, Wilkes believed that good design is a skill set with many dimensions, well worth cultivating.

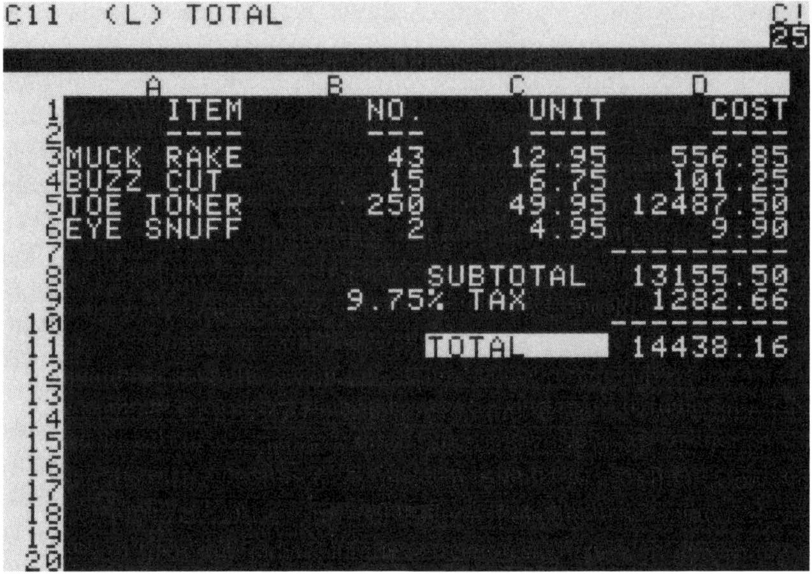

Figure 10.2
VisiCalc, the first spreadsheet program, was introduced in 1979 for the Apple II personal computer. Its designers, Bob Frankston and Dan Bricklin, adopted standard accounting practices into their spreadsheets. Numbers could be displayed in rows and columns. Labels could be placed anywhere. Standard arithmetic operations were specified by formulas placed in spreadsheet cells; the screen display showed result of the formula, not the formula. Business users found it completely natural to set up spreadsheets and found that the automation of formulas greatly accelerated their work. VisiCalc demonstrated an important design principle: align the design with practices familiar to users. (Photo source: Wikipedia Creative Commons)

Many designers aim to automate existing practices rather than create new practices. The automated spreadsheet, invented in 1979, is an example. It imitated standard business practices for tallying and displaying numbers and, through automation, greatly speeded up the calculations (see figure 10.2). The ATM (automatic teller machine), introduced in 1971, is another example; ATMs simply offered automated versions of deposits and withdrawals, actions familiar to every bank customer.

Criteria for Software Systems

In chapter 5 on Programming we discussed the error problem, which is the universal tendency of programmers to make mistakes in programming.

There are many opportunities for mistakes along the path from the designer's conception to the perceptions of users of the final product. This problem has been a major challenge for programmers since the beginning and has motivated the heavy use of the engineering design process to reduce errors. Even so it has been an uphill battle (Neumann 1995).

Despite the difficulties, the engineering design process is the backbone of most software development. To maximize its chances of success, designers work with five success criteria:

1. *Requirements* Does it have a clear purpose?
2. *Correctness* Does it work properly?
3. *Fault tolerance* Does it keep working?
4. *Timeliness* Does it complete its work in time to be useful?
5. *Fitness* Does it align well with the environment?

The principles for achieving these criteria have been embodied into structures in languages, tools, operating systems, and networks.

Requirements

The designer knows what job the machine is intended to perform and can state the requirements precisely as a specification. This is easier said than done. Articulating requirements is a challenge because interviewing the intended users about what they want is notoriously unreliable. Many designers succumb to the temptation to focus on technology rather than to listen to users (Norman 2010). Letting intended users interact with prototypes is often a more reliable way to learn what mistakes they are likely to make and what aspects of the system are most valuable.

Correctness

The behavior of a source or machine code program provably meets precise specifications. Correctness is challenging because requirements are often fuzzy and proofs are often computationally infeasible. Experimental methods are often the only practical way to test whether functions meet specifications and avoid intractability.

The dream of correct computation goes back to Charles Babbage (1791–1871), who was deeply concerned about errors in mathematical tables such as tabulations of sines, tangents, or logarithms. These tables were calculated using "difference methods"—each line of the table was computed from the previous by adding a small "difference." All this was done by hand. A small error at one line could propagate forward and magnify into large errors in all the subsequent lines. Babbage demonstrated that errors in navigation tables caused shipwrecks. In 1823 he persuaded the British government to sponsor him in building a Difference Engine that would calculate navigation tables very quickly without making the kinds of errors that tired or distracted humans can make. Unfortunately, Babbage made little progress, and the government abandoned the project in 1842. The Swedish engineers Georg and Edvard Scheutz built two copies of a Difference Engine in 1843, but the machines were temperamental and difficult to set up, and few people wanted to use them.

This small history lesson reminds us that computing machines have never been error-free. They provide new sources of errors. The designers must prove that the machine code implements the desired function. If the machine only approximates the desired function (as for the Difference Engine), the designers need additional analyses and proofs that rounding errors cannot build up and sabotage the results.

Computing designers have always been interested in the possibility that machines themselves could construct the needed correctness proofs. The most advanced form of automatic verification is model checking (Clark and Emerson 1981, Quielle and Sifakis 1982, Clark 2008). The idea is to model the system with a finite-state machine and verify that the model satisfies a set of temporal-logic formulas. The machine model represents the observable states of the real machine and the transitions that can occur between them. The logic formulas represent the formal specification. Model-checking technology has been successful in verifying real-time systems with a large number of states.[4]

Fault Tolerance

The software and its host systems can continue to function despite small errors and will refuse to function in case of a large error. Redundancy supports fault tolerance by duplicating hardware and data so that a failed component can be bypassed by other still-working components and data sets. Error confinement supports fault tolerance by structuring the operating environment so that no process has access to any object other than those it needs for its computation and by limiting (or eliminating) the super user state.[5]

The related principle of least privilege means that the designer sets the default access of each process to the smallest possible set of objects needed for that process to do its job. It supports error confinement by limiting the number of objects that an error can influence.

Mechanisms for error confinement are of three kinds:

1. *Static checks in the software* Primary examples are type checks performed by the compiler: floating-point operations apply to floating-point data

only, character strings can only be passed to subroutines expecting string arguments, file handles are passed only to file system functions, and so on.
2. *Dynamic checks in the software* A primary example is array bounds checking, which verifies that each value of an array index is within range declared for the array. Another example is buffer overflow protection, which verifies that the size of an argument to a procedure may not exceed the storage allocated for the argument. A compiler can add code to do such checks automatically.
3. *Dynamic checks in the host environment in which the software runs* For example, an operating system enforces that a handle passed to the file manager is tagged "file." Another example is an operating system that enforces storage partitioning: a process cannot execute an instruction that changes the memory bounds of another process or access a page belonging to another process.

Static checks are the cheapest, but they do not catch dynamic errors such as erroneous input, data corruption, or equipment failure. Dynamic internal checks are often avoided because of their overhead—imagine adding code to a fast loop to check that an array index remains in bounds. Therefore, we need help from the operating environment. We give examples of operational structures below.

Another important approach to fault tolerance is the "end-to-end argument," commonly used in distributed systems and networks (Saltzer et al. 1984). The idea is to concentrate error checking at the two ends rather than the middle of a communication channel; an error is corrected by asking the transmitter to resend a portion of the communication. This approach is at the heart of the TCP protocol of the Internet (Tanenbaum 1980, Comer 2013).

Timeliness

The system completes its tasks within the expected deadlines. Supporting techniques include algorithm analysis, queueing network analysis, and real-time system deadline analysis.

Fitness

The dynamic behavior of a system aligns with its environment of use. Fitness is challenging because the DRUSS objectives are context sensitive and much of the context is not obvious even to the experienced designer.

The ATM, mentioned earlier, is an example of an excellent fit between a machine and the standard practices of its user community. Experienced software designers understand that they are not designing just a mechanism but also a practice for users to engage in. The closer the practice is to other practices the users are familiar with, the easier it will be for them to use the software.

Other examples of good fit include games, spreadsheets, Amazon.com, Bayesian spam filters, semantic web, Google, linkers and loaders, thrashing controllers in operating systems, and forensics tools. Examples of poor fit include unidentified error codes from operating systems, automated voice menus at business phone numbers, and online technical support and help systems.

Design Principles, Patterns, and Hints

Designers have accumulated much practical wisdom to meet the challenges described above. The wisdom is expressed as design principles, design patterns, and design hints.[6]

Design principles are descriptions of skills and strategies that software designers follow when making design decisions. The strategies almost always lead them in the direction of designs that meet the five criteria.

Design patterns are descriptions of common situations a programmer is likely to encounter. They offer guidance on how to structure the program, or the process of writing it, for best results.

Design hints are useful rules of thumb, morsels of advice, but are not as compelling as principles or patterns.

We give examples of principles, patterns, and hints in the next three subsections. Be warned that the number of published principles, patterns, and hints is large; we counted 115 in the examples below. This is not an indication of immaturity of the field but rather of the high level of skill that good designers embody.

Principles

The now-classic paper by Jerome Saltzer and Michael Schroeder (1975) about information protection is an excellent example of design principles (see table 10.1). Many years later Saltzer and his colleague Frans Kaashoek published a monumental work that took them nearly 30 years to perfect (2009). They presented twenty-five validated system design principles and many more subsidiary principles. We do not go into any of them here.

Patterns

Within computing various schools of thought have developed around specific approaches to the five criteria. These schools have advanced "process

Table 10.1
Information Protection Principles of Saltzer and Schroeder

Principle	Directive
Economy of mechanism	Keep the design simple and small.
Fail-safe defaults	Deny access by default; grant access only by explicit permission.
Complete mediation	Check every access to every object.
Open design	Do not depend on attackers being ignorant of the design.
Separation of privilege	Grant access based on more than one piece of information.
Least privilege	Force every process to operate with the minimum privileges needed for its task.
Least common mechanism	Make shared state information inaccessible to individual processes, lest one corrupt it.
Psychological acceptability	Protection should be easy to use, at least as easy as not using it.

models" such as waterfall or spiral, or "design approaches" such as participatory, user centered, agile, or pattern. They are all after the same thing, but they weigh the criteria in different ways. Barry Boehm (2002) argued that the standard engineering design approach of careful, almost rigid process was at the strict end of a planning spectrum, and agile methods were at the flexible end. He thought that careful planning is needed when reliability, safety, and security are important and that agility is needed when usability and evolvability are important. He exhorted the careful-planning schools to collaborate with the agile schools to find the common ground for better systems.

In the early 1990s a group of programmers from the agile school founded the "software pattern community" movement, inspired by the design-pattern idea of architect Chrisopher Alexander (1979). A *software pattern* characterizes a large number of situations a programmer is likely to encounter and offers guidance on how to structure the program to best fit the pattern. One of their first works was a compendium of software patterns (Coplien and Schmidt 1995). The community has produced many other patterns since then. A compilation in Wikipedia lists forty-eight patterns in four categories[7]:

1. *Creational: patterns for managing the creation of new objects and interfaces* An example is "avoid expensive acquisition and release of resources by recycling objects no longer in use."

2. *Structural: patterns for organizing code* An example is "group related elements into a single conceptual entity."
3. *Behavioral: patterns of desirable behaviors of modules* An example is "avoid null references by providing a default null object."
4. *Concurrency: patterns for managing concurrent objects* An example is "use a monitor when an object's methods are subject to mutual exclusion."

The pattern community appeals to our sense of empiricism because its members are relentless about testing ideas with potential users and learning from the feedback.

Hints

Butler Lampson, a superb and accomplished designer, summarized a number of guidelines that help designers (1983). He called his statements "design hints" because none works for all cases. They are a sense of direction that good designers develop over time. Table 10.2 summarizes his hints as slogans. We do not explain them. The point is that there is considerable art in designing. Lampson has outlined the best practices of his art.

Table 10.2
Lampson's Design Hints

	Correctness & Fit	Speed	Fault Tolerance
Use cases	Separate normal and worst cases	Safety first Shed load End-to-end	End-to-end
Interface	Keep it simple Do one thing well Don't generalize Get it right Don't hide power Use procedure arguments Leave it to the client Keep interface stable Keep a place to stand	Make it fast Split resources Static analysis Dynamic translation	End-to-end Log updates Make actions atomic
Implementation	Plan to throw one away Keep secrets Reuse a good idea Divide and conquer	Cache answers Use hints Use brute force Compute in background Batch processing	Make actions atomic Use hints

Design Principles for Software Systems

As suggested above, the software engineering literature records a large number of design principles that have been widely studied and found to be strongly supportive of good design. The very best of these principles have been encoded as structures that appear in languages, application programs, and operating systems. The most popular structures include:

modularity	class hierarchies
interfaces	layering
abstraction	virtual machines
information hiding	reuse
encapsulation	objects and packages
decomposition	version control
separate compilation	client server
functional levels	

These structures are intended as tools to help with recurrent patterns that designers encounter. It is easy to lose sight of the patterns that the structures are supporting. We describe six patterns that encompass everything on the list above: hierarchical aggregation, encapsulation, levels, virtual machines, objects, and client servers.

Hierarchical Aggregation

Hierarchical aggregation means that objects (identifiable software and hardware components) consist of interconnected groups of smaller objects and are themselves components of larger objects. You can interact with an object as a unity and not be concerned with its individual parts. When you do look inside, you focus on the interactions among components and are not concerned with what is going on in the external environment. Thus, there is a hierarchy with smaller aggregates making up larger aggregates. Aggregates at every level of the hierarchy are insulated from lower- and higher-level details.

Hierarchical aggregation is common in nature. Physical objects can be aggregated at many levels according to their sizes. Quarks, electrons, protons, atoms, and molecules are at the lowest dimensions with scales as small as 10^{-18} meters; planets, solar systems, galaxies, clusters, and quasars are at the highest dimensions with scales as high as 10^{26} meters. Nature encompasses forty-five levels in a natural hierarchy of aggregate sizes.

In biology, living organisms have hierarchies with levels including DNA, genes, cells, organs, nervous systems, plants, animals, and social systems. In mathematics, fractals are sets whose subsets follow the same structure rules as the set: the same structure is observed at all levels of aggregation. In computing, the principle of locality is a consequence of hierarchical aggregation: neighboring components interact more frequently than components at a distance, and a single interaction with an object can trigger a long sequence of internal actions among the object's components.

In the list of design structures, modularity, abstraction, information hiding, and decomposition are complementary aspects of hierarchical aggregation.

Modularity is a process of dividing a large system into a hierarchy of smaller aggregates (modules) that interact across precisely defined interfaces.

Abstraction means to define a simplified version of something and to state the operations (functions) that apply to it. For example, the bit (0 or 1) is an abstraction of all sorts of media that rely on two states to store or transmit information; computing involves the physical actions of reading or writing bits. Abstraction is one of the most fundamental powers of the human brain. By bringing out the essence and suppressing detail, an abstraction offers a simple set of operations that apply to all the cases. An abstraction corresponds to an aggregate in a hierarchy; forming a hierarchy is a process of abstraction. Abstractions in classical science are mostly explanatory—they define fundamental laws and describe how things work. Abstractions in computing do more: not only do they define computational objects, they also perform actions.

A file (a named sequence of bits) is a common abstraction for named containers of digital objects—for example, text documents, graphs, spreadsheets, images, movies, sounds, directories, and more. A file system provides create, delete, open, close, read, and write operations that work on any file. Any program's output (already represented as bits) can be stored in a file. The file system does not have to understand the differences between file formats assigned by applications—it just stores and retrieves the bits.

Information hiding means to hide the details of an implementation from users (Parnas 1972). It protects against errors caused by changes in the details that do not concern users. It protects the details by preventing users of the abstraction from accessing them. In a hierarchy it is a decision to hide the internal component structure of an aggregate, allowing that structure to be rearranged without changing the behavior of the aggregate. A software module hides the implementation details of a function behind a simple interface.

File systems illustrate information hiding. The users see only files but not the complex nest of internal details including disks, disk drivers, disk addresses, records, index tables, buffers, caches, open file control blocks, and RAM copies of files. The user benefits in two ways. First, all the user does is open, close, read, or write files and never has to worry about which disks hold the files, how the file is decomposed into blocks stored randomly on the disk, how buffers are managed, and so on. Second, the software engineers who maintain the file system can make internal improvements without forcing users to change anything.

It is possible to have abstraction without information hiding. An organizational hierarchy, for example, is a set of abstractions that group people by functions. But executives can micromanage, a practice of reaching into a group and overriding its local leaders.

Decomposition means to subdivide a large problem into components that can be designed separately and then assembled into the full system. In a hierarchy, identifying the components of an aggregate is an act of decomposition. A module is an abstraction of the components that compose it.

Designing by decomposing a system into modules and interfaces is often insufficient in large systems. When the independently designed modules are plugged together, the system often does not work even though the module designers insist that the individual modules meet specifications. The problem is that the interactions among the modules are as important as the internal computations of the modules; independent module designers do not see or test the interactions. Considerable testing of the system as a whole is needed, leading to redesign of individual modules until the entire system works.

Encapsulation

An example of a support in the operating environment is the encapsulation of software into minimum-privilege domains (Dennis and Van Horn 1966, Fabry 1974, Saltzer and Schroeder 1975). This mechanism is especially useful when running untrusted software. A process's protection domain is represented by a *capability list*, a table of pointers to all the objects a process is authorized to access. (Capability lists were discussed in chapter 7 on Memory.) Because the operating system maps all references to objects through the capability list, a process can access only the objects explicitly shown in its capability list. All other objects are inaccessible simply because there is no way for a process to generate their addresses.

Normally a process uses just one capability list during its life. However, when a process needs to use an untrusted procedure, it can switch into a small, separate domain that calls the procedure code and contains just the objects the procedure needs for its advertised job. The encapsulated procedure has no access to any other objects of its caller. When the procedure is done, its return restores the original domain of the caller. No matter what errors or malicious intents the encapsulated software might have, it cannot damage any object outside its restricted domain (see figure 10.3).

Levels

Levels are a form of hierarchical aggregation that stratifies components. All objects in the same level are treated as peers with respect to how they interact with each other and with the higher levels. The levels structure of the universe, mentioned earlier, illustrates this. At the level of atoms, we are concerned with issues such as chemical bonding, electron deficiencies, and molecular shapes but not with what materials the atoms belong to or with what holds the protons and neutrons together inside atoms.

The levels principle has been used in computing to structure very complex, provably correct software systems. Its first use was to structure an operating system. In 1968 Edsger Dijkstra completed an operating system at Technische Hogeschool Eindhoven, known to posterity as "THE operating system." He organized it into seven levels, each containing software components that realized a particular abstraction. The "processes" level, for example, abstracted away from the processor by creating an abstraction of a computation that always moved forward except when it was waiting for a signal. All software components above the process level could be programmed with processes instead of subroutine calls and "CPU context switches." The process level solved once and for all the problem of multiplexing the CPU among programs to give the illusion of joint parallel processes. A decade later, a group at SRI, Inc., built a "provably secure operating system" of fourteen levels in which they were able to prove that a level is secure given that all levels below it are secure (Neumann et al. 1980) (see figure 10.4).

Internet engineers have structured protocol software as layers. Layers are like levels in that they stratify software so that higher-level functions are built from lower-level functions. The file transfer protocol TCP, for example, is built on several lower-level layers including IP protocol, routing protocol, data link protocol, and physical signal protocols (Tanenbaum 1980, Comer 2013). Layers differ from levels in an important way. Layers access each other by passing data downward or upward through intervening layers; levels access only lower levels by direct procedure calls.

Whether applied in operating systems or networks, the levels principle facilitates system construction, correctness proofs, and testing because a system can be built up one level or layer at a time.

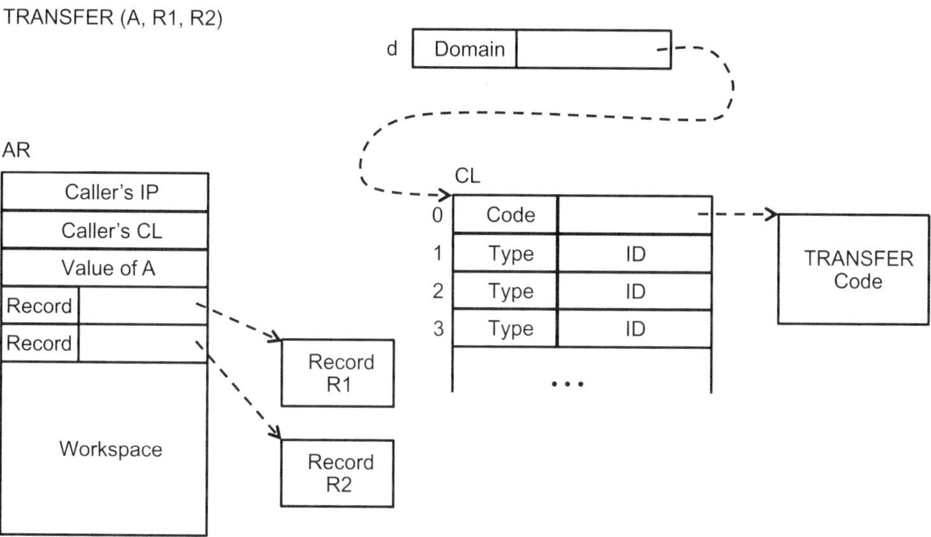

Figure 10.3
Capability-based operating systems provide structures that aid error confinement. The structure shown here encapsulates an untrusted funds transfer program, which moves an amount *A* from account record *R1* to account record *R2*. When TRANSFER is called, its capability list is the one pointed to by the domain capability *d* at the top. Its domain contains the code for TRANSFER plus any internal other objects packaged with that code by the compiler of TRANSFER. The normal call instruction is replaced by a new instruction "ENTER *d*" that takes a domain capability *d* as argument. ENTER creates an activation record (AR), changes the current capability list (a CPU register) to *d*, and sets the instruction pointer to the location 0 of capability 0 of that list. The TRANSFER code comes into execution in the restricted domain *d*. The activation record now includes a domain capability for the caller's capability list, allowing it to be restored on return. The AR also contains capabilities pointing to the two records passed as parameters. While it executes, the only external objects TRANSFER can access are the two records passed into its AR during the call; it has no capabilities for anything else.

Level	Name	Objects
9	Shell	Interface language that runs application programs and manages windows and user - generated events
8	Directories	Directories, trees of directories, path-names
7	Streams	Files, devices, pipes
6	Virtual machines	Virtual machines
5	Threads	Multiple threads in address space
4	Inter-process communication (IPC)	Messages, ports, sockets
3	Virtual memory	Address space, page
2	Processes	Process, ready list, semaphore
1	Low-level I/O	Device, driver
0	Hardware levels	Interrupts, procedures, call stacks, instruction set, logic gates

Figure 10.4
This example of 10 levels comes from a composite model of many operating systems (Denning et al. 2000). The hardware is at the lowest level. Each level above that adds a new function as a subsystem that implements a small set of operations on a particular type of object, for example, read and write on files. The functions of a level are composed of operations on objects of lower levels but not higher levels. Levels 1–5 make up the *microkernel,* the smallest set of functions that must be executed in supervisor mode. Microkernels can be implemented in surprisingly small amount of memory. Levels 5–9 are usually distributed, which means that all machines on the mutually trusting network can access any object in the network regardless of its physical location. The difference of time scales from the user level to the hardware level is about 10^{15}, making operating systems among the most complex artificial systems.

Virtual Machines

A virtual machine is a simulation of one computer by another. The idea comes from the simulation principle behind Alan Turing's Universal Machine. The term virtual machine is used in four ways.

First, it means the simulation of any abstract computing machine. An abstract computer has a set of operations that apply to values in the machine's memory. Each operation is like an instruction of a hardware computer. The set of operations is often called the Application Program Interface (API). The user of the abstract machine interacts only via its API and cannot bypass it to look or affect what goes on inside. The subsystems of an operating system that manage classes of objects, such as files, are organized this way. Figure 10.5 illustrates the example of a file system.

Second, virtual machines are simulations of hardware computers. The virtual machine has subroutines that carry out the effect of the machine instructions on the hardware computer. This idea came into practice in the late 1950s when a second generation of computers began to replace the first generation. The new computer had to run all the software written for previous versions of the computer. Accordingly, the new computer's instruction set contained microcode that simulated the old computer's instruction set. The "emulation mode" of these new machines allowed old programs to run with the old instruction set. As old programs were brought up to date and were recompiled for the new instruction set, they would run faster. This mode can be found today in such programs as Parallels, VMware, and Hyper-V, which simulate entire computers running their own operating systems. The ubiquitous Java Virtual Machines (JVM) emulate Java on any commercial machine by executing the Java "byte code" produced by Java compilers. This allows great portability of Java programs.

Third, virtual machines are simulations of computers within separate memory partitions of the machine. This was the organizing principle of the IBM VM 370 and later operating systems. The IBM virtual machine was a complete simulation of an IBM mainframe identical in every way to the original except that it had a reduced main memory (see figure 10.6). A similar idea is used today in the multitasking features of operating systems such as Mac OS and Windows. This approach allows the virtual machine to run at nearly the same speed as the real machine; there is no significant performance loss.

Fourth, a virtual machine is a standard environment for implementing any program within an operating system. This idea was pioneered in the Multics system at MIT (Organick 1972) and the UNIX system at Bell Labs (Ritchie and Thompson 1974). These systems defined a "process" as a program in execution on a virtual machine. The virtual machine was simply a standard template for providing input and output to a running program and connecting with any submachines it may have spawned. Every user program would be embedded into the standard virtual machine for execution (see figure 10.7).

Objects

Objects are a virtual machine structure that originated with a programming practice called "data abstraction" in the 1960s and evolved into over 120 sophisticated "object-oriented languages" today. An object is an abstract

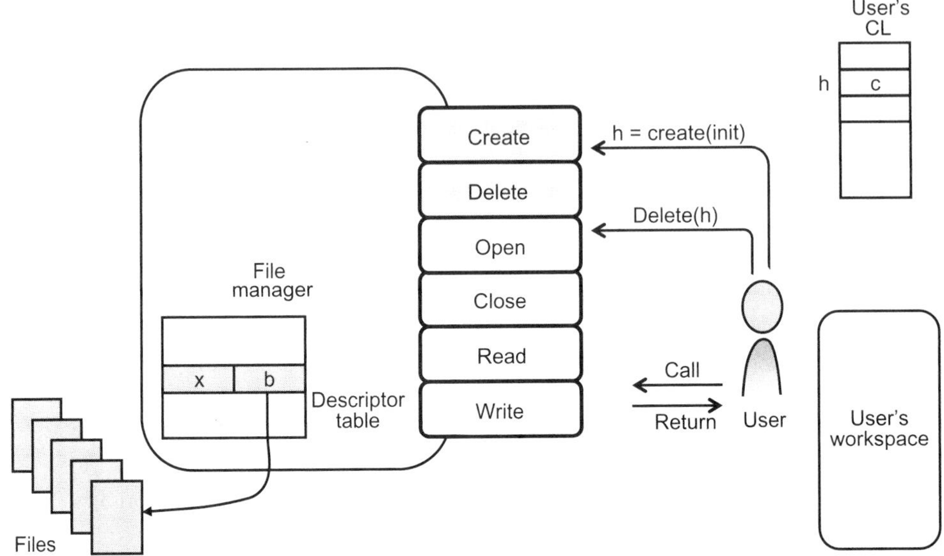

Figure 10.5

A file manager looks like a virtual machine with a simple six-operation instruction set and a memory that holds files. The internal structures of the file manager are hidden (encapsulated)—users cannot see file structures, descriptor tables, buffers, or code of the operations. The six operations work as follows. *Create* generates a new file at location *b* in the memory, assigns a unique identifier *x*, and embeds *x* in a new capability *c*. It returns the new capability *c* to the user's capability list at a convenient position *h*. It records the association (*x*,*b*) in its internal descriptor table. Thereafter, the user refers to the file by its local name *h*. The operation *delete*(*h*) removes the file *h*. *Open*(*h*) makes a copy of the file in a RAM buffer (for fast access), and *close*(*h*) writes the buffer back to disk and deletes it. *Read*(*h*) and *write*(*h*) transfer bytes between the buffer and the user's workspace. The five file system operations with parameter *h* extract the unique identifier *x* from the file capability *h*, find entry *(x,b)* in the descriptor table, and apply the operation the file at location *b*.

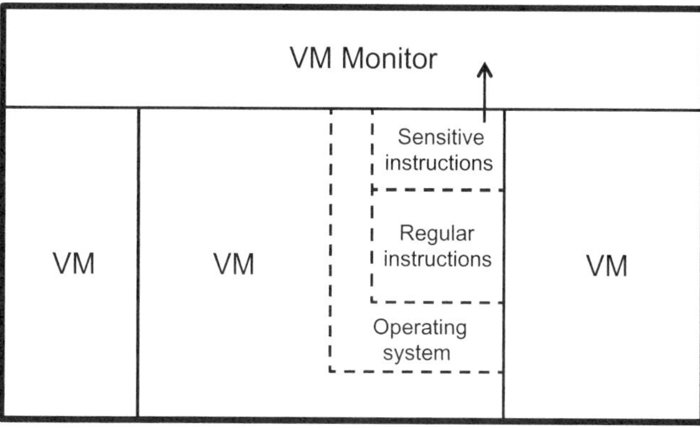

Figure 10.6
A virtual machine operating system partitions the RAM into disjoint blocks, one for each virtual machine (VM). A virtual machine is an exact copy of the CPU, and its memory contains its own copy of an operating system; thus, virtual machines can run different operating systems. The Virtual Machine Monitor is a global operating system that allocates virtual machines and maintains their separateness and integrity. To do this the CPU instruction set is divided into two parts. The regular instructions apply only to the contents of the VM's assigned memory and can be directly executed. The sensitive instructions affect the state of the system seen by other VMs and may not be directly executed. Examples of sensitive instructions are "increase the memory allocation" or "shut off the interrupts." If the CPU attempts a sensitive instruction, it is interrupted, and the VM Monitor takes over. For example, a sensitive instruction to change memory allocation would be intercepted by the VM Monitor, which would grant the allocation after verifying that it does not overlap with any other VM's assigned memory. Most of the time, this type of virtual machine is running the regular CPU instructions at full machine speed.

entity that can be viewed and altered only through a defined set of operations. Its internal structure is hidden. For example, as discussed above, a file is a container of a sequence of bits and can be acted on only with the open, close, read, or write operations; its structure as a set of records scattered across a disk is hidden.

Some object languages present objects as data structures that can be manipulated only by procedures associated with the class of objects; examples are Python, Java, and C++. Other object languages present them as autonomous entities that are activated by sending them request messages and that return their results in response messages; examples are SmallTalk and Squeak. The message view is often used when objects are used in distributed computing systems.

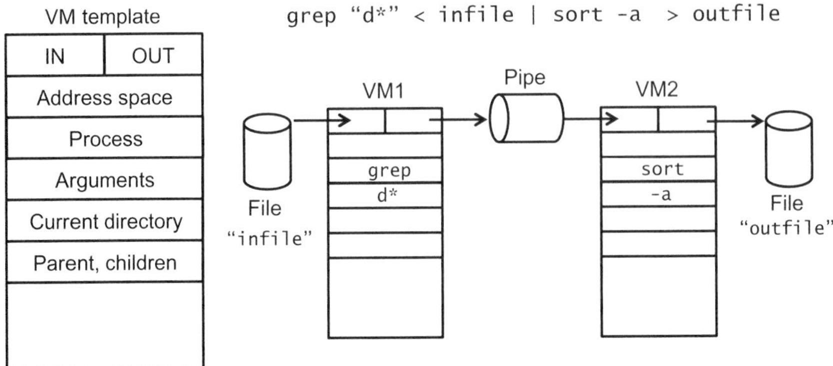

Figure 10.7
The operating systems Multics and UNIX introduced a virtual machine model to execute user commands. The template of a virtual machine (*left*) is a standard form providing an IN port, an OUT port, a pointer to an address space, a pointer to a process in that address space, the set of arguments passed to the process in the virtual machine, the current directory in use by the virtual machine, and pointers to the parent virtual machine and any children virtual machines. When a user types a command to the shell interface (*upper right*), the shell parses it into a set of components and creates a virtual machine pipeline to execute the command (*lower right*). In this example, "grep," a search program, takes its input from a file "infile" and outputs only the lines beginning with the letter "d." That output flows to the "sort" program, which arranges its input lines into alphabetic order and places its results in the file "outfile." By standardizing the form of virtual machines, allowing any file to be input or output, and providing a "pipe" structure to flow one VM's output into another VM's input, these systems made it possible to provide rich functionality with a simple command language.

Objects are grouped into *classes* (also called types) with similar properties and the same set of operations. For example, a file is a member of the class of all files. An abstract machine called a class manager can be the environment for implementing the class operations; for instance, the file manager can open, close, read, or write any file and can locate all the components of a file in the disk storage system (refer again to figure 10.5).

Object classes are usually organized into *inheritance hierarchies* so that properties of an object propagate down the tree into its "children." For example, a byte file might be a subclass of bit files, and a directory might be a subclass of byte files formatted to associate strings with handles.

Objects also come with mutual exclusion locks so that only one process at a time can use a particular object. This prevents race conditions.

Objects are sometimes presented as a first principle because they manifest the fundamental principle of abstraction. However, they are actually an advanced concept because they provide a unified way to deal with a host of structural and synchronization problems. Novice programmers often find objects confusing because they do not yet understand abstract machines, information hiding, inheritance, and synchronization.

Clients and Servers

The client server model is a conceptually simple way to organize interactions between processes in a distributed (networked) computing system.[8] A server is a process dedicated to performing a particular service on request. A client is another process that makes requests. Clients and servers are usually (but not always) on different hosts in a network. Their requests and responses are passed as messages through the network. For example, a network file server stores all the files of the network's users; client processes on user workstations send it requests to read and write files. An authentication server interacts with the login client on a user's workstation to process the user's credentials during login. A web server interacts with client browsers to send them web pages.

Although the client server idea is simple, its implementations are often far from simple. Designers must master many subtle details to get communications, error control, and synchronization working correctly (Birrell and Nelson 1984).

In some systems pairs of interacting servers can play either role (client or server) with each other. In that case they are called peer-to-peer (P2P) processes. Many network services are organized this way. For example, the Internet TCP protocol runs in a local process on every machine of the network; a local TCP process can request remote connections to other TCP processes or receive remote requests for connections from them.

Conclusions

Design has been a central issue of computing since the beginning. The first designers in computing had to figure out how to arrange electronic circuits and memory for efficient, reliable computation. They gave us a remarkable plan, the stored-program computer, also called the von Neumann architecture, which is still in use today.

The machine's instruction set is the user interface for a stored-program computer. Programmers designed algorithms and encoded them in the instruction set. From the earliest days, programmers found themselves spending much of their time hunting for mistakes in their programs: they discovered debugging. They found that programming is inherently complex and error-prone. They set out on a quest, which goes on to this day, to design programs that are dependable, reliable, usable, safe, and secure (DRUSS). Over the years they have developed a programming profession and software industry that relies on a wide range of technologies to prevent errors in programs and confine them if they occur. Even with all this technology, errors in programs are a major problem.

Designing is not just about the arrangements of hardware components and instructions to solve problems. It is about providing value to the users of the computing machines. Designers have to understand how users will use programs and anticipate what will delight or infuriate them. Designers must become competent at the skill of design.[9]

In their quest for systematic ways to design good software, designers work with five success criteria: requirements, correctness, fault tolerance, speed, and fitness. Requirements are concerned with formulating precise statements of the job the system will perform, correctness with preventing errors during construction, fault tolerance with minimizing the effects of errors until they can be corrected and expunged, speed with configuring systems to get results on time, and fitness with user satisfaction.

Five design patterns are particularly useful in designing computing systems and software: hierarchical aggregation (bringing in abstraction, decomposition, modularity, information hiding), encapsulation, levels, virtual machines, and objects. These patterns appear as structures in languages, application programs, and operating systems. Although none is a panacea, there is a broad consensus that these structures help meet the five design criteria and support the general DRUSS goals.

There are numerous other principles of software design that we cannot cover here because of space limitations. There are more principles for project management, error confinement, fault tolerance, network structure, operating system structure, and correctness than we have been able to discuss. Design is a rich field. It makes all the difference between successful and failed computing systems. Designing well is perhaps the greatest challenge in computing.

11 Networking

Human brains and computers will be coupled together very tightly; the resulting partnership will think as no brain has ever thought and process in a way not approached by information handling machines today.

—J. C. R. Licklider

New digital computer techniques using redundancy make cheap unreliable links potentially usable. The network is best designed for data transmission and survivability at the outset.

—Paul Baran

As networks grow up, we will probably see the spread of "computer utilities," which, like present electric and telephone utilities, will service individual homes and offices across the country.

—Leonard Kleinrock

It is hard to imagine that a network connecting all computers in the world was just a dream in 1960. In the mid-1960s the US Defense Department took the first steps toward this dream. It started planning the ARPANET, an experiment in resource sharing. It began operating the ARPANET in 1969 with two hosts, the networking term for attached computer systems.[1]

The ARPANET was the first in a chain of technologies that evolved to the current Internet. Because the original design did not scale to a large network, the idea of an expandable "Internet," or network of networks, was introduced in 1973. After a decade of testing and improvements, the Internet design became official; hardly anyone noticed when the ARPANET was decommissioned in 1989. The World Wide Web was overlaid on the Internet in the early 1990s. The growth of networking technologies has been phenomenal. About 200 hosts were connected in 1981, 200 thousand in 1990, 200 million in 2004, and 1 billion hosts in 2014. Today's Internet includes millions of component networks. It is a convincing demonstration of the tremendous value a network can generate for its members.[2]

This remarkable technical achievement is the result of its designers cleverly combining computing principles from all six categories named in chapter 1. The design enabled the Internet to scale seven orders of magnitude over 30 years of reliable operation. As a case study, we examine here each major aspect of the Internet and show which computing principles it relies on.

The concept of a network is much older than the Internet. Around 1750 mathematician Leonhard Euler drew the first network graphs to prove that there is no tour of the city of Königsberg crossing each of its seven bridges just once. Since that time graph theory emerged as a major area of mathematics for studying relationships between objects. A network consists of a set of nodes (also called vertices) and a set of links (also called edges) connecting some of them. The links often represent flow paths by which some entity moves from one node to another—for example, signals, messages, commodities, requests, and promises. Electrical engineers developed flow, energy, current, and voltage conservation laws and applied them to design electrical networks with desired signal transfer functions. Industrial engineers and operations researchers developed network models of many kinds of systems including manufacturing, transportation, inventory, communication, and queueing; the models enabled accurate performance predictions of those networks. Today social scientists use networks to map communication relationships among members of a community and draw inferences about power and influence. The Internet exhibits features of these different networks: it is a communication system, a transportation system (of messages), an information retrieval system (of data), a queueing system (of services), an inventory system (of storage subsystems), and a social network support system.

Resilient Networks

In the early 1960s defense communications engineers began searching for alternatives to the telephone network. Defense officials were very concerned about using the telephone network for their communications. The telephone network was based on the principle of *circuit switching*, which meant that dialing a phone number caused a series of mechanical crossbar switches to provide a direct electrical connection from a calling station to a receiving station. The telephone network had evolved into a small set of regional switching offices connected by "trunks"; the regional centers were connected to local switching offices, in turn connected to individual homes and offices. The network could be severely disrupted by a natural disaster (such as a fire or flood) or a manmade disaster (such as a terror attack) because disabling one or a few nodes could completely sever the network. Not only was the network insecure—a telephone line could be tapped fairly easily—but it was unreliable in the face of hostile operations. The telephone network was seen as a serious weak spot in national defenses.

Leonard Kleinrock (1961, 1964) and Paul Baran (1964a,b) were the first to examine alternatives. Kleinrock formulated and analyzed a stochastic model of a message-switching system. Baran proposed a new design for telephone communication, in which analog voice would be digitized and the resulting bitstreams broken into packets that would travel through a store-and-forward system to their destinations, where they would be reassembled into the original bitstream.[3] A digital file can be transmitted similarly by clustering its bits into a sequence of packets. The network itself would contain many redundant paths so that packets could move to their destinations by alternate routes in case some part of the network was down. Reconfigurable routers handle the routing; they receive messages and then forward them to the next router one hop (link) closer to the destination host. Modern networks are a combination of a mesh structure for the long-distance backbone and hub-and-spoke structure for local connections (see figure 11.1). Local networks can take a variety of forms (see figure 11.2).

Packet Switching

A *packet* is a sequence of bits consisting of a few headers and a chunk of data (see figure 11.3).[4] *Packet switching* is a mode of operating a network so that a subnet of devices called routers, like the backbone of figure 11.1, transport packets to their destination hosts. The discussion below examines the principles of packet networks.

Packet switching is an instance of the multiplexing principle mentioned in earlier chapters. *Multiplexing* means to divide a resource into chunks and then allocate the chunks to various individuals. For example, main memory is multiplexed by dividing it into pages; pages can be quickly placed anywhere convenient and can be removed when they are unused. Disks are multiplexed among many files by dividing all files into records and allowing records to be scattered around the disk. A channel is multiplexed by dividing each signal stream into packets and transmitting the packets on the channel; several streams can share the same channel.

Packet multiplexing was one of several "time division multiplexing" methods used in telephone systems in the 1950s. For example, voice is

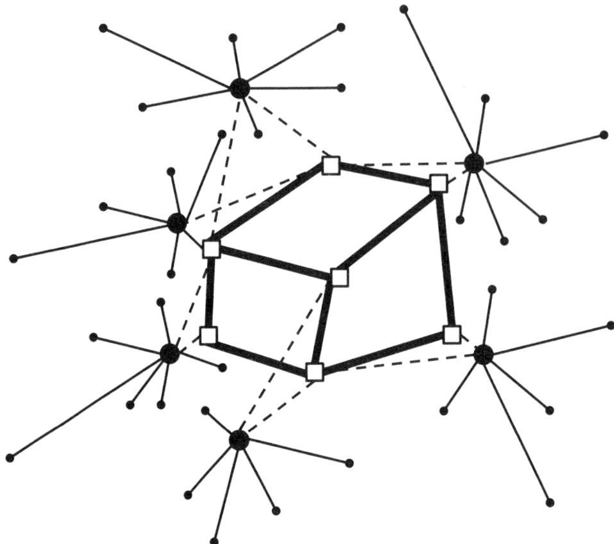

Figure 11.1
Engineered networks such as the telephone network or Internet have linkages much like this highly simplified diagram. A backbone network (*white boxes*) serves a collection of local networks (*large black circles*) connected to a set of computers such as desktops, servers, or mobile devices (*small black circles*). The local networks are multiply connected to the mesh (*dotted links*). The backbone is structured as a mesh so that the loss of any backbone node does not partition the network into isolated, unconnected pieces. The backbone and local network nodes are implemented as packet routers. In the Internet, local networks are called LANs (local area networks), and the backbone is called a WAN (wide area network). The connection points between LAN and WAN (*large black circles*) are implemented by gateway routers that translate packets from the WAN signaling format to the LAN signaling format.

typically low bandwidth. Analog voice digitized and compressed into packets can be sent in a fraction of the time needed for the analog signal. Telephone engineers were able to get several digitized conversations over a single wire with no loss of information or fidelity.

The packet network is attractive for three main reasons. First, it accommodates different types of traffic simultaneously. For example, voice traffic comes in bitstreams of a constant rate, typically 44,000 samples per second, lasting many minutes. Web traffic comes in short, high-intensity bursts when web servers transfer pages to requesting clients. The network transmits packets without regard to what to whether they contain continuous voice or bursty data traffic.

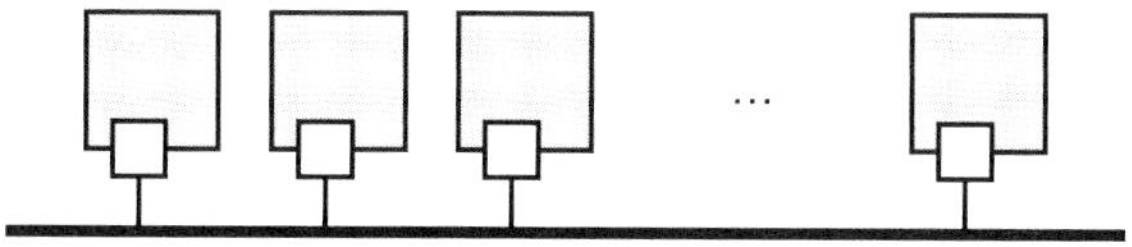

(a) Hosts connected by Ethernet

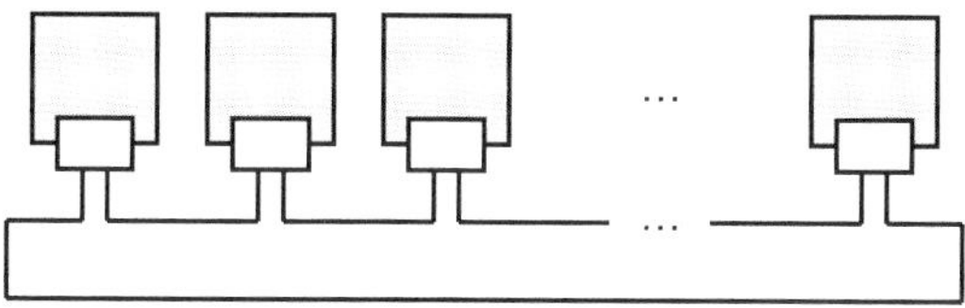

(b) Hosts connected by ring

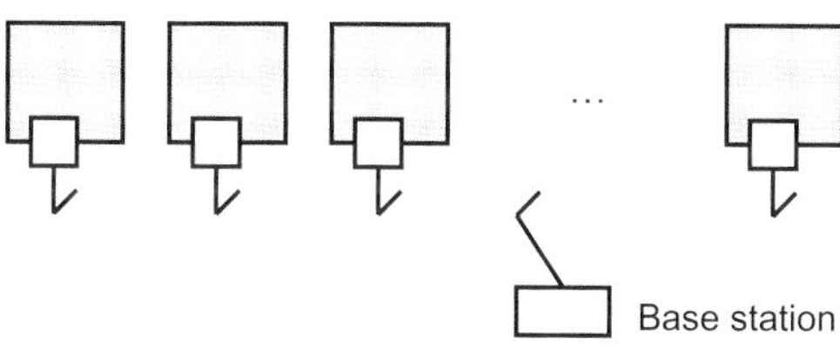

(c) Hosts connected by wireless

Figure 11.2

A local network (LAN) connects a set of computers by short-distance links. LANs are used in homes, offices, and buildings. One of the computers serves as a gateway to the Internet. The Ethernet configuration (a) attaches all the computers to a shared switch that sends packets to their target computers. The ring configuration (b) circulates packets from one computer to the next. The wireless configuration (c) uses radio signals and the 802.11 protocol to exchange packets via a base station. In these configurations no routers are needed because each computer sees all packets but selects only packets addressed to it. However, the ability to see all packets is a security vulnerability because a rogue computer can listen to other packets or send spoofed packets.

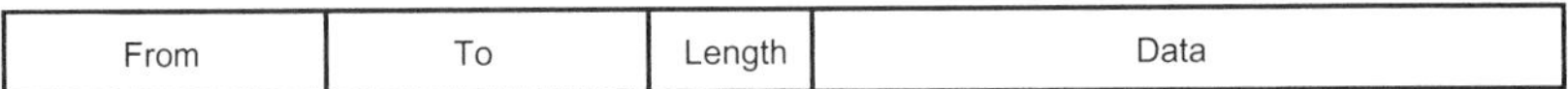

Figure 11.3
In packet switching the source station's data stream is broken into chunks, which are inserted into packets. In this simplified view of an Internet packet, the *from* field contains the address of the sending station, the *to* field contains the address of the receiving station, and the *length* field specifies the total size of the packet. The *data* field contains a block of data from the original stream; that block may include a sequence number so that the receiving protocol can reassemble the data chunks into their original order. A packet is shipped from one router to another, moving closer to the receiver at each "hop." If an internal network node or link fails, the routers will reconfigure and send the packets by other routes.

Second, the packet network is inherently more efficient than a telephone-based data network. The telephone network handles calls in two phases:

1. call set up (dialing) to establish a circuit
2. transmission (speaking back and forth) on the circuit

Early networking mechanisms such as the original ARPANET protocols and the X.25 protocols set up a virtual circuit before transmitting the data on it, mirroring the practice of the telephone network. But the designers soon realized that with packets they did not need any concept of setting up a reserved circuit. Senders simply transmit packets, the network routes them individually, and the receiver reacts to them as they arrive. Moreover, reserved circuits keep a channel open even when no packets flow, whereas without circuits, packets can be sent whenever bandwidth is available. Packets thus utilize the available bandwidth better. In his CYCLADES network in France, Louis Pouzin used the term *datagram* for a packet that carried part of a data stream without a prior setup protocol. Vinton Cerf and Robert Kahn designed a similar idea into the TCP protocol, which is discussed shortly.

Third, the packet network enables dynamic reconfiguration when links or routers fail. A router receives packets and forwards them to a next router one hop closer to the destination. If a router detects that the forwarding link (or the next router) is down, it can send the packet by a different link. Occasionally, a packet will be lost if the link (or router) goes down while the packet is in transit; but this is not a problem because transmission protocols can detect lost packets and resend them.

A router stores incoming packets in a queue and then, using a routing table, forwards them to a next router closer to the destination. The routing algorithm, which generates the routing tables, finds the shortest paths (measured by hops between routers) to the targeted hosts. Routing algorithms are generally run in the background so that routing tables are continuously updated to represent the current network connectivity (see figure 11.4). Edsger Dijkstra (1959) is credited with creating the efficient algorithm now used to find the shortest paths in hops between nodes. Other algorithms are used when path lengths are measured with delays or costs instead of hops.

Because of the store-and-forward design of the network, routers are potential congestion points. What happens if the traffic coming to a router overflows its queue? One possibility is to drop the packets and let the transmission protocol detect and resend the lost packets and back off on transmissions if the loss rate is too high. A less common possibility is to use link protocols that prevent a router from sending a packet unless there is room in the queue to receive it. That prevents packets from being lost but backs up the congestion to the points at which hosts attach to the network, slowing them down. The latter strategy is used under the name "flow control" in link management protocols.

It should come as no surprise that queueing network models (chapter 9) have been very effective for predicting mean throughput and transmission times in store-and-forward networks.

The Internet Protocol

The principles of packet switching and reconfigurability are not enough to make a network workable. The Internet consists of a billion hosts and millions of local networks. Users are interested in services offered by these hosts. How does a user's process address the desired server, so that it can send packets requesting the service and receive response packets? The method of addressing a service should not depend on the vagaries of the local networks or on the routes available in the network. Without some uniform method of addressing services, the local differences and constant churn of available services would make the network so chaotic that it would not be usable.

Vint Cerf and Bob Kahn offered a solution to this problem in 1974. They proposed a very large address space with enough bits in the addresses that every computer in the Internet could have its own unique address. They

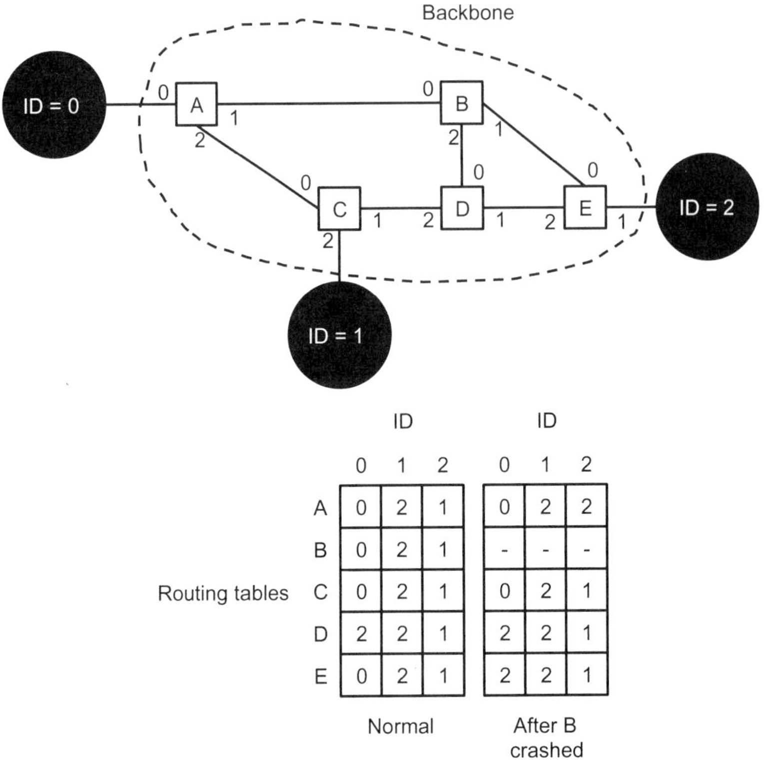

Normal:

	ID 0	ID 1	ID 2
A	0	2	1
B	0	2	1
C	0	2	1
D	2	2	1
E	0	2	1

After B crashed:

	ID 0	ID 1	ID 2
A	0	2	2
B	-	-	-
C	0	2	1
D	2	2	1
E	2	2	1

Figure 11.4
This example shows a backbone network connecting to three local network access hosts with ID numbers 0, 1, and 2. Each backbone router (*square boxes*) has three ports (numbered 0, 1, 2) that can send or receive packets. The normal routing table (*lower right, left column*) tells the router which link to use for a packet addressed a particular destination. For example, a packet from host 0 to host 1 would follow the route A, C; a packet from host 0 to host 2 would follow A, B, E. If router B fails, the reconfiguration algorithm modifies the table to route all traffic around B (*lower right*); now packets from host 0 to host 2 follow the route A, C, D, E. Note that if A, C, or E fails one of the hosts is cut off from the backbone. If D fails, packets from host 2 to host 1 follow the route E, B, A, C.

designed a protocol called Internet Protocol (IP) that would locate a server given its unique address. The unique addresses are called IP addresses.

An IP address is a 32-bit quantity. It is represented as four 8-bit bytes. Each byte can encode an integer from 0 to 255 ($2^8 - 1$). The standard notation for an IP address is four integers (from 0 to 255) separated by dots, for example, 192.168.3.55. The total number of Internet addresses is 2^{32}, or approximately 4 billion. With the rapid growth of the Internet to allow mobile devices, home appliances, and indeed anything with an embedded computer, 128-bit IP addresses are now allowed.[5]

Many local networks include a service called *dynamic host configuration protocol* (DHCP) to reduce the demand for fixed IP addresses within the network. When a computer is powered up it requests an IP address from a local computer called the DHCP server. The DHCP server assigns a temporary IP address from a pool of local subnet addresses. Because the number of hosts that are actually logged in is often much smaller than the total connected to the local network, this strategy permits a much larger set of hosts to share a given set of IP addresses.

The IP protocol gives no assurance that a packet will get to its destination. Many things could go wrong anywhere along the route. For example, a router might not be informed that the link selected to forward a packet is not operating. Packets incoming to a router might be dropped because the router's buffer is already full with other packets. Noise on a link may garble some bits in the packet, and the receiving router cannot decode the header fields. These and other errors can cause a packet to be lost or corrupted before it reaches its destination. The IP is called a "best effort datagram protocol" because it delivers packets as datagrams when they encounter no errors and makes no attempt to retransmit lost or corrupted packets.

Vint Cerf draws an analogy between the IP and a version of the Postal Service that deals only with postcards. A postcard is like a packet: to-field, from-field, and a limited area for the message. When you mail a postcard, you know it may not be delivered, or it may be damaged in transit. You do not know exactly how long it will take for delivery. There is no guarantee that a series of postcards will be received in the same order they were sent: each postcard can follow a different route on different mail trucks or planes.

The principle of best-effort datagram delivery is simple and efficient. It was used in the CYCLADES network (Pouzin 1973, 1974) and in the original design of the transmission control protocol (TCP), which encapsulated each chunk of data into an IP packet that functioned as a datagram (Cerf and Kahn 1974, Cerf et al. 1974). In 1977 the datagram function was split out of TCP into a separate user datagram protocol (UDP). TCP and UDP are parallel services operating on top of the basic IP protocol. The 1981 specifications for IP, TCP, and UDP form the basis of today's standards.

The Transmission Control Protocol

For many applications we need a more complex protocol than IP so that we can move data with a very high probability of accurate delivery in a network that can lose packets. The transmission control protocol (TCP), designed by Vinton Cerf and Robert Kahn (1974), does this. It enables reliable delivery of files, even if the datagrams carrying their components are unreliable.

TCP uses the end-to-end error-correction principle to achieve reliability across a lossy network (Saltzer et al. 1984). The idea is that the receiver sends acknowledgment packets to the sender, which can then tell how much of the data stream has been successfully received. Because acknowledgments can be lost, the sender automatically resends a packet if it has not received an acknowledgment within a set deadline. The receiver ignores duplicate packets that may result from resends. This scheme detects and replaces lost packets at the ends of the connection without having to assume that any error detection or correction is happening in the network. Of course, any error correction inside the network, such as Hamming codes on links, reduces packet lost and speeds up the TCP transmission.

TCP's principle of operation can be further understood by continuing Vint Cerf's analogy with the Postal Service. How would a shipper send a book using only postcards? This can be done if the shipper and receiver have agreements about disassembling the book before transmission and reassembling it after. The sender cuts up the pages of the book into small pieces and pastes them on postcards. The sender labels the postcards with sequence numbers and keeps backup copies of all postcards. The receiver puts the received postcards into proper order (as determined by their numbers), then removes the page snippets and pastes them back into a book.

So that the sender knows which postcards have been received, the receiver returns an acknowledgment (ACK) postcard from time to time summarizing the postcards that have been so far received; on receipt of ACKs, the sender discards the backup copies of acknowledged postcards. Here is the important step: if the sender receives no ACK within a time-out limit since the previous send, the sender automatically resends the postcard. The sender repeats this until finally an ACK comes for the card—or until the sender "times out" and reports that a transmission failure has occurred. This method overcomes possible loss of ACKs in the network. The receiver ignores duplicate postcards from the sender.

This scheme would be clumsy and messy with a real (paper) book, but with digital documents it is simple, clean, and fast. TCP takes longer to send a file over a noisy network because resends and acknowledgments slow it down. But as long as the probability that a packet will get through is non-zero, TCP will eventually deliver the entire file.

Clients and Servers

TCP enables a large variety of network services organized as "clients" and "servers." Clients and servers are autonomous, continuously running processes supported by the operating systems of their hosts. A client process on one system connects via TCP with a server process on another system. Using the connection the client makes requests and the server returns responses.

TCP can also be used for "peer-to-peer" interactions in which the processes on both ends can send requests and make responses.

The processes attached to the network interfaces rely on the multiplexing facilities of their local operating systems to handle many incoming packets and direct them to their proper service processes. These interfaces can also deal with multiple connections from the same host, such as a user accessing two different web pages at the same time.

TCP supports connections to specific processes with "ports." A *port* is a local designation of a client or server process (Pullen 2000). For instance, a host's web server is assigned to port 80. A client seeking a web page from host *H* packages the request as a packet, which it asks TCP to deliver to "*H* port 80." The receiver on host *H* passes the packet to the local process connected to port 80. The combination of host address and port number ("*H* port 80") is called a *socket.* TCP is designed to transmit packets to sockets, not just hosts. Over time, thousands of other services have been defined and assigned port numbers.[6]

The file transfer protocol (FTP) illustrates the client-server relationship in a more complex case. FTP is assigned to port 21. It is designed for users with accounts on two hosts. The user on host *A* calls the local FTP program and asks FTP to open a TCP connection to socket "*B* port 21." The FTP server on host *B* requests the host *A* FTP to get and return the user's login credentials for host *B*. Once logged in, the user changes to the desired directory and issues a "put" command giving the local and remote names. Once the file is completely received into the remote directory, host *B*'s acknowledgment is seen as a completion message by the user on *A*. The user can now exit the local host *A* FTP program, closing the session with the remote host *B* FTP process.

TCP and its companion UDP (user datagram protocol) are not client-server systems. They are simply channels for connecting processes, such as clients and servers, or peers, on two hosts.

Domain Name System

The TCP and IP described above use IP addresses to identify the senders and receivers of packets. A 32-bit IP (version 4) address is rendered in a more human readable way by expressing each of its four bytes as an integer in the range 0 to 255. For example, the IP address

10000001101011100000000100011100

is displayed as

129.174.1.28

These numerical representations are notoriously more difficult to remember than 10-digit telephone numbers. (It gets even worse for the hexadecimal representation of the 128-bit IP version 6 addresses.) The Internet, therefore, has adopted a system of easily remembered symbolic names for all the hosts. For example, "gmu.edu" has IP address 129.174.1.28. It is much easier to remember "gmu.edu" than its IP address.

We can translate symbolic host names to IP addresses with the help of a name server. Name servers act much like telephone white pages. In the Internet, host symbolic names are called domain names, and the name servers are part of the Domain Name Service (DNS). Ask the DNS to look up a domain name, and it responds with the corresponding IP address(es).

The TCP software is set up to automatically request translations of domain names to IP addresses. For example, the user request "Send file *F* to gmu.edu" would be translated to "Send file *F* to 129.174.1.28" by the domain name resolver associated with the network of the sending host.[7] The DNS is not implemented as a single server. It is a network of servers and caches that reduce the chance of bottlenecks and congestion in looking up domain names.

The Internet designers thought carefully about how to generate unique symbolic names. The original ARPANET had a master file at SRI International containing all the host names and their ARPANET addresses. Distributing this file to all hosts became a bottleneck for a growing Internet. In

1983 Paul Mockapetris designed the DNS, a distributed service for the registry of domain names. DNS automated the translation process from names to IP addresses and allowed for arbitrarily large expansion of the domain name space.

In the DNS, symbolic names are partitioned into fields separated by dots, as in "www.gmu.edu". The last field is the top-level domain, which represents a sector of industry or government, a generic grouping of organizations, or a country code. A single authority, the Internet Corporation for Assigned Names and Numbers (ICANN), administers top-level names.[8] In 1985 there were just a few top-level domains including .com, .mil, .gov, .edu, .org, and .net. In 2014 the number had grown to around 350 (including country codes), and another 2000 names were under consideration.

Each top-level domain has a registry that assigns names to individual organizations within the domain. Each organization has a registry that assigns names within the organization. The names assigned by this hierarchy of registries are strung together from the lowest to highest registrar. With the name www.cs.gmu.edu, for example:

- "www" is assigned by the registry in CS at GMU.
- "cs" is assigned by GMU's registry.
- "gmu" is assigned by the .edu domain registry.
- "edu" is assigned by ICANN.

This method pushes the authority to assign names down to local organizations, which can choose more meaningful names, and it reduces bottlenecks and congestion at individual registrars. Notice that domain names may not be independent of geographical location; for example, cnri.reston.va.us belongs to the Corporation for National Infrastructure Initiatives in Reston, VA, USA, and inria.fr belongs to Institut National de Recherche en Informatique et en Automatique in France.

Domain name mapping is an instance of the dynamic name translation principle (chapter 7), in which a system automatically translates a name at a higher level to a name a lower level. The two primary benefits of this principle in domain name mapping are, first, the ability to assign any IP address to any domain name and, second, the ability to change the IP address of a server without changing its domain name. In some address translation systems the lower-level name is hidden from the higher level—but not in the Internet, which does not hide IP addresses from those who want to use them. Domain name translation systems improve their performance by caching portions of the DNS database on local name servers, bypassing the delays of sending messages to a more distant, congestion-prone, centralized name server. The same is true for many services accessible on the Internet. Popular services would be bottlenecks were not it for networks of caches called content delivery networks (CDN).

Organization of Network Software

The descriptions above reveal the Internet as a vast system of great complexity. Its true extent can only be estimated. It has a billion hosts and millions of local networks. Its routers, links, servers, appliances, data centers, service providers, and more are so numerous that *The Economist* reported in 2012 that they collectively consume around 3 percent of the world's electricity; the International Energy Agency (iea.org) put consumption at nearly 6 percent in 2014. Much of the international economy has come to depend on the Internet as a way of communicating and doing business.

The ability of the Internet to accomplish so much and be so ubiquitous and reliable is a testimony to the foresight and vision of the engineers who designed it. They exploited the design "principle of layers" to structure the components in a way that expands to large networks and can be understood by most people.[9] Let us briefly review the organization of the Internet software.

In discussing TCP/IP we used an extended analogy of shipping a book via the Postal Service. Let us reexamine the process to see how all the components come together into a working system.

- The customer, wishing to send a book to a friend, gives it to the shipper along with the friend's address.
- The shipper cuts the pages of the book into pieces and pastes the pieces on numbered postcards, makes backup copies, and gives the originals to the Post Office. The shipper waits for acknowledgment postcards to know when to discard the backup copies. The shipper resends postcards that have not been acknowledged after a time-out limit.
- The Post Office packs postcards into pouches and marks the pouches with routes and carriers.
- The carriers place the pouches on trucks (or planes) to get them to their destinations.
- At the destination the pouch is taken off the truck and delivered to the Post Office.
- The Post Office removes the postcards, sorts them by address, and delivers to the shipper.

Software	Analogy
Client software	Customer
TCP	Shipper
IP	Post Office
Links	Routes
Signals	Trucks, planes

Figure 11.5
The Internet protocol software is arranged in a series of layers (*left*). These layers are analogous to the infrastructure levels used by shippers to deliver books to customers (*right*). The services of a layer are composed from simpler services at lower levels. The TCP layer manages reliable data-stream transfers. The IP layer manages best-effort delivery of packets. The links layer selects routes between routers and performs simple error corrections on links. The signals layer encodes packets into signals along selected links.

- The shipper removes book pieces from the postcards, pastes them back together, sends acknowledgment postcards, and waits occasionally for replacements of lost cards.
- The shipper gives the completely reassembled book to the friend.

Figure 11.5 shows the correspondence between the layers of the postal analogy and the layers of the Internet software. Exactly the same sequence of actions occurs in the Internet software, as a file moves down through the layers until it is encoded as signals in a physical medium and then up through the layers at the receiver until it is decoded and reassembled into a file.

In this arrangement each level on the sending side can see itself as communicating with the same level on the receiving side. For example, the shipper sees its job as getting the book to the receiving shipping agent. The Post Office sees its job as getting postcards to the receiving Post Office. The carriers see their job as getting pouches to delivery locations. In the same way the sending-side TCP sees itself as communicating directly with the receiving-side TCP. Although the actual flow is down to the physical level and back up to the receiving TCP, the *apparent* flow is direct from sending to receiving TCP (see figure 11.6). This apparent direct connection of a layer

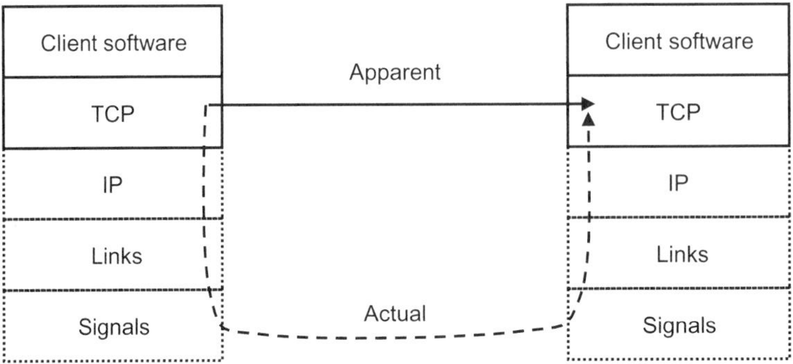

Figure 11.6
The same Internet protocol software is placed on every host of the network. The layers of the software give the appearance that a level is communicating directly with its counterpart on the other host. The apparent connection is implemented by lower-level functions. For example, TCP sends a file as a series of packets passed to IP, which uses dynamically reconfigurable routers that send packets as signals over physical links. On the receiver the physical signals are decoded into packets, which flow through the local IP to TCP, which reassembles the packets into a file. Network engineers call the set of software layers the *protocol stack* because they are implemented as software modules stacked up on one another.

to its counterpart on another host is characteristic of Internet software. It enables the designers of a layer to ignore the details of lower levels of software.

World Wide Web

The World Wide Web (WWW) was first proposed by Tim Berners-Lee in 1989 as a document-sharing system at the CERN Laboratory in Switzerland, supporting the exchange of research papers and other digital objects (Berners-Lee 2000). Its first implementation went live in late 1991. In 1993 the National Center for Supercomputing Applications of the University of Illinois at Champaign-Urbana released Mosaic, the first graphical user interface for the WWW; suddenly many people were able to quickly grasp the import of automated information sharing in the Internet. The WWW took off like wildfire, and the age of the Internet "dot com" companies was born. Today the WWW is seen as an information-sharing overlay for the Internet. Any sort of digital object including text, pictures, voice, music, and video can be accessed, transferred, and displayed or played within the one WWW system.

The WWW technology came from the convergence of several existing technologies to solve the problem of information sharing:

- The Internet—especially the TCP/IP protocol in supporting client-server applications
- Domain naming—the unique, hierarchical names for hosts in the Internet
- Hypertext—the construction of documents from text blocks linked in nonlinear structures
- Markup languages—the annotations of digital documents with tags that tell other programs how to display or render the documents

These technologies came together because Tim Berners-Lee was a practitioner in all of them. His inventions include these:

- URL—the uniform resource locator, which is the concatenation of the host's domain name with the pathname of a file in the directories of the host. Because pathnames are hierarchical, the URL is also hierarchical. URLs are globally unique symbolic names for digital objects in the Internet.
- HTML—the hypertext markup language, which is used to annotate digital object files with tags that indicate how to render the components of the digital object. For example, text blocks in a file can be marked as headers, paragraphs, or list elements, and the display program will show them appropriately. Hyperlinks, which encode the URLs of digital objects, are among the elements marked by tags. Although hyperlinks can be citations to other documents, they can also point to any objects whatsoever in the Internet, for example image or sound files.
- HTTP—the hypertext transfer protocol, which is automatically invoked by the browser when the cursor selects a hyperlink. HTTP opens a TCP connection to port 80 of the host designated in the link's URL and passes the file pathname to the HTTP server; the server finds the file, sends a copy back to the sender, and closes the TCP connection.

The public WWW was hardly two years old when the first web search engines began to appear. Users wanted to find information made available through the web. A search engine is a service that takes keywords and searches the Internet for web pages containing them; it returns the pages' URLs and some of the matching text to the person requesting the search. To make the search fast the search engine runs a subprogram, variously called an "indexer" or "web crawler," that systematically enumerates hostnames, opens connections to port 80 on those hosts, finds all the URLs on the pages accessed, and follows them. It captures a copy of each page into a master database, and creates a master index that finds URLs for given keywords. Dozens of web search engines have appeared since 1993.

In the mid-2000s Google became the biggest search engine service. Using web-crawlers, Google maintains a continuously updated snapshot of the entire World Wide Web and constructs an index that enables high-speed lookup of pages given strings that might appear on them. Other popular search services include Yahoo, Bing, and Wolfram Alpha.

Search engines are limited in what they can see. They query databases filled by web crawlers. Any content that is not the target of a URL will not be found. URLs pointing to web pages requiring a user login or offering a query interface to a database cannot be cataloged. Some servers are accessible only by protocols such as FTP and TELNET but are not part of the WWW. Sometimes web crawlers get stuck in Internet "islands"—portions of the web whose connection graphs are not connected to the rest of the web graph. Web experts believe that at most 10 percent of the web content is seen by search engines.

Even though search engines are mostly blind, the amount of web content they can see is still staggering. In 2013 the World Wide Web Foundation estimated there were over a trillion web pages. Even if a search engine indexed only 10 percent of them, a query would have to search 100 billion records. This is why it is all too easy to get an overwhelming number of "hits" to a set of keywords. For example, after the 9/11 attacks, the keywords "Osama bin Laden" typically yielded nearly 3 million hits. No human being has the capacity to go through more than a few dozen of them. Thus, the amount of the web a human can actually locate is tiny indeed. Hubert Dreyfus (2001) commented that finding something in the web is like searching for a needle in a stack of needles. John MacCormick (2012) likened web searches to searching the world's largest haystack.

To add to the challenge it is almost impossible to tell if the information retrieved is the best answer to a query. It can be very difficult to independently verify new information. Yet people do find web searches valuable because even meager information can be useful. It is truly remarkable that web searches consistently find valuable information. It is even more remarkable that millions of people spend untold hours putting up web pages for others to find.

The web has become the medium for e-commerce: business transactions conducted electronically in the Internet. Businesses and their clients increase security and protect privacy with protocols that encipher data before sending them on the Internet. The first such protocol, secure socket layer (SSL) in 1996, was superseded by transport layer security (TLS) in

1999. TLS allows two hosts to negotiate encryption parameters and then encipher traffic between them. TLS protects passwords, payments, bank account numbers, credit-card numbers, and other data that are passed over the web interfaces as part of business transactions. Users can tell when the protocol is being used because a lock icon and the string "https" will appear in their browser's address fields.[10]

In addition to new protocols e-commerce has given us new business models for shopping (the online store and shopping cart), for coordinating across enterprises (workflow), and for setting prices (eBay auctions). The euphoria that accompanied the development of these new concepts stoked hype about a "new economy" and led to the "dot com bust" at the turn of the century.

In addition to these innovations in business practice, the Internet has also stimulated dark innovations—spam, viruses, worms, hijackings, denial of service attacks, intrusions, and other nasties that make the Internet harder and hazardous to use. Technical solutions to these problems have been hard to find, and the few that have been proposed (such as "Internet caller ID") have met with fierce opposition.

The Internet has indeed given us a new world and a new conception of reality. One day it may be listed among the great inventions along with the others cited by James Burke in *The Day the Universe Changed* (1985).

Network Science

As the Internet and web grew, scientists became interested in studying the connections between persons and objects recorded in the Internet. Researchers studied the statistics of citations. Organizational analysts examined the patterns of email connections to discover who were the "hubs" and "brokers" of organizations. Law enforcement officials correlated conversation and payments histories of suspected criminals. Counterterrorists mapped terrorist networks in hopes of disrupting them. The modelers came to the Internet and started mining the data about connections. When they started to find interesting patterns and make startling predictions, they launched a new field called network science.

Alberto Barabasi applied methods from statistical physics to network graphs derived from the data (Barabasi 2002). In the web, for example, a node might represent a page and a link a URL connecting two pages. The degree of a node is the number of incoming links. Barabasi found that the data fit a "power law," meaning that $P(x)$, the fraction of nodes of degree x, is proportional to x^{-a} for an exponent a in the range 1 to 3. He also noted

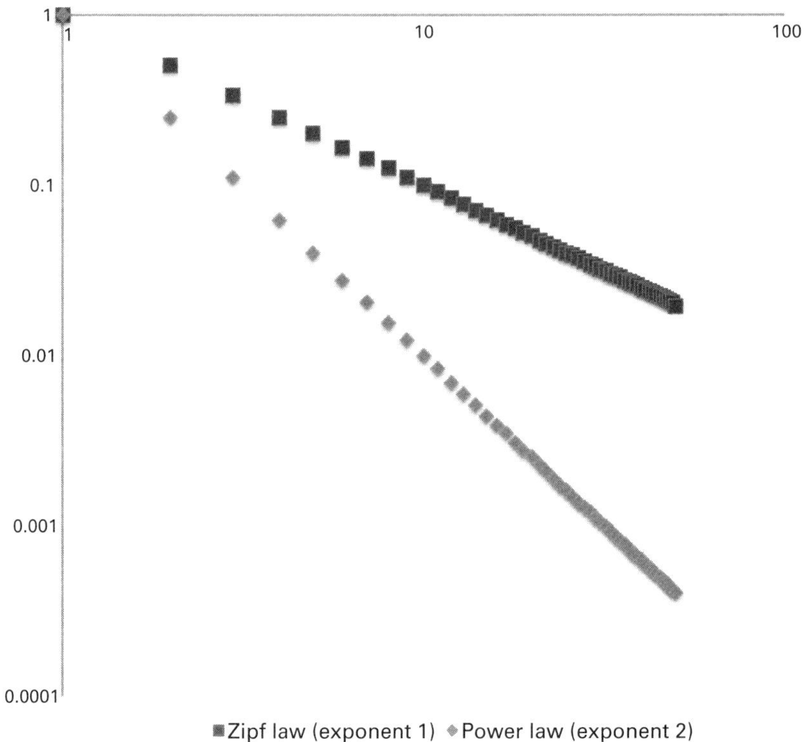

Figure 11.7
Node degree data from web connections tend to follow straight lines on log-log plots. That means $P(x)$, the number of nodes of degree x, is proportional to x^{-a} for a constant a. Exponent $a = 1$ is the well-known Zipf law in which $P(x)$ is proportion to $1/x$. The exponent $a = 2$ is common in many web connection graphs.

that data following power laws are "scale free" because scaling x scales $P(x)$ by the same factor for any x. For example, the number of nodes of degree $2x$ is $(2x)^{-a} = 2^{-a} \cdot P(x)$ (see figure 11.7). In addition, Barabasi found that networks that grow by preferential attachment are scale-free. Preferential attachment means that the probability that a new link will attach to a node is proportional to the degree of the node. This is often true in the web: a popular site is more likely to accumulate new links than an obscure one.

When applied to router connectivity in the Internet, the scale-free claim led to two conclusions. One was that the Internet should be highly resistant to random node failures because the vast majority of nodes have low degree; disrupting one would hardly affect anything. The other was more serious: the Internet should be vulnerable to severe disruption because the model said it has a small number of high-degree hubs. This vulnerability was called the "Achilles heel of the Internet" because it implied that an attacker could bring down much of the Internet by finding and disabling a few hubs.

The Achilles heel claim did not square with Internet engineers' own vulnerability assessments or with the actual experience of no major Internet disruptions. In 2009 several researchers openly questioned this claim (Willinger et al. 2009). They noted that the claim of power-law-degree connectivity came from "traceroute" data. *Traceroute* is an Internet tool that returns a list of the IP addresses traversed as a probe packet moves to its destination. Traceroute data do not represent actual physical connections. The reason is the protocol stack: the IP layer cannot see into the routing and link layers, where the physical connectivity would be visible.

Even more telling, the engineering design of subnets and of backbone links is driven by two main factors: the need for link and node redundancy to avoid connectivity losses and the need for capacity to handle the expected traffic. These engineering objectives steer engineers well clear of preferential attachment. They lead to structures like those suggested in figure 11.1, where local networks attach to a large backbone mesh. The higher-degree nodes tend to be in the local networks and not in the mesh. Willinger and colleagues (2009) were highly critical of those who accepted the claim "Internet router connectivity is scale-free" without verifying it. The Internet does not have the scale-free Achilles heel after all.

To put this another way, scale-free claims may apply to the network graphs but not to the engineered physical networks that host the connections represented in the graphs.

What about the connectivity data for social networks, web pages, or email networks? Does the scale-free idea apply to them? Yes, because those data directly measure the nodes and their degrees. However, we must be careful when translating conclusions to the physical Internet. For example, it would appear that very popular sites such as google.com are hubs and are highly vulnerable to disruption. However, Google engineers have implemented their data warehousing and query engines as highly distributed mesh networks, precisely to avoid that kind of vulnerability.

David Clark (1988) believed that the biggest vulnerability of the Internet was the original design decision to trust other nodes. Malware, botnets, denial-of-service, and intruders have been the biggest source of Internet connectivity and capacity problems. For example, arguably the most disruptive incident was the 1988 Morris Worm, which took down about 10 percent of the then relatively small Internet for a few days; most of the downed nodes were taken off line voluntarily by their administrators to halt the spread of the worm until they could eradicate it.

Despite the challenges of modeling the physical Internet, network science may still hold a promise to help make better models of the Internet and to design critical network infrastructures that cannot easily be disrupted.

Acknowledgment

We are grateful to Internet experts Vint Cerf and Robert Beverly for detailed reviews of this chapter.

12 Afterword

Our aim in this book has been to demonstrate that computing science is founded on a rich set of principles. The principles tell us how to manipulate matter and energy to perform computations. The principles help us to understand what computers can and cannot do and where the limits to computing technology are. The principles can help us locate connections between technologies and opportunities for innovation. The principles can help us evaluate risks and avoid making life worse for people using computing. The principles are timeless and will continue to be relevant long after current technologies have become museum exhibits.

We would like to close this book with some reflections on some key lessons from this project.

Mindless Machines

In writing this book we have had to immerse ourselves in the principles of computing for a long time. We constantly found ourselves confronting the pervasiveness of matter and energy in computation. In one way or another, all the principles concern how to control matter and energy to perform computations. There is no such thing as a bit without a physical manifestation behind it. Every program ultimately controls the flows of signals though electronic circuits or other media. Every designer seeks programs that channel matter and energy into the intended outcomes.

We believe that the popular notion that "bits not atoms" power computing discounts the importance of matter and energy in performing computations. Remember that the International Energy Agency estimated in 2014 that nearly 6 percent of the world's electricity powers the connections and data centers of the Internet. Even so, a substantive change has occurred in the past decade with the explosion of digital technologies and digitization of almost everything. It is now possible to produce new digital artifacts (for example “apps”) with low development costs, no-cost error-free copying, worldwide distribution, and dirt-cheap consumer prices. The resulting digital economy is one of abundance, not scarcity. This change is not the result of bits but of our having learned how to control large numbers of signals and atoms cheaply.

Although we have become adept at using abstractions to explain and design computations, there is nothing abstract about computation itself. It is always the movement of signals and the changing of states of matter. Every one of these movements or changes is purely physical, following some law of physics. There is no intelligence anywhere in computing machines. It is astounding how mindless and mechanical computing machines are.

Intelligent Machines

How then do computers seem intelligent? For us, the answer is profoundly simple: they were designed that way. Human designers shape the software or the machine itself to produce the responses they want. Designers often experiment with prototypes to learn how users will respond to various aspects of the machine’s behavior. If they do not like a response, they alter the design. On their side, most users do not think of an errant result as a lapse of intelligence; they simply think the machine is broken. When you encounter a computer whose behavior seems intelligent, you are responding to a designer’s intent. The machine itself is not intelligent.

Some people believe that large networks of unintelligent machines can develop emergent behavior that, in fact, becomes intelligent.[1] Much “emergent behavior” is the result of intentional design. For example, a designer iteratively shapes local behaviors of a computation after observing previous responses to the computation. In these cases the “emergent intelligence” is really a reflection of the designer’s intent. More generally, technologies are always embedded into social systems; they follow the actions of the humans in the system. For instance, it might seem that robot telemarketers are invading homes when in fact companies are choosing to use those machines because they produce results. It is possible to explain many apparently emergent intelligent behaviors without having to assume that the machines or networks are intelligent.

Computers can also seem intelligent because of their speed. Even though you may realize that billions of computational steps have produced an answer to your question, it is still amazing when the machine does it in the blink of an eye. Computing machines today are about 10^{14} times faster than those built in the 1940s, and they can do things that would amaze the pioneers. Who would have thought that a machine could, in under half a second, find a million documents from around the world that match your query? Science fiction writer Arthur C. Clarke put it well when he said, "Any sufficiently advanced technology looks like magic."

However, these observations are not comforting to some observers. In 2000 Bill Joy of Sun Microsystems worried that some sort of dangerous intelligence might emerge, go out of control, and thwart or overwhelm human attempts to stop it.[2] In 2014 physicist Stephen Hawking similarly warned, "artificial intelligence could be the worst thing to happen to humanity."[3] Google set up an AI Ethics Board to oversee its work in artificial intelligence to help it avoid contributing to the extinction of humanity in the twenty-first century. We see no computing principles that would rule this future out, and we agree that designers should pay a lot of attention to the risks of large networked computing systems.

However, it is not a foregone conclusion that machines will eventually outpace humans. In 1997 it appeared that an IBM supercomputer had achieved greater chess mastery than Garry Kasparov. Just a few years later Freestyle Chess tournaments sprang up in which teams of chess players consulting with chess programs on laptops easily beat the chess supercomputer. When collaborating humans race "with" the machines rather than "against" them, the combination can be surprisingly more intelligent than a machine.

Architecture and Algorithms

We have encountered a common view that all the great advances of computing are due to algorithms. For example, it looks as though Google's success relies on its clever page-ranking algorithm. Or database resiliency relies on the clever algorithms for atomic transactions. Or that online business transactions are secured by numerical algorithms in the RSA code. Behind every significant advance in computing it seems there is a clever algorithm.

As a consequence, it appears to many that algorithm analysis and programming are the heart of computer science.

This conclusion does not seem right to us. There is more to the story. Consider Moore's law. Moore's law says that the number of transistors on a computer chip doubles every two years. It has been an industry trend since the beginning. It gives us nearly a hundredfold increase of computing power every decade. There is an industry rule of thumb that any technology that can make an important process go ten times faster is potentially disruptive.

Moore's law goes well beyond that and keeps the computing industry in a constant process of disruption. It is a very important phenomenon.

But the improvements of Moore's law are not due simply to algorithms. They are due to design of materials, new understandings of physics, architecture of circuits on the chip, and improvements in lithography, circuit simulators, testers, clean manufacturing, and more.

Google's page-rank algorithm would not work without the underlying infrastructure of Google's worldwide data warehouses, which mobilizes tens of thousands of processors to find matches to queries in under half a second.

What of quantum computing? Physics labs are looking for ways to implement computations over "qubits" representing superimposed quantum states of atoms. These advances will flow from a new physics, not from algorithms. If they succeed, much of modern cryptography could become obsolete.

And what of multicore chips? In effort to wrest more computation from chips, designers have built chips containing dozens of CPUs, requiring programmers to write multithreaded algorithms to get the most speed. If they succeed they will not only push Moore's law forward a few more generations, they will start a revolution in programming.

These are just a few of the many examples in which the computer architecture itself has changed. New architectures enable faster algorithms and make some infeasible algorithms feasible. They enable new algorithms that best exploit the architecture.

So it appears to us that the architecture of computers is as important as the algorithms they run. This is abundantly evident in the principles of computing. Many principles are about the systems on which computations run. We cannot give a complete picture of computing if we limit our principles to algorithms and ignore the principles of architecture.

That is why there are so many systems principles in this book.

Empirical Mindset

Critics of computer science have traditionally maintained that computer science is mostly mathematics (for example, algorithm analysis) and engineering (for example, design of architectures and development of software). They objected to computer science calling itself science partly because they did not see a deep commitment to experimental methods and partly because the objects of study, information processes, appear to be artificial rather than natural.

Much has changed in the past two decades. Computer scientists have embraced empirical methods in many areas including software prototyping, security, debugging, quantitative design of architecture, predicting network response times, artificial intelligence, validation of heuristic algorithms, and much more. Computer scientists have not given up on modeling and analysis, but they have come a long way in experimentally validating models and analyses.

Moreover, scientists in many fields have discovered information processes occurring in nature and have invited computer scientists to help them understand those processes. Although much of computer science is concerned with artificial (machine produced) information processes, many of the same principles apply to natural information processes. A growing segment of the computing field is concerned with natural information processes.

Computer science is growing up and earning a reputation for being a science as well as engineering and mathematics.

Because of the pervasive influence of computing and computation throughout science and the large and growing number of interactions between computer scientists and other fields, Paul Rosenbloom has argued that computing is not just a field of science, it is a new domain of science on par with the physical, life, and social sciences.[4]

A New Machine Age Dawns

Just as the steam engine was an inflection point for automating and amplifying manual work in the 1780s, the networked computer has become an inflection point for automating and amplifying cognitive work.[5] This has happened from a convergence of all the things covered in this book: algorithmics, systems, and design. Algorithmics has produced ingenious new methods of solving cognitive problems. Systems and networks have developed the reach and capacity to provide seemingly universal computing power to run those methods. And designers have become extremely adept at finding new combinations of algorithmic principles and systems to provide great value to human communities.

The economics of information differs in a profound way from the economics of things. Physical artifacts such as smartphones require a lot of up-front development costs and large sales to amortize those costs. Digital artifacts can now be designed cheaply and distributed even more cheaply—witness the explosion of apps, app development tools, and app markets. The world of digital objects is characterized by abundance rather than scarcity.

The app is the software workhorse in this new economy. Apps perform jobs that make life a whole lot easier for their users. Are you a hiker? Get a GPS record to track your treks. Want to read your morning paper? Get your local paper's app. Want to check in quickly to your flight? Get your airline's app. Need a taxi? Get the taxi finder app for your area of the city. The smartphones and tablets are not producing the revolution; the apps transform those devices into immensely useful cognitive job doers.

One of the most troubling disruptions of the new age of computing machines is the rapidly changing job market. People whose jobs are subject to automation by a machine are at risk of losing their jobs. Jobs for designers and software engineers are expanding even while their artifacts displace workers whose jobs become automated. Our education system has not yet caught up with the need to help the displaced find new skill sets and jobs. Educators and policy makers have their work cut out for them.

Our Way of Thinking Is Transforming

Imagine two images that are easily found in Internet searches. One is a photograph of a modern supercomputer. For example, the IBM Blue Gene supercomputer at Argonne Labs has 250,000 processors in 72 cabinets and can perform 10^{15} operations per second—a million times faster than the chip in a smartphone. This machine is very good at processing large data sets with deterministic algorithms. It has no intelligence.

The other image is an Internet graph, a strikingly beautiful snapshot of connection data among Internet sites. Sites with more incoming connections are shown larger and brighter in the graph. The Internet is an organism with humans and machines in a never-ending dance of interactions amplifying each other's capabilities. It is constantly changing its structure, and some of the changes are disruptive. The graph represents a supercomputer grown from a billion machines and several billion people. The organism has intelligence—the collected, amplified, collaborative intelligence of everyone who participates in it.

The Internet organism is not replacing the machine. It is a new system built on machines, mobile devices, their connections, and their interaction with humans. The network of machines is the infrastructure of the organic system.

The two images also represent different approaches to understanding the world. The machine view represents the advancement of science, which seems poised to know all data, predict what will happen, and exert controls. The organism view exposes an unruly, ever-evolving world rife in uncertainties, unpredictable events, and disruptions. Our attitudes toward design and architecture were formed in the machine age. New design and architecture principles will doubtless emerge for the Internet organism age. Our education systems will also have to adapt to prepare people for living in this emerging world and taking care that technologies leave the world a better place for generations that follow.

Centrality of Design

Taken together, these considerations place designers and their work at the center of the progress and innovation in computing. The apparent intelligence of machines comes not from architectures or algorithms but from the work of designers. Designers pay a lot of attention to the meaning that software and machines will generate for their users. They craft their designs so that the meaning they intend is actually present for users. Programmers have the largest impact when they are designers; otherwise, they are just coders for someone else's design.

To emphasize this, we included chapter 10 on Design. Experienced designers work with design principles that guide them toward dependable, reliable, usable, safe, and secure computing systems. Although these principles are not laws of nature, they are every bit as important in realizing computation.

Let us celebrate the designers, for they enable us to do our work.

Summary of This Book

Chapter 1: Computing

Computing is a relatively young discipline. It started as an academic field of study in the 1930s with a cluster of remarkable papers by Kurt Gödel, Alonzo Church, Emil Post, and Alan Turing. These men saw the importance of automatic computation and sought to give it solid mathematical foundations. They answered the question, "What is computation?" and discussed schemes for implementing computations. The first forty years of the new field were focused on developing and perfecting computing technology and networks. In the 1980s the field started seriously to turn its attentions outward. It developed strong interactions with computational sciences and many other fields. Recognizing that the computer itself is just a tool for studying information processes, the field shifted its focus from the machine itself to information transformations.

Chapter 2: Domains

The real work of computing comes from people designing and using computing. Computing people have organized into numerous communities of practice, which we call computing domains. There are dozens of domains. The members of these domains share similar concerns, skill sets, methods, and interactions with other communities. They are empowered and constrained by computing principles. We examine four computing domains of contemporary importance—security, artificial intelligence, cloud computing, and big data. For each one, we give a brief history of its evolution and then show who is involved, what they are concerned with, what principles they mobilize from the six categories, and what principles they mobilize from other fields. The same method of analysis can be used with any of the other computing domains.

Chapter 3: Information

Computing machines are said to store, transform, and transmit information. This claim puzzles many people because information seems abstract and at least partially subjective, whereas machines process definite signals and states of matter. So what is information? Signals and states? Meanings chosen by humans? A mixture: information is meaningful patterns (codes) of signals and states of matter. The word "meaningful" calls attention to the fact that patterns are encoded interpretations set by designers; the machine processes the codes according to rules set by the designers, and the designers make sure that the results will be interpreted as intended. Information theory, which deals with the codes forming the patterns, tells us that entropy defines the minimum number of bits in a decipherable code, that we can add enough redundant bits to a code to guarantee 100% reliable transmission in the presence of noise, and that we can compress files by shortening the codes representing the information in them. One of the seeming paradoxes of computing is that machines process information without regard to its meaning, and yet human users find meaning in their interactions with the machines. The paradox disappears when we remember that the meaning comes from the intentions of designers.

Chapter 4: Machines

Computing machines are information transformers. They execute a series of computational steps, each carried out by a simple instruction implemented with electronic circuits. The stored-program computer, which was invented in 1944, has instructions for arithmetic and logical operations, conditional choices, and looping iterations. Such a simple instruction set is powerful enough to enable a computer to be programmed for any computable function. The simplicity has a price: even relatively straightforward functions can require programs whose execution takes billions of instructions. We are able to afford the price because computers are so fast. Tasks that would have taken weeks in 1950 can now be done in the blink of an eye. Programming languages were developed so that programmers could describe, with short expressions, what they wanted done; compilers translate programs into machine instructions while preserving the exact meaning of the original expressions. Programming languages revealed additional concepts that needed support from machine instructions, notably the calling of subroutines and the fielding of interrupt signals. Designers of computational electronic circuits discovered that machine design may not always have a happy ending because of an uncertainty principle—circuits that must distinguish between two near-simultaneous signals within a deadline can hang up and crash the computer. This risk worsens at fast clock speeds (shorter deadlines). The risk can be mitigated by slowing the clock rate and eliminated with self-timed circuits that wait until near-simultaneous signals can be distinguished.

Chapter 5: Programming

From the earliest days programmers realized they would be spending a considerable portion of their lives searching for errors in their own programs or in the machines that run them. They invented programming languages to help overcome the error problem. A programming language allows a programmer to say, with simple expressions following a precise grammar, what is to be done; then a compiler translates the program into machine instructions that preserve the exact meanings of the original expressions. There are thousands of programming languages, each customized for a particular domain of problem solving. Each one has a precise grammar and a compiler. The power of the machine can be extended by a virtual machine, which adds new instructions in as subroutines. Virtual machines have enabled the execution of Java programs on any computing system, the execution of multiple versions of the operating system on the same CPU-RAM hardware, and the implementation of functional levels of operating systems and network protocols.

Chapter 6: Computation

How long do computing machines take to solve the problems they are designed for? To answer this, we count the number of steps executed by an algorithm. Every step requires a definite, nonzero amount of time; the totality of steps adds up to a noticeable delay regardless of how fast computers run individual steps. Algorithms can be classified into groups according to how long they take. Some algorithms require time linearly proportional to the size of the data set they work with, some quadratic, some exponential, and some much worse. Algorithms that require exponential processing time get the bulk of our attention because they solve important problems and are essentially undoable for large data sets. Even if every particle in the universe were a memory location, there would not be enough memory for the algorithm to solve large problems in this class. Moreover, even if we had the memory, the time needed to achieve a solution would be longer than the expected remaining life of the solar system. We examine why computer scientists believe that the set of problems solvable by fast algorithms ("P" for polynomial time) is not the same as the problems for which the only known algorithms are exponential or worse but that can be verified by fast algorithms ("NP" for nondeterministic polynomial time). Many common, everyday problems suffer from this limitation. Examples are distributing goods in a transportation network or finding the optimal subset within large data sets. In many cases we have discovered amazing heuristic algorithms (ones that give approximate answers) that can come within a fraction of a percent of the optimal solution within a reasonable time. The worst cases of all are the problems that cannot be solved by any computational machine—for example, whether a program contains an infinite loop, or a malicious virus. This limitation is imposed by the logic of information itself.

Chapter 7: Memory

We cannot compute unless we can store and retrieve information efficiently. The four main principles of storage and retrieval are naming, mapping, authenticating, and positioning. Naming refers to methods of designating items to which a computation applies; these methods include addresses, queries of databases, and keyword searches of unstructured data. Mapping refers to associating an access path from a name to an object and using that map to transfer information. Authentication refers to validating that the user requesting an access has rights allowing the access; unauthorized users are denied access. Positioning refers to arranging information in a storage hierarchy or network so that the apparent distance from a processor is minimum. Positioning is critical in the common cases where the access-time gap between a CPU cache and a hard disk is on the order of a million, or when a popular server in the network develops a long queue. The principle of locality, which says computations cluster their references to small subsets of objects over extended periods of time, underlies all methods of efficient positioning. The locality principle is deeply connected to the notion of computation itself: every algorithm is constrained on every operation to reading or modifying a bounded amount of its data structure. Without locality, computation cannot be.

Chapter 8: Parallelism

Although we traditionally emphasize sequential algorithms in computing, most actions in the world are done in parallel by autonomous agents acting with occasional synchronization. Parallel processing is by far the most common mode of computation. There are two broad classes of parallelism: cooperative and competitive. Cooperative parallelism occurs when many processes synchronize together to accomplish a common goal, such as speeding up a weather forecast by using 10,000 processors. Competitive parallelism occurs when many processes with little or no synchronization queue up for access to finite network resources. This chapter examines the issues of cooperative parallelism, which include avoiding race conditions, locking shared items during use, and avoiding deadlocks. In large systems there is no way to guarantee the execution order of independent constituent tasks. Their order can vary from one run to the next, making results unpredictable and behavior potentially unsafe. Debugging is nearly impossible in these environments because there is no way to reproduce the buggy behavior. The only solution is to obey design protocols that prevent unsafe race conditions and deadlocks from ever happening. Many of these methods have been hidden within operating systems, and the average programmer did not have to deal with them. However, multicore chip technology is forcing all programmers to become conversant in the methods of cooperative parallelism—a major paradigm shift for programmers.

Chapter 9: Queueing

This chapter examines the issues of competitive parallelism. A computing system is modeled as a set of servers connected by a network. When users submit jobs (work requests) to the system, their jobs move from one server to another, collecting portions of service until they are done. However, queues of jobs form at individual servers, especially when a server cannot keep up with the demand. The queueing delays are likely to add significantly to the system's response time to a job. How can we predict the response time and throughput of a networked system? Simply counting the steps of an algorithm barely begins to answer this question. We need to invoke principles from queueing theory to answer performance prediction questions and to find and eliminate bottlenecks. Computer scientists discovered how to use queueing networks to model large computing systems accurately, and they developed very fast algorithms to calculate predictions with these models. The same models work for many industrial problems and business workflow problems. When they apply thousands of processors to answer a query quickly, search engines illustrate the queueing network principle that parallelism eliminates bottlenecks.

Chapter 10: Design

Design has been a central issue of computing since the beginning. The first designers gave us a remarkable plan, the stored-program computer, also called the von Neumann architecture, which is still in use today. The stored-program computer made the instruction set the user interface and gave birth to the profession of programming. It also gave birth to debugging, the systematic search for mistakes in programs. Software designers work with five success criteria: requirements, correctness, fault tolerance, timeliness, and fitness. *Requirements* are concerned with making precise statements about the job a system does for its users, *correctness* with preventing errors during construction, *fault tolerance* with minimizing the effects of errors until they can be corrected and expunged, *timeliness* with configuring systems to get results on time, and *fitness* with user satisfaction. Five design patterns are particularly useful in satisfying these criteria: hierarchical aggregation (which blends abstraction, decomposition, modularity, and information hiding), encapsulation, levels (layers), virtual machines, and objects. These patterns show up as structures in languages, application programs, and operating systems. Design is a rich field. It makes all the difference between successful and failed computing systems. Designing well is perhaps the greatest challenge in computing.

Chapter 11: Networking

This chapter is a case study of the Internet, one of the most important computing technologies. Each major component of the Internet draws on principles from the six categories named in chapter 1. The components are all knit together with such coherence that the Internet is able to be an enormous system, yet reliable, dependable, and continuously expandable. The Internet is based on packet-switched messaging rather than circuit switching as in the telephone networks that preceded it. Packet switching enables the Internet to survive the inevitable loss of nodes and links by automatically rerouting packets around the damaged region of the network. The Internet protocol (IP) transcends the millions of local networks by assigning each host a single address recognizable throughout the network. The transmission control protocol (TCP) divides a stream of bits from a sender into sequentially numbered packets, which are reassembled into the original stream at the receiver; acknowledgments assure the sender that packets are received, and time-outs tell the parties to resend unacknowledged packets. The Domain Name Service (DNS) gives every host a unique symbolic name and translates host names to their IP addresses. A client-server model uses TCP for connections to access basic networking services; an internationally administered system assigns standard port numbers to the services. The World Wide Web adds functions to link any document on any host to any digital object in the network and bring a copy of an object to a user who clicks on a link. This vast system uses principles of communication (coding and error correction), computation (secure encryption, routing tables), coordination (protocols, multiplexing), recollection (naming, addressing, and caching), evaluation (flow controls, traffic analysis), and design (layers, client servers, end-to-end protocols). Studies of the connections in the web have led to new models of network connectivity and a new field called "network science."

Afterword

We conclude the book with a summary of our personal observations on several key issues that have permeated this project: mindless machines, intelligent machines, architecture and algorithms, empirical mindset, a new machine age, transforming our thinking, and centrality of design.

Notes

Preface

1. Brynjolfsson, Erik, and Andrew McAfee. 2014. *The Second Machine Age: Work, Progress, and Prosperity in a Time of Brilliant Technologies.* W. W. Norton.

2. See Rosenbloom, Paul. 2012. *On Computing: The Fourth Great Scientific Domain.* MIT Press.

3. Moore's law is the empirical observation that the power of computer chips doubles about every two years at the same price, giving ten times increase of computing power every decade.

4. See Bacon, Dave. 2010. Computation and fundamental physics. http://ubiquity.acm.org/article.cfm?id=1920826.

5. See Snyder, Lawrence. 2012. *Fluency with Information Technology: Skills, Concepts, and Capabilities,* 5th ed. Addison-Wesley. http://www.fluencywithinformationtechnology.org/

6. http://www.csprinciples.org/

7. See Wing, Jeannette. 2006. Computational thinking. *Communications of ACM* 49 (3):33–35. http://doi.acm.org/10.1145/1118178.1118215.

8. The outreach books are:

- Eck, David. 1995. *The Most Complex Machine.* CRC Press.
- Biermann, Alan. 1997. *Great Ideas in Computer Science* (2nd ed.). MIT Press.
- Hillis, Danny. 1999. *The Pattern on the Stone: The Simple Ideas That Make Computers Work.* Basic Books.
- Harel, David. 2000. *Computers Ltd: What They Really Can't Do.* Oxford.
- Petzold, Charles. 2000. *Code: The Hidden Language of Computer Hardware and Software.* Microsoft Press.
- Berlinski, David. 2001. *The Advent of the Algorithm: The 300-Year Journey from Idea to the Computer.* Mariner Books.

• Witten, Ian, Marco Gori, and Teresa Numerico. 2006. *Web Dragons.* Morgan Kaufman.
• Abelson, Hal, Ken Ledeen, and Harry Lewis. 2008. *Blown to Bits: Your Life, Liberty, and Happiness After the Digital Explosion.* Addison-Wesley.
• Reed, David. 2010. *A Balanced Introduction to Computer Science,* 3rd ed. Addison-Wesley.
• Rushkoff, Douglas, and Leland Purvis. 2011. *Program or Be Programmed: Ten Commands for a Digital Age.* Soft Skull Press.
• Blum, Andrew. 2012. *Tubes: A Journey to the Center of the Internet.* Harper Collins Ecco.
• Brynjolfsson, Erik, and Andrew McAfee. 2012. *Race Against the Machine: How the Digital Revolution Is Accelerating Innovation, Driving Productivity, and Irreversibly Transforming Employment and the Economy.* Digital Frontier Press.
• Gleick, James. 2012. *The Information: A History, A Theory, A Flood.* Vintage.
• MacCormick, John. 2012. *Nine Algorithms That Changed the Future.* Princeton University Press.
• Fortnow, Lance. 2013. *The Golden Ticket: P, NP, and the Search for the Impossible.* Princeton University Press.
• Brynjolfsson, Erik, and Andrew McAfee. 2014. *The Second Machine Age: Work, Progress, and Prosperity in a Time of Brilliant Technologies.* Norton.

9. See Denning, Peter. 2003. Great Principles of Computing. *Communications of ACM 46* (11):15–20.

10. Our colleague, the late Jim Gray, an ACM Turing Award recipient, strongly endorsed our search for the deepest principles of computing science. He advocated that we focus on "cosmic principles"—those that will be true at all times in all parts of the universe—and avoid confusing good ideas with such principles. He believed, for example, that virtual memory is an unbelievably good idea and locality is a deep principle.

11. Williams, Archibald. 1911. *How It Works: Dealing in Simple Language with Steam, Electricity, Light, Heat, Sound, Hydraulics, Optics, etc. and with Their Application to Apparatus in Common Use.* Thomas Nelson and Sons. (Available free on the Internet)

Chapter 1

1. Matti Tedre (2014) has given an excellent, detailed historical account of what the traditions of mathematics, engineering, and science brought to computing. Through the 1980s these traditions occasionally clashed. For example, mathematicians thought the theory of computation was the true computer science and that computer engineering was a branch of technology. Engineers thought that the mathematics prepared no one for the rigors of building computers and networks that worked. For a while they even fought over whether software engineering should be part of computer science or a separate engineering discipline. These clashes have

largely been resolved as computing has developed its own unique blend of these traditions, achieving its own identity in its service to so many other fields.

2. We reduced the seven categories of the original formulation to six in this book. One of the prior categories, automation, is a higher-level domain of computing, focusing on how and when to automate human cognitive tasks. That domain is called "artificial intelligence" in chapter 2.

Chapter 3

1. James Carse (1986) makes a similar distinction for games. He said, "There are at least two kinds of games. One could be called finite; the other infinite. A finite game is played for the purpose of winning, an infinite game for the purpose of continuing the play." These two kinds of games are profoundly different. Although he was not discussing computing, the distinction further highlights the profound difference between a finite algorithm and a never-ending interaction system.

2. A sender can encipher a message with a one-time pad, which uses the logical operation XOR (exclusive-or) to combine each bit of a long random sequence (the pad) with a corresponding message bit. (XOR has the value 1 if the two inputs bits are different, and 0 if they are the same.) A receiver recovers by XORing the same sequence of random bits with the ciphertext. Shannon showed that the entropy of the ciphertext is maximum, meaning that it contains no information for the eavesdropper. Where did the message and its information go? It is not in the key or the cipher stream. It is in the transformations chosen by the designer. The encoding and decoding transformations, taken as a pair, preserve the original meaning. Other cipher systems use shorter keys, in which case there may be some residual information in the ciphertext that a cryptanalyst can exploit.

Chapter 4

1. The book by Hennessey and Patterson (2011) has excellent coverage of all aspects of computer architecture. The original architecture of the stored program computer is frequently attributed to John von Neumann (1945), who published notes of his meetings with Eckert, Mauchly, Burks, and Goldstine. Most of that architecture came from Eckert and Mauchly, not from von Neumann.

2. IBM may have been the first to describe memory access as "random" with its new disk storage system RAMAC (Random Access Memory Accounting Machine) in 1956. Random meant that the time to complete an access was a random variable composed of seek time (arm positioning) and latency (rotational positioning). Today RAM refers to the main memory of a computer chip, but random means that the access time for any randomly chosen address is fixed, a different use of the word "random."

3. Corrado Bohm and Giuseppe Jacopini (1966) proved that any computable function can be computed by a program limited to these three structures. This theorem was used as the basis of "structured programming," a movement to make programs easier to understand and prove correct. Some years later David Harel (1980) traced this claim all the way back to the design of the von Neumann architecture itself and to a normal-form theorem proved by Stephen Kleene in the 1930s.

4. Jan Lukasiewicz (1957) notes that he first came upon the notation in 1924. Arthur Burks, Don Warren, and Jesse Wright (1954) are credited with being the first to notice that reverse Polish notation simplified mechanical evaluation of expressions. Fritz Bauer and Edsger Dijkstra are credited with independently discovering this in the early 1960s (Wikipedia).

5. Recursion can lead to simpler programs. For example, it is possible to write a sort routine in the form SORT(list) = {SORT(left half of list); SORT(right half of list); MERGE(left half, right half)}, with the boundary condition SORT(empty list)=empty list. Each inner call to SORT must have a smaller input than the outer call.

6. There is a superficial similarity with the Heisenberg uncertainty principle of quantum physics. That principle says that product of the standard deviations of position and momentum is at least 10^{-34} joule-seconds. Trying to reduce the uncertainty of one forces greater uncertainty of the other. Part of the reason for the Heisenberg principle is that the very act of observing either adds or removes energy from the particle being observed. But this holds only at atomic scales of electrons and not at the macro scales of currents in wires. The choice uncertainty principle is not an instance of Heisenberg's principle.

7. Asynchronous circuits (see chapter 8, Parallelism) are made of modules that interact with ready-acknowledge signals. They can be designed so that they will not generate ready or acknowledge signals while in a metastable state. They need no clocks. They are often faster than clocked circuits because modules "fire when ready" and do not have to wait for a next clock tick.

Chapter 5

1. Good general texts about programming languages are Pierce (2002) and Louden (2011).

2. Google searches turned up a claim that a group at Murdock University in Perth, Australia, had compiled a database of 8500 languages, but we have not been able to verify that claim.

3. These estimates can be found in Wikipedia and in many other sources by simple Internet searches. A *Harvard Business Review* article (Flyvbjerg and Budzier 2011) says that the average IT budget overrun is 27 percent and that one-sixth of projects have major overruns of over 200 percent on cost and over 70 percent on schedule.

4. Automatic translation of high-level programs to machine code goes back to the 1950s. It took many years of research to learn how to parse programming languages and generate efficient machine code. Today it is a specialized subfield. The book by Aho, Lam, Sethi, and Ullman (2006) is an excellent study of all the theory and how it translated into practice. We have distilled the essence of a rich, complex theory. The book by Brown et al. (2012) discusses two famous Unix programs, Lex and Yacc, that generate compilers from BNF descriptions of programming languages.

5. This happens a lot with standardized languages that work on many platforms. For example, HTML, Java, and Javascript have precise international standards, and yet web designers need to test their pages and sites on each platform because language constructs do not work exactly the same on every operating system.

Chapter 6

1. $O(n^3)$ is not the best for matrix multiplication. Volker Strassen (1969) found a trick to make it $O(n^{2.807})$, and later Coppersmith and Winograd (1990) found another trick to make it $O(n^{2.37})$. These faster algorithms are complex and nonobvious.

2. Variations of the knapsack problem have been studied as far back as 1897. However, the mathematician Tobias Dantzig gave it a name in 1930 in an essay "Numbers: The Language of Science."

3. See http://www.math.uwaterloo.ca/tsp/sweden/ and http://chern.ie.nthu.edu.tw/gen/12.pdf.

Chapter 7

1. The mapping function is performed by a hardware component in the CPU called the memory mapping unit (MMU). The MMU contains a small cache called a Translation Lookaside Buffer (TLB) that holds copies of the most recently mapped page-to-frame pairs. The MMU can bypass the page table lookup, which costs another memory reference, if its target page is listed in the TLB. The TLB typically speeds up the mapping process to within 1–3 percent of what it would be if page table accesses cost no delay.

2. The following are examples from a rich literature on capability systems. Jack Dennis and Earl Van Horn (1966) proposed the idea. Robert Fabry (1974) showed capability addressing to be the best solution for the shared data problem. Bill Wulf and colleagues (1974) implemented a capability kernel linked to objects. Maurice Wilkes and Roger Needham (1979) built a capability machine and operating system at University of Cambridge. Henry Levy (1984) wrote a summary and overview of capability systems and their operating principles. Mark Miller (2003) wrote a rebuttal of several false myths about capability systems.

3. Tahoe Least Authority File System (https://tahoe-lafs.org) is an open source file system that uses capability addressing. No server can exceed its authority because it gets a set of capabilities exactly equal to what it needs to do its advertised job. Errors are confined to those objects and cannot spread to other objects.

4. MIN is the optimal policy first defined by Belady (1966) for virtual memory. At a page fault, the incoming page replaces the loaded page whose reuse time is farthest in the future. No fixed-partition memory policy can generate fewer page faults for any given memory size. However, MIN can never change its RAM allocation. It is constrained to wait until the next page load before it can remove a page. In contrast, VMIN can remove a page immediately after its current use if it foresees no use for that page before the threshold time expires. When VMIN's threshold is adjusted to make its average allocation equal to MIN's fixed allocation, VMIN always generates fewer faults for that amount of memory use.

5. Les Belady of IBM Research and Peter Denning of MIT independently proposed the locality principle in 1966 and then collaborated on some of the research to validate it. Belady (1966) proposed it to explain the nonrandom performance of paging algorithms, and Denning (1968a) to characterize intrinsic memory demands of programs. Many researchers have since studied the principle in many systems. The locality principle is one of the most extensively validated models in computer science (Denning 1980). It continues to be the subject of research on cache performance optimization (Xiang et al. 2013).

6. The measurement must be conducted in the virtual time of the program. Virtual time counts memory references at one per time unit. Virtual time omits delays caused by interruptions such as disk requests; those delays can be added in if they are relevant to a performance analysis (Denning 1980).

7. Thrashing is a sudden collapse of system throughput when the multiprogramming load exceeds a volatile and changing critical value. It occurs when RAM is too small to hold the working sets of all the active programs. Programs starved for space generate significantly more page faults and steal pages from other working sets. Soon none of them has its working set present, and all of them are queued up at the disk waiting for their page faults to be satisfied (Denning 1968b).Queueing network models showed that the onset of thrashing occurs when increasing demand for paging forces the paging disk to become the bottleneck of the system (Denning et al. 1976).

Chapter 8

1. Real weather prediction is much more complex. It would use three-dimensional cubes touching at six sides and would allow contributions from neighboring cubes touching only at corners. The pressure equation would be more complicated, accounting for the influence of wind speed and direction as well.

2. Modula, a revision of Pascal, was designed and developed by Niklaus Wirth between 1977 and 1985. Smalltalk was created in 1980 by Adele Goldberg (1983),

Alan Kay, Dan Ingalls, and others at Xerox PARC and became an ANSI standard in 1988. CLU was developed at MIT by Barbara Liskov (1977) and her students. Occam, which implemented Hoare's CSP model (1985), was developed in 1984 by David May at INMOS Corp., a maker of chips called transputers for parallel supercomputers.

3. Jerry Saltzer (1965) of MIT defined a process as "a program in execution on a processor." Jack Dennis and Earl Van Horn (1966) of MIT defined a process as "locus of control in an instruction sequence" and Vic Vyssotsky of Bell Labs as a "thread." Edsger Dijkstra (1968a, 1968b) of Technische Hogeschool Eindhoven defined process as "a sequence of CPU states following executions of instructions of a program."

4. In CSP, Hoare replaced Dijkstra's semaphores with a simpler coordination mechanism, rendezvous, in which two processes wanting to exchange data visit their respective rendezvous points, at which moment the data flows between them over a channel.

5. Nico Habermann (1969) is often credited with the first formal model of deadlock. He showed that an operating system can enter unsafe states in which there is no deadlock, but a future deadlock is certain. He showed a "Banker's Algorithm" that would decide whether a proposed resource allocation would be safe. Other algorithms for safety are discussed by Coffman and Denning (1973). These algorithms are not much used because of their overhead.

6. To visualize this, assume that the constraint is followed and yet there is a set of deadlocked processes. The highest-numbered lock held by the deadlocked processes cannot be released because a deadlocked process is holding it. The holder of that lock must itself be waiting for a lock, which by the constraint must be numbered higher. This contradicts the assumption that deadlock exists.

7. Dijkstra's famous Dining Philosophers problem can be solved with this method. Imagine a round table with 5 plates in front of 5 seats and one fork between each pair of plates. Every so often a philosopher comes and sits down to eat from a bowl of spaghetti in the middle. To eat, the philosopher needs to pick up the two forks adjacent to his plate. A deadlock is possible when they all try to pick up one fork (say the right) at the same time; now each will be waiting for a neighbor to release a fork. If each one philosopher picks up the lower numbered fork first, this circular wait cannot happen.

8. Richard Karp and Raymond Miller (1966, 1969) were the first to prove such a theorem. Coffman and Denning (1973) proved it in the context of operating systems. Brinch Hansen (1973) declared it an important principle of operating systems.

Chapter 9

1. For readers interested in full coverage of the queueing theory and methods applied to computer systems and networks, we recommend the books by Kleinrock

(1975, 1976), Kobayahsi and Mark (2008), Lazowska et al (1984), Menascé and Almeida (2002), Menascé et al (1994), and Stewart (2009).

2. The utilization law and Little's law are counterparts of well-known limit theorems for stochastic queueing systems in a steady state. The limit theorems will usually be verified in actual measurements, not because a steady state has been attained but because the measured quantities obey operational laws (Buzen 1976).

3. Designate a series of cells called $H[n]$ for $n = 0, 1, \ldots, N$. These cells will hold trial values of $p(n)$ on the (incorrect) assumption that $p(0) = 1$. Insert the balance equation as the formula for computing $H[n]$ from $H[n-1]$. The trial values obey the balance equation but do not sum to 1. We can make them sum to 1 as follows. First, create a new cell "*sum*" for $H[0] + \ldots + H[N]$. Next, create a new set of cells $p[n]$ for $n = 0, 1, \ldots, N$. Finally, put the formula $p[n] = H[n]/sum$ into those p-cells. Now the values in the p-cells will sum to 1 and obey the balance equation.

4. A state is a vector $(n_1, \ldots, n_K)$ where n_i is the state of server i and the sum of all the n_i is the system load N. We could represent a vector with a string of N 1's with $K-1$ 0's. The 0's are placed so that the length of each group of 1's equals one of the components. The number of possible such strings is $(N + K - 1)!/N!(K - 1)!$

Chapter 10

1. It is sometimes said that Ada Lovelace, who collaborated with Charles Babbage on the Analytic Engine in the early 1840s, was the first programmer of a digital computer. Babbage never completed his Engine, and Lovelace never ran her programs. Programming did not become a profession until there were many people doing it beginning in the 1940s, a hundred years later. The practice of programming generated new designers—of languages, editors, translators, debuggers, version control systems, graphical interfaces, applications, and more.

2. Christopher Alexander, who started the school of architecture known as "the timeless way of building" (1979), said that experienced designers follow a relatively small set of timeless patterns when making their design choices.

3. These ten aspects of good design were formulated by German industrial designer Dieter Rams and are often known as the "Rams's principles" (source: Wikipedia).

4. In 2007 the originators of modeling checking—Edmund Clark, E. Allen Emerson, and Joseph Sifakis—received an ACM Turing Award for their work.

5. Error confinement is familiar in other domains. Ships are compartmented into sections separated by water-tight doors to lower risk of sinking in case of a hull breach. Hot-air balloons are compartmented into sections to lower risks of failure from a puncture. Bridges are trussed into thousands of triangular sections to protect against collapse if any one section breaks.

6. Carl Mitcham (1994), a philosopher of technology, described "technical knowledge" as (1) skills of making ("know-how"), (2) descriptive laws (rules stating actions to take when the right conditions apply), (3) technical maxims (rules of thumb and other heuristics), and (4) technological theories (applications of scientific theories to practice). In our terminology a principle is a description of a skill of making, a pattern is a description law, and a hint is a technical maxim. The scientific knowledge that constrains practice must be part of the background awareness of the designer.

7. http://en.wikipedia.org/wiki/Software_design_pattern. In 2014 the page listed nine creational, nine structural, fifteen behavioral, and fifteen concurrency patterns.

8. Jay Israel, James Mitchell, and Howard Sturgis (1978) at Xerox Palo Alto Research Center developed the client-server model. Alfred Spector (1982) and Andrew Birrell and Bruce Nelson (1984) implemented the idea as remote procedure call (RPC). In 1984 Robert Sheifler and James Gettys developed the X-Window system at MIT (Scheifler et al 1988). X-Windows is a generic client server hosting system; users provide the code for clients and servers and X-Windows provides the communication through the network.

9. The talent and skill of designers are not trivial points. Simple web searches will reveal numerous studies showing that the best programmers are at least ten times more productive than entry-level programmers. Elite programmers can "see" large systems at all levels of detail in their heads and transform their vision into working code very quickly. It is well worthwhile for a software company to find a 10× programmer and pay twice the normal salary. This is far superior to hiring ten entry-level programmers and then trying to manage them well.

Chapter 11

1. Internet engineers distinguish between the network and the hosts. The network is the set of routers and links that move packets. The hosts are systems attached to the network through standard interfaces. The original ARPANET (1970s) was a network of packet switches called Interface Message Processors (IMPs); they formed the so-called subnet to which the hosts were attached. The IMPs did the real networking; the hosts appeared as sources and sinks of messages. The first-version Internet software (1980s) used computers called "gateways" to connect packet networks to each other. Eventually, gateways were renamed "routers." Hosts connected to the network via a router.

2. What follows is a brief history of the early Internet. Much more detailed treatments can be found in the document by Barry Leiner et al. (1996) and the book by Katie Hafner and Matthew Lyon (1999).

J. C. R. Licklider of MIT in 1960 described a visionary future with a worldwide network connecting all computers (Licklider 1960). The network would support resource sharing, ubiquitous computing, computing utilities, intelligent interfaces, new approaches to research, and new kinds of businesses (Licklider 1962, 1963). In 1961 Leonard Kleinrock of UCLA analyzed a stochastic communication network model in which discrete messages flowed to their destinations and queued at intermediate nodes (Kleinrock 1961, 1964). In 1964 Paul Baran of the RAND Corporation published a series of papers on the architecture of a new kind of network, a distributed voice communication system, which could survive link and node disruptions (Baran 1964a, 1964b). Digitized voice bitstreams were broken into small message blocks that could be routed (and rerouted) over alternative paths en route to their destinations. In 1966 Donald Davies of the National Physical Laboratory in the UK started using the term "packet" for those message-blocks (Davies et al 1967), and that term stuck as the standard.

In 1967 Bob Taylor of DARPA asked Larry Roberts to lead a research project to build a distributed network to realize these visions (Roberts 1967, Roberts and Merrill 1966). Roberts collaborated with Len Kleinrock and Wesley Clark. Clark suggested that the network be configured as a subnet of identical small computers, called interface message processors (IMPs), which transmitted packets and served as interfaces to the heterogeneous host computers. Nobody built Baran's design. The first two nodes of the ARPANET were operating in late 1969.

Steve Crocker led the development of the Network Control Protocol (NCP), ARPANET's host-to-host protocol from 1970 to 1983. Protocols for file transfer (FTP), remote login (TELNET), and mail (SMTP) were developed as companions to NCP. In 1973 Vinton Cerf and Robert Kahn proposed the transmission control protocol (TCP), which later became the TCP/IP protocol suite. They also designed the addressing structure and the gateway architecture for connecting distinct networks. In their positions at ARPA they oversaw the evolution and development the Internet until its formal initiation in January 1983. The TCP gave a uniform method for connecting many subnets into a network of networks (the Internet). TCP gave reliable, efficient file and message transfer in the Internet. NCP was retired in 1983 when TCP/IP became the standard protocol. The period 1973–1983 was a time of experimental development of the new protocols. By 1981 the ARPANET had standardized the basic suite of protocols for an Internet (RFCs 791, 792, 783): IP for addressing and basic packet transfer, TCP for sequenced data transport, UDP for datagram transfer, FTP for manual file transfer between hosts, TELNET for remote login, and SMTP for mail exchange.

The British and French governments also sponsored early research projects in networking. In 1967 Donald Davies in the UK built a one-node packet switch and simulated packet networks. In 1972 Louis Pouzin in France created a network called CYCLADES, for which he coined the term "datagram" for packets used to transfer data (Pouzin 1973, 1974). The datagram idea was incorporated into the TCP/IP protocol suite. However, the French government was more interested in preserving the familiar structures of telephony in its data communications; it backed the X.25 protocol and let the CYCLADES project lapse. The X.25 work is less known in the United States because only one company, GTE Telenet, offered the service. The prime movers of X.25 were Rémi Després and Paul Gulnaudeau at CCETT in France, David Horton and Anton Rybczynsky at TCTS in Canada, Larry Roberts and Barry Wessler at Telenet in the United States, Philip Kelly and John Wedlake at the Post Office in the United Kingdom, and Masao Kato at NTT in Japan. They got the X.25 standard adopted by CCITT in 1976. Chris Bloomfield at the UK Post Office and Bernard Jamet at the CCETT in France contributed shortly after that the character-mode-interface recommendations for X.3, X.28, and X.29. For more detail, see Després (2010).

In 1981 the US National Science Foundation (NSF) entered the network business by sponsoring CSNET, a community network connecting research-oriented CS departments and labs around the world. The CSNET project involved a large number of people under the leadership of a university consortium led by Principal Investigators Larry Landweber, David Farber, Tony Hearn, and Peter Denning. CSNET developed versions of the ARPANET TCP/IP protocols that ran over telephone dial-up connections and X.25 connections, departing from the ARPANET's standard of leased telephone lines. In 1986 the NSF expanded its presence in networking by sponsoring a backbone, NSFNET, connecting the NSF supercomputing centers. They connected regional networks to the backbone and opened the network to commercial traffic. By 1990 the emerging Internet had grown to over 150,000 hosts and was doubling every year.

In parallel with the US networking efforts, the Organization for International Standardization (ISO) designed the Open Systems Interconnection (OSI) protocol suite built initially atop the European X.25 protocol. The first OSI reference model paper appeared in 1978 (see Zimmerman 1980), and the standard itself was published by the ISO in 1984. For the next fifteen years there was an international debate between advocates of the TCP/IP suite and the OSI suite. TCP/IP became the Internet standard around 1993, when the US government, via NIST (National Institute for Standards and Technology), accepted that TCP/IP was a reasonable alternative to OSI.

The Internet was initially slow to evolve into a medium for commercial transactions. In the mid-1970s ARPA encouraged IBM, DEC, and HP to participate in the research project. In 1985 ARPA and NSF agreed to allow industry members of CSNET to send traffic on the ARPANET; however, those members did not try sales or marketing with their CSNET connections. In 1989 the NSF permitted the first commercial vendors to serve the NSFNET infrastructure—Internet Service Providers (ISPs) UUNET, PSINET, CERFNET, and the first email providers including MCI Mail, Compuserve, OnTyme, Telemail, and GENIE. In 1989 a team at CERN Laboratory in Switzerland, led by computer scientist Tim Berners-Lee, developed the World Wide Web technology to enable easy sharing of documents in the Internet. The WWW took off in 1993 with the release of Marc Andreessen's Mosaic browser by the University of Illinois; Mosaic was the first graphical interface to the WWW. After that, various commercial firms started developing web pages and offering to do business transactions via the web.

The first ideas of a worldwide web can be found in Ted Nelson's proposals in the 1960s for digital publication in a shared network (Nelson 1980). Authors would make digital documents available by a system he called *Xanadu*, which would automatically handle publication, distribution, royalties, and copyrights. Authors would use hypertext instead of linear writing. Nelson's vision remained in the status of a dream well into the 1980s, when AutoDesk bought his company, Xanadu, and made the software public.

Also in the 1960s Douglas Engelbart of SRI began a project to augment human intelligence by supporting cooperative work. His NLS (oNLine System) supported hypertext document organization, textual interaction with the screen, group collaboration on a document, embedded video, a chord keyset, and the first mouse. His demo made it obvious that NLS could be extended to networks, which would amplify its power to augment intelligence.

In 1980 the American National Standards Institute (ANSI) formed a committee on computer languages for processing of text. Publishers traditionally marked up author's manuscripts with special symbols to tell the printers how to set up the typesetting machines properly. In 1985 the ANSI group proposed a standard generalized markup language (SGML), a meta-language to describe the grammars of individual markup languages. With SGML, it became possible for authors, editors, and publishers to process and exchange documents automatically. Tim Berners-Lee, a member of the SGML users group, used the SGML principles to define HTML, the markup language for web pages. He included tags for URLs (uniform resource locators) of digital objects anywhere in the Internet, and he defined the protocol HTTP to automatically fetch a document designated by a URL link. The combination of a browser, HTML, HTTP, the URL, and a web server was the initial World Wide Web. Berners-Lee founded the World Wide Web Consortium (W3C) in 1985 to oversee the orderly development of the web.

3. Kleinrock and Baran spoke of messages and message blocks. The term "packet" was introduced by Donald Davies in 1967 and was soon accepted as the standard.

4. Whether all packets are of the same size or can be of different sizes has been a constant source of debate. Fixed-size packets are subject to fragmentation, which means that the final packet of a sequence has an unused portion of its data field; on average half the last packet's data field will be lost to fragmentation. Variable packets can be sized to exactly fit the data, without fragmentation. Protocol engineers weigh the cost of the headers against the cost of the fragmentation. There are no easy answers because the costs depend on the network and the distribution of file or communication sizes.

5. In Internet terminology the most recent version of 32-bit addressing is called "IP version 4" or IPv4. The revised protocol for 128-bit addressing is called "IP version 6" or IPv6. As of 2014 many network administrators had not upgraded to support IPv6 in parallel with IPv4.

6. An article "List of TCP and UDP port numbers" in Wikipedia lists hundreds of "well-known ports" in the range 0–1023. Thousands of other services and their port numbers in the range 1024 to 49151 have been registered with IANA.

7. The network control panel on your computer has a field containing the IP address of the DNS server your computer uses for translating domain names to IP addresses. TCP uses that DNS server.

8. Administration of domain names and IP addresses is complicated and is structured to reflect the hierarchical methods of constructing domain names and IP addresses. The Internet Corporation for Assigned Names and Numbers (ICANN, icann.org) has overall responsibility for determining the top-level domains and setting the policies for administering domains at the lower levels of the hierarchy. The primary root servers, which contain the top-level domain database, are updated by a complex but secure process. ICANN sends proposed updates to National Technical Information Agency (NTIA), which confirms the changes to Verisign; Verisign generates the new root zone and sends copies of it to 13 root zone operators, including ICANN (one root server) and Verisign (two root servers). Each root server is implemented at multiple redundant locations to protect against failure or attack and to provide faster response in all parts of the world; in 2014 there were 385 root server locations (see www.iana.org/domains/root/servers). ICANN is global in scope but is actually a nonprofit organization incorporated in California, with a very international board and operations in Singapore, Istanbul, and Los Angeles. One of the functions of ICANN is the allocation of blocks of addresses to regional Internet registries (RIRs), a function performed by the Internet Assigned Numbers Authority (IANA, iana.org). The RIRs formulate global rules that are adopted by ICANN and administered by IANA. The Internet Engineering Task Force (IETF, ietf.org) sets technical standards that can affect IP address formats, allocations, and assignments. IETF is hosted by the Internet Society, a nonprofit incorporated in Washington, DC, with offices and chapters around the world.

9. The same principle is known in software engineering as the *principle of levels* and is discussed in chapter 10 on design. Levels and layers are strata of software that add functions to the levels below. In networking, data flow up and down through the levels in the form of packets, with each level performing its unique operation on a packet. In software engineering, data flow as parameters to procedure calls, which are allowed only to lower levels; data flow upward via procedure returns.

10. In 2014, a flaw was discovered in the OpenSSL implementation of TLS. This so-called Heartbleed bug affected about 17 percent of hosts using https connections and would allow an intruder to steal passwords and encryption keys. A patch was quickly distributed, but many users had to change passwords on the affected web sites. Even with careful design, flaws still get into software!

Afterword

1. An example is Kelly, Kevin. 2010. *What Technology Wants.* Viking.

2. Joy, Bill. 2000. Why the future doesn't need us. *Wired* magazine, issue 8.04 (April). Available at http://archive.wired.com/wired/archive/8.04/joy.html.

3. In May 2014 Stephen Hawking discussed a new film "Transcendence" about operating systems developing intelligence and threatening humanity. He was not convinced that computing experts are working to control the risks that accompany the bounty. He believed that autonomous military technology could easily get out of hand.

4. Rosenbloom, Paul. 2012. *On Computing: The Fourth Great Scientific Domain.* MIT Press.

5. Brynjolfsson, Erik, and Andrew McAfee. 2014. *The Second Machine Age: Work, Progress, and Prosperity in a Time of Brilliant Technologies.* W. W. Norton.

References

Abrams, Robert. 2011. *Encyclopedia of Computer Sciences*. Nova Science Publishers.

ACM Education Board. 2001. Curriculum 2001 recommendations. http://www.acm.org/education/curric_vols/cc2001.pdf

ACM Education Board. 2013. Curriculum 2013 recommendations. http://www.acm.org/education/CS2013-final-report.pdf

Aho, Alfred, Peter Denning, and Jeffrey Ullman. 1971. Principles of optimal page replacement. *Journal of the ACM* 18 (1):80–93.

Aho, Alfred, Monica Lam, Ravi Sethi, and Jeffrey Ullman. 2006. *Compilers: Principles, Techniques, and Tools*. Addison-Wesley.

Alexander, Christopher. 1979. *The Timeless Way of Building*. Oxford University Press.

Alfke, Peter. 2005. Metastable recovery in Virtex-II Pro FPGAs. Technical Report xapp094 (February), available from Xilinx.com website.

Arden, Bruce W. (ed.) 1983. *What Can Be Automated: Computer Science and Engineering Research Study (COSERS)*. MIT Press.

Bachman, Charles. 1973. The programmer as navigator. *Communications of the ACM* 16 (11):653–658.

Backus, John. 1959. The syntax and semantics of the proposed international algebraic languages of the Zurich ACM-GAMM Conference. *Proceedings of the International Conference on Information Processing*, pp. 125–132. UNESCO.

Bacon, Dave, and Wim van Dam. 2010. Recent progress in quantum algorithms. *Communications of the ACM* 53 (2):84–93.

Baltimore, David. 2001. How biology became an information science. In *The Invisible Future*, ed. P. Denning, 43–56. McGraw-Hill.

Barabasi, Albert-Laszlo. 2002. *Linked: The New Science of Networks*. Perseus.

Baran, Paul. 1964a. *On distributed communications: Introduction to distributed communications networks.* Rand Corp memorandum RM-3420-PR, available from http://rand.org/pubs/research_memoranda/RM3420.html

Baran, Paul. 1964b. On distributed communications networks. *IEEE Transactions on Communications Systems* 12(1).

Bard, Y. 1979. Some extensions to multiclass queueing network analysis. *Proceedings of the Fourth International Symposium on Computer Performance Modeling, Measurement, and Evaluation* (H. Beilner and E. Gelenbe, eds.). North-Holland.

Basket, F., R. Muntz, M. Chandy, and F. Palacios. 1975. Open, closed, and mixed networks of queues with different classes of customers. *Journal of the ACM* 22 (2):248–260.

Belady, Les A. 1966. A study of replacement algorithms for a virtual-storage computer. *IBM Systems Journal* 5 (2):78–101.

Bell, David, and Leonard LaPadula. 1976. Secure Computing System: Unified Exposition and Multics Interpretation. MITRE Technical Report 2547.

Bell, T., and M. Fellows. CSunplugged.org website. Video presentation of a workshop. http://csunplugged.org/videos.

Berners-Lee, Tim. 2000. *Weaving the Web: The Original Design and Ultimate Destiny of the World Wide Web.* Harper Business.

Birrell, Andrew, and Bruce Nelson. 1984. Implementing remote procedure calls. *ACM Transactions on Computer Systems* 2 (1):39–59.

Boehm, Barry. 2002. Get ready for agile methods, with care. *IEEE Computer* (January):64–69.

Bohm, Corrado, and Giuseppe Jacopini. 1966. Flow diagrams, Turing machines, and languages with only two formation rules. *Communications of the ACM* 9 (5):366–371.

Brooks, Frederick. 1975. *The Mythical Man Month.* Addison-Wesley. Second edition published 1995.

Brooks, Frederick. 1986. No silver bullet—Essence and accident in software engineering. *Proceedings of the 10th IFIP World Congress*, pp. 1069–1076. Reprinted 1987 in *IEEE Computer* 20 (4):10–19.

Brooks, Frederick P. 1995. *The Mythical Man Month*, 2nd ed. Addison-Wesley. (Original work published 1975)

Brown, Doug, John Levine, and Tony Mason. 2012. *Lex & Yacc*, 2nd ed. O'Reilly Media. (Original work published 1992)

Brynjolfsson, Erik, and Andrew McAfee. 2012. *Race against the Machine: How the Digital Revolution Is Accelerating Innovation, Driving Productivity, and Irreversibly Transforming Employment and the Economy.* Digital Frontier Press.

Burke, James. 1985. *The Day the Universe Changed.* Little, Brown.

Burks, Arthur, Don Warren, and Jesse Wright. 1954. An analysis of a logical machine using parenthesis-free notation. *Mathematical Tables and Other Aids to Computation* 8:53–57.

Buzen, Jeffrey P. 1973. Computational algorithms for closed queueing networks. *Communications of the ACM* 16 (9):527–531.

Buzen, Jeffrey P. 1976. Fundamental operational laws of computer system performance. *Acta Informatica* 7:167–182.

Buzen, Jeffrey P. 2011. Computation, uncertainty, and risk. *ACM Ubiquity Symposium on Computation.* http://ubiquity.acm.org/article.cfm?id=1936886.

Carse, J. 1986. *Finite and Infinite Games.* Ballantine Books, Random House.

Cerf, Vinton, Yogen Dalal, and Carl Sunshine. 1974. Specification of Internet Transmission Control Program. RFC 675 (December). Available as https://tools.ietf.org/html/rfc675.

Cerf, Vinton, and Robert Kahn. 1974. A protocol for packet network interconnection. *IEEE Transactions on Communication Technology COM-22* (5):627–641.

Chaitin, Gregory. 2006. *Meta Math!: The Quest for Omega.* Vintage.

Chan, Tony, and Yousef Saad. 1986. Multigrid algorithms on the hypercube multiprocessor. *IEEE Transactions on Computers* C-35 (11):969–977.

Chaney, T. J., and C. E. Molnor. 1973. Anomalous behavior of synchronizer and arbiter circuits. *IEEE Transactions on Computers* 22 (April):421–422.

Cisco. 2012. Visual Networking Index (VNI) Forecast (2011–2016). http://cisco.com/en/US/netsol/ns827/networking_solutions_sub_solution.html.

Clark, David. 1988. The design philosophy of the DARPA Internet Protocol. *ACM Computer Communication Review* 18 (4):106–114.

Clark, Edmund. 2008. *The Birth of Model Checking. In 25 Years of Model Checking,* vol. 5000, ed. O. Grumberg and H. Veith, pp. 1–26. Lecture Notes in Computer Science. Springer Verlag.

Clark, Edmund, and E. Allen Emerson. 1981. Design and synthesis of synchronization skeletons using branching time temporal logic. In *Logic of Programs: Workshop, Yorktown Heights, NY.* Lecture Notes on Computer Science, Springer Verlag.

Clark, Richard. 2012. *Cyber War: The Next Threat to National Security and What to Do about It.* Ecco.

Codd, Edgar. 1970. A relational model of data for large shared databanks. *Communications of the ACM* 25 (2):109–117.

Codd, Edgar. 1990. *The Relational Model for Database Management,* 2nd ed. Addison-Wesley.

Coffman, Edward G. Jr., and Peter Denning. 1973. *Operating Systems Theory.* Prentice-Hall.

Comer, Douglas. 2013. *Internetworking with TCP/IP,* 6th ed., vol. 1. Addison-Wesley.

Cook, Stephen. 1971. The complexity of theorem proving procedures. *Proceedings of the 3rd ACM Symposium on Theory of Computation,* pp. 151–158. ACM Press.

Coplien, James, and Douglas Schmidt. 1995. *Pattern Languages of Program Design.* Addison-Wesley.

Coppersmith, Donald, and Shmuel Winograd. 1990. Matrix multiplication via arithmetic progressions. *Journal of Symbolic Computation* 9:251–280.

Cormen, Thomas, Charles Leiserson, Ronald Rivest, and Clifford Stein. 2009. *Introduction to Algorithms.* MIT Press.

Davies, Donald W., K. A. Bartlett, R. A. Scantlebury, and P. T. Wilkinson. 1967. A digital communication network for computers giving rapid response at remote terminals. *Proceedings of the ACM Symposium on Operating System Principles* (SOSP). http://doi.acm.org/10.1145/800001.811669

Dean, Jeffrey, and Sanjay Ghemawat. 2004. MapReduce: Simplified data processing on large clusters. *Proceedings of the 6th Symposium on Operating System Design and Implementation 6* (OSDI'74). USENIX Association.

Dean, Jeffrey, and Sanjay Ghemawat. 2008. MapReduce: Simplified data processing on large clusters. *Communications of the ACM* 51 (1):107–113.

Denning, Dorothy. 1976. A lattice model for secure information flow. *Communications of the ACM* 19 (5):236–243.

Denning, Dorothy. 1982. *Cryptography and Data Security.* Addison-Wesley.

Denning, Dorothy. 1998. *Information Warfare and Security.* Addison-Wesley.

Denning, Peter. 1968a. The working set model for program behavior. *Communications of the ACM* 11 (5):323–333.

Denning, Peter. 1968b. Thrashing: Its causes and prevention. *Proceedings of the AFIPS Conference* 32:915–922.

Denning, Peter. 1970. Virtual memory. *ACM Computing Surveys* 2 (3):153–189.

Denning, Peter. 1971. Third generation computer systems. *ACM Computing Surveys* 3 (4):175–216.

Denning, Peter. 1980. Working sets past and present. *IEEE Transactions on Software Engineering* SE-6 (1):64–84.

Denning, Peter. 1985. The arbitration problem. *American Scientist* 73 (Nov–Dec): 516–518.

Denning, Peter. 1987. Multigrids and hypercubes. *American Scientist* 75 (3):234–238.

Denning, Peter. 2001. Who are we? *Communications of the ACM* 44 (2): 15–19.

Denning, Peter. 2003. Great principles of computing. *Communications of the ACM* 46 (11):15–20.

Denning, Peter. 2007a. Computing is a natural science. *Communications of the ACM* 50 (7):15–18.

Denning, Peter. 2007b. The choice uncertainty principle. *Communications of the ACM* 50 (11):9–14.

Denning, Peter. 2013. Design thinking. *Communications of the ACM* 58:12.

Denning, Peter, Douglas Comer, David Gries, Michael Mulder, Allen Tucker, A. Joe Turner, and Paul Young. 1989. Computing as a discipline. *Communications of the ACM* 32 (1):9–23.

Denning, Peter, and Dennis Frailey. 2011. Who are we—now? *Communications of the ACM* 54 (6):27–29.

Denning, Peter, and Peter Freeman. 2009. Computing's paradigm. *Communications of the ACM* 52 (12):28–30.

Denning, Peter, Kevin Kahn, Jacques Leroudier, Dominique Potier, and Rajan Suri. 1976. Optimal multiprogramming. *Acta Informatica* 7 (2):197–216.

Denning, Peter, and Robert Kahn. 2010. The long quest for universal information access. *ACM Communications of the ACM* 53 (12):34–36.

Denning, Peter, and Craig Martell. 2004. Great Principles of Computing Web site. http://greatprinciples.org.

Denning, Peter, Walter Tichy, and James Hunt. 2000. Operating systems. In *Encyclopedia of Computer Science*, ed. A. Ralston, E. O'Reilly, and D. Hemmendinger, pp. 1290–1311. Nature Publishing Group, Grove's Dictionaries.

Denning, Peter J. 1991a. Queueing in networks of computers. *American Scientist* 79 (3):8–10.

Denning, Peter J. 1991b. In the queue: Mean values. *American Scientist* 79 (5):402–403.

Denning, Peter J., and Jeffrey P. Buzen. 1977. Operational analysis of queueing networks. *Modeling and Performance Evaluation of Computer Systems* (H. Beilner and E. Gelenbe, eds.), pp. 151–172. North-Holland.

Denning, Peter J., and Jeffrey P. Buzen. 1978. The operational analysis of queueing network models. *ACM Computing Surveys* 10 (3):225–261.

Denning, Peter J., and Tim Bell. 2012. The information paradox. *American Scientist* 100:470–477.

Dennis, Jack, and David Misunas. 1975. A preliminary architecture for a basic data-flow processor. *ACM 2nd Symposium on Computer Architecture,* pp. 126–132, ACM Press.

Dennis, Jack, and Earl Van Horn. 1966. Programming semantics for multiprogrammed computations. *Communications of the ACM* 9 (3):143–155.

Dennis, Jack, and Earl C. Van Horn. 1966. Programming semantics for multiprogrammed computations. *Communications of the ACM* 9 (3):143–155.

Després, Rémi. 2010. X.25 virtual circuits: Transpac in France—pre-Internet data networking. *IEEE Communications Magazine* 40 (11):40–46.

Dijkstra, Edsger. 1959. A note on two problems in connection with graphs. *Numerische Mathematik* 1:269–271.

Dijkstra, Edsger. 1965. Solution of a problem in concurrent program control. *Communications of the ACM* 8 (9):569.

Dijkstra, Edsger. 1968. The structure of the THE-multiprogramming system. *Communications of the ACM* 11 (5):341–346.

Dijkstra, Edsger. 1968a. Cooperating sequential processes. In *Programming Languages,* ed. F. Genuys, pp. 43–112. Academic Press.

Dijkstra, Edsger. 1968b. The structure of the "THE" multiprogramming system. *ACM Communications* 11 (5):341–346.

Dretske, F. 1981. *Knowledge and the Flow of Information.* MIT Press.

Dreyfus, Hubert. 1972. *What Computers Can't Do.* MIT Press.

Dreyfus, Hubert. 1992. What Computers Still Can't Do. MIT Press. See also the Wikipedia summary at http://en.wikipedia.org/wiki/Hubert_Dreyfus%27s_views_on_artificial_intelligence.

Dreyfus, Hubert. 2001. *On the Internet.* Routledge.

Erlang, A. K. 1909. Theory of probabilities and telephone conversations. *Nyt Tidsskrift for Matematik B* 20.

Erlang, A. K. 1917. Solution of some problems in the theory of probabilities of significance in automatic telephone exchanges. *Electroteknikeren,* 13.

Fabry, Robert. 1974. Capability-based addressing. *Communications the ACM* 17 (7):403–412.

Flynn, Michael. 1972. Some computer organizations and their effectiveness. *IEEE Transactions on Computers* C-21:948–960.

Flyvbjerg, Bent, and Alexander Budzier. 2011. Why your IT project may be riskier than you think. *Harvard Business Review* (September):23–25.

Fortnow, Lance. 2009. The status of the P versus NP problem. *Communications of the ACM* 52 (9):78–86.

Fortnow, Lance. 2013. *The Golden Ticket: P, NP, and the Search for the Impossible.* Princeton University Press.

Garey, Michael, and David Johnson. 1979. *Computers and Intractability: A Guide to the Theory of NP-Completeness.* W. H. Freeman.

Garfinkel, Simson. 2001. *Database nation: The Death of Privacy in the 21st Century.* O'Reilly.

Gelenbe, Erol. 2011. Natural computation. *ACM Ubiquity* (February). Available at http://ubiquity.acm.org/article.cfm?id=1940722.

Ginosar, R. 2003. Fourteen ways to fool your synchronizer. *Proceedings of the 9th International Symposium on Asynchronous Circuits and Systems,* IEEE. Available at http://www.ee.technion.ac.il/~ran/papers/Sync_Errors_Feb03.pdf.

Gleick, J. 2011. *The Information: A History, a Theory, a Flood.* Random House.

Goldberg, Adele. 1983. *Smalltalk-80: The Interactive Programming Environment.* Addison-Wesley.

Goldin, D., S. Smolka, and P. Wegner. 2010. *Interactive Computation: The New Paradigm.* Springer.

Goldstine, Herman. 1993. *The Computer from Pascal to von Neumann.* Princeton University Press.

Gordon, W. J., and G. F. Newell. 1967. Closed queueing systems with exponential servers. *Operations Research* 15 (2):254–265.

Graefe, Goetz. 2007. The five-minute rule twenty years later, and how flash memory changes the rules. *Proceedings of the 3rd International Workshop on Data Management on New Hardware,* article 6. ACM.

Gray, Jim, and Franco Putzolu. 1985. The 5 minute rule for trading memory for disk accesses. *Tandem Corporation Technical Report 86.1.* (Available at http://www.hpl.hp.com/techreports/tandem/TR-86.1.pdf)

Gries, David. 1971. *Compiler Construction for Digital Computers.* Wiley.

Gurevich, Yuri. 2012. What is an algorithm? In *Proceedings of the 38th International Conference on Current Trends in Theory and Practice of Computer Science* (SOFSEM'12), Mária Bieliková, Gerhard Friedrich, Georg Gottlob, and Stefan Katzenbeisser, Eds., pp. 31–42. Springer-Verlag.

Habermann, A. Nico. 1969. Prevention of system deadlock. *Communications of the ACM* 12 (7):373–377.

Hafner, Katie, and Matthew Lyon. 1998. *Where Wizards Stay Up Late: The Origins of the Internet.* Simon & Schuster.

Brinch Hansen, Per. 1973. *Operating System Principles.* Prentice-Hall.

Harel, David. 1980. On folk theorems. *Communications of the ACM* 23 (7):379–389.

Hazen, Robert. 2007. *Genesis: The Scientific Quest for Life's Origins.* Joseph Henry Press.

Henderson, Harry. 2008. *Encyclopedia of Computer Science and Technology.* Facts on File.

Hennessey, John, and David Patterson. 2011. *Computer Architecture: A Quantitative Approach,* 5th ed. Morgan Kaufman.

Hoare, C. A. R. 1974. Monitors: An operating system structuring concept. *Communications of the ACM* 17 (10):549–557.

Hoare, C. A. R. 1978. Communicating sequential processes. *Communications of the ACM* 21 (8):666–677.

Hoare, Tony. 1961. Algorithm 64: Quicksort. *Communications of the ACM* 4 (7):321.

Hoare, Tony. 1985. *Communicating Sequential Processes.* Prentice-Hall.

Hofstadter, Douglas. 1985. *Metamagical Themas: Questing for the Essence of Mind and Pattern.* Basic Books. See his essay "The genetic code: Arbitrary?"

Israel, Jay, James Mitchell, and Howard Sturgis. 1978. *Separating Data from Function in a Distributed File System.* Xerox Palo Alto Research Center Technical Report Series.

Jackson, J. R. 1957. Networks of waiting lines. *Operations Research* 5 (4):131–142.

Kahn, Robert, and Robert Wilensky. 1995. A framework for distributed digital object services. CNRI technical report, available as http://www.cnri.reston.va.us/cstr/arch/k-w.html. Reprinted 2006. *International Journal on Digital Libraries* 6 (2):115–123.

Kanerva, Pentti. 2003. *Sparse Distributed Memory.* MIT Press.

Karnaugh, Maurice. 1953. The map method for synthesis of combinational logic circuits. *Transactions of AIEE, Part 1,* 72 (9):593–599.

Karp, Richard. 1972. Reducibility among combinatorial problems. In *Complexity of Computer Computations,* ed. R. E. Miller and J. W. Thatcher, pp. 85–103. Plenum.

Karp, Richard. 1993. Mapping the genome: Some combinatorial problems arising in molecular biology. *Proceedings of the 25th ACM Symposium on Theory of Computing,* ACM Press, 278–285.

Karp, Richard, and Raymond Miller. 1966. Properties of a model for parallel computations: Determinacy, termination, and queueing. *SIAM Journal of Applied Math* 14 (6):1390–1411.

Karp, Richard, and Raymond Miller. 1969. Parallel program schemata. *Journal of Computer and Systems Sciences* 3 (2):147–195.

Kilburn, T., D. B. G. Edwards, M. J. Lanigan, and F. H. Sumner. 1962. One level storage system. *IRE Transactions on Electronic Communication* (April):223–235.

Kinniment, D. J., and J. V. Woods. 1976. Synchronization and arbitration circuits in digital systems. *IEEE Proceedings* (October):961–966.

Kleene, Stephen. 1936. General recursive functions of natural numbers. *Mathematische Annalen* 112:727–742.

Kleinrock, Leonard. 1961. *Information flow in large communication nets.* RLE Quarterly Progress Report (July).

Kleinrock, Leonard. 1964. *Communication Nets: Stochastic Message Flow and Delay.* McGraw-Hill.

Kleinrock, Leonard. 1975. *Queueing Systems: Theory*, vol. 1. Wiley.

Kleinrock, Leonard. 1976. *Queueing Systems: Computer Applications*, vol. 2. Wiley.

Knuth, Donald. 1964. Backus Normal Form vs. Backus Naur Form. *Communications of the ACM* 7 (12):735–736.

Kobayashi, H., and B. L. Mark. 2008. *System Modeling and Analysis*. Prentice-Hall.

Kurzweil, Ray. 2005. *The Singularity Is Near.* Viking.

Lamport, L. 1984. Buridan's principle. Technical report available from http://research.microsoft.com/users/lamport/pubs/buridan.pdf.

Lampson, Butler. 1974. Protection. *ACM SIGOPS Operating Systems Review* 8 (1):18–24.

Lampson, Butler. 1983. Hints for computer system design. *Proceedings of the ACM Symposium on Operating Systems Principles*, pp. 33–48.

Lazowska, Edward D., John Zahorjan. G. Scott Graham, and Kenneth C. Sevcik. 1984.. *Quantitative System Performance.* Prentice-Hall.

Leiner, Barry, Vinton Cerf, David Clark, Robert Kahn, Leonard Kleinrock, Dan Lynch, Jon Postel, Larry Roberts, and Stephen Wolff. 1996. *Brief History of the Internet.* http://www.internetsociety.org/internet/what-internet/history-internet/brief-history-internet (retrieved March 2014).

Levy, Steven. 1984. *Capability-Based Computer Systems.* Digital Press.

Licklider, J. C. R. 1960. Man-computer symbiosis. *IRE Transactions on Human Factors in Electronics HFE-1* (March):4–11. Available at http://groups.csail.mit.edu/medg/people/psz/Licklider.html.

Licklider, J. C. R. 1963. *Memorandum for Members and Affiliates of the Intergallactic Computer Network*. DARPA memorandum (April). Available at http://worrydream.com/refs/Licklider-IntergalacticNetwork.pdf

Licklider, J. C. R., and Welden Clark. 1962. On-line man computer communication. *Proceedings of the AFIPS Conference SJCC* (May). Available from ACM at http://doi.acm.org/10.1145/1460833.1460847.

Liskov, Barbara, Alan Snyder, Russell Atkinson, and Craig Schaffert. 1977. Abstraction mechanisms in CLU. *Communications of the ACM* 20 (8):564–576.

Little, J. D. C. 1961. A proof for the queueing formula L = λW. *Operations Research* 9 (3):383–387.

Louden, Kenneth. 2011. *Programming Languages: Principles and Practice*, 3rd ed. Cengage Learning. (Original work published 2002)

Lukasiewicz, Jan. 1957. Aristotle's Syllogistic from the Standpoint of Modern Formal Logic. Oxford University Press.

MacCormick, John. 2012. *Nine Algorithms That Changed the Future*. Princeton University Press.

Madison, A. Wayne, and Alan P. Batson. 1976. Characteristics of program localities. *Communications of the ACM* 19 (5):285–294.

McMenamin, Adrian. 2011. *Applying Working Set Heuristics to the Linux Kernel*. Masters Thesis, Birkbeck College, University of London. Available at: http://cartesianproduct.files.wordpress.com/2011/12/main.pdf.

Menasce, Daniel A., and Virgilio A. F. Almeida. 2002. *Capacity Planning for Web Services*. Prentice-Hall.

Menasce, Daniel A., Virgilio A. F. Almeida, and Lawrence W. Dowdy. 1994. *Capacity Planning and Performance Modeling*. Prentice-Hall.

Metcalfe, Robert, and David Boggs. 1983. Ethernet: Distributed packet switching for local computer networks. *Communications of ACM* 26 (1):90–95.

Miller, Mark. 2003. Capability myths demolished. Johns Hopkins University, Systems Research Laboratory. Available at http://srl.cs.jhu.edu/pubs/SRL2003-02.pdf.

Mitcham, Carl. 1994. *Thinking Through Technology: The Path Between Engineering and Philosophy*. University of Chicago Press.

Mockapetris, Paul. 1983. *Domain Names—Implementation and Specification*. Internet Engineering Task Force memoranda RFC 883 and 884 (November). Available at http://tools.ietf.org/html/rfc883, http://tools.ietf.org/html/rfc884

Moore, G. 1965. Cramming more components onto integrated circuits. *Electronics* 38 (8):4–6.

Negroponte, Nicholas. 1996. *Being Digital*. Vintage.

Nelson, Ted. 1980. *Literary Machines*. Mindful Press.

Neumann, Peter. 1995. *Computer-Related Risks*. ACM Press: Addison-Wesley.

Neumann, Peter G., Robert Boyer, Richard Feiertag, Karl Levitt, and Lawrence Robinson. 1980. A Provably Secure Operating System, its Applications, and Proofs. CSL-116 (2nd edition), SRI International, Menlo Park, CA (May).

Newell, Allen, Alan J. Perlis, and Herbert A. Simon. 1967. "Computer Science" [letter] *Science* 157 (3795):1373–1374.

Newell, Allen, and Herbert Simon. 1963. GPS: A program that simulates human thought. In *Computers and Thought*, ed. E. Feigenbaum and J. Feldman. McGraw-Hill.

Nilsson, Nils. 2010. *The Quest for Artificial Intelligence: A History of Ideas and Achievements*. Cambridge University Press.

Norman, Donald. 2010. Technology first, needs last: The research-product gulf. *Interactions (New York)* 17 (2):38–42.

Norman, Donald. 2013. *The Design of Everyday Things*, 2nd ed. Basic Books. (Previously published as *The Psychology of Everyday Things*, Basic, 1998)

Nyquist, Harry. 1928. Certain topics in telegraph transmission theory. *Transactions of AIEE* 47:617–644. Reprinted 2002 in *Proceedings of the IEEE* 90 (2).

Organick, Elliott. 1972. *The Multics System: An Examination of Its Structure*. MIT Press.

Organick, Elliott. 1973. *Computer System Organization: B5700–B6700 Series*. Academic Press.

Parnas, David. 1972. On the criteria to be used in decomposing systems into modules. *Communications of the ACM* 15 (12):1053–1058.

Pierce, Benjamin. 2002. *Types and Programming Languages*. MIT Press.

Pouzin, Louis. 1973. Presentation and major design aspects of the CYCLADES computer network. *Proceedings of the NATO Advanced Study Institute on Computer Communication Networks*, pp. 415–434. Noordhoff International Publishing.

Pouzin, Louis. 1974. CIGALE, the packet switching machine of the CYCLADES computer network. *Proceedings of the IFIP Congress*, pp. 155–159.

Prieve, Barton, and Robert Fabry. 1976. VMIN—An optimal variable-space page replacement algorithm. *Communications of the ACM* 19 (5):295–297.

Pullen, J. Mark. 2000. *Understanding Network Protocols*. Wiley.

Quielle, J. P., and J. Sifakis. 1982. Specification and verification of concurrent systems in DESAR. In *Proceedings of the 5th International Symposium on Programming*, 337–250.

Ralston, Anthony, Edwin Reilly, and David Hemmengdinger. 2003. *Encyclopedia of Computer Science*. 4th ed., Wiley.

Reiser, Martin, and Stephen Lavenberg. 1980. Mean value analysis of closed multichain queueing networks. *Journal of the ACM* 27:313–322.

Rice, John. 1976. Algorithmic progress in solving partial differential equations. CS Technical Report CSD-TR-173 (Jan). Available at http://docs.lib.purdue.edu/cgi/viewcontent.cgi?article=1117&context=cstech.

Ritchie, Dennis, and Kenneth Thompson. 1974. The UNIX Time-Sharing System. *Communications of the ACM* 17 (7):365–375.

Rivest, Ronald, Adi Shamir, and Len Adleman. 1978. A method for obtaining digital signatures and public-key cryptosystems. *Communications of the ACM* 21 (2):120–126.

Roberts, Larry. 1967. Multiple computer networks and intercomputer communication. *Proceedings of the ACM Symposium on Operating Systems Principles* (Gatlinburg, October).

Roberts, Larry, and T. Merrill. 1966. Toward a cooperative network of time-shared computers. *AFIPS Conference Proceedings FJCC* (October).

Rocchi, Paolo. 2010. *Logic of Analog and Digital Machines*. Nova Publishers.

Rocchi, P. 2012. *The Logic of Digital and Analog Machines*. Nova Publishers.

Rosenbloom, Paul S. (November 2004). A new framework for computer science and engineering. *IEEE Computer* 31–36.

Rosenbloom, Paul S. 2012. *On Computing: The Fourth Great Domain of Science*. MIT Press.

Russell, Stuart, and Peter Norvig. 2010. *Artificial Intelligence: A Modern Approach*, 3rd ed. Prentice Hall.

Saltzer, Jerome. 1965. *Traffic Control in a Multiplexed Computer System*. MIT Project MAC-TR-30 (Sc.D. thesis). Available at http://web.mit.edu/Saltzer/www/publications/MIT-MAC-TR-030.ocr.pdf.

Saltzer, Jerry, and Frans Kaashoek. 2009. *Principles of Computer System Design*. Morgan-Kaufman.

Saltzer, Jerry, David Reed, and David Clark. 1984. End-to-end arguments in system design. *ACM Transactions on Computer Systems* 2 (4):277–288.

Saltzer, Jerome, and Michael Schroeder. 1975. Protection of information computer systems. *Proceedings of the IEEE* 63 (9):1278–1308.

Sayre, David. 1969. Is automatic "folding" of programs efficient enough to displace manual? *Communications of the ACM* 12 (12):656–660.

Scheifler, Robert, Ron Newman, and James Gettys. 1988. *X Window System: C Library and Protocol Reference*. Digital Press.

Scherr, Allan. 1965. *An Analysis of Time-Shared Computer Systems*. MIT Technical report MIT-LCS-TR-018. Available at http://publications.csail.mit.edu/lcs/pubs/pdf/MIT-LCS-TR-018.pdf.

Schneier, Bruce. 2004. *Secrets and Lies: Digital Security in a Networked World*. Wiley.

Schneier, Bruce. 2008. *Schneier on Security*. Wiley.

Searle, John. 1984. *Minds, Brains and Science*. Harvard University Press.

Seitz, C. L. 1980. System timing. In *Introduction to VLSI Systems*, ed. C. Mead and L. Conway, 218–262. Addison-Wesley.

Shannon, Claude. 1948. The mathematical theory of communication. *Bell System Technical Journal* 27:379–423, 623–656.

Shannon, Claude, and Warren Weaver. 1949. *The Mathematical Theory of Communication*. University of Illinois Press (reprinted 1998). Shannon's original paper is available on the Web: http://cm.bell-labs.com/cm/ms/what/shannonday/paper.html

Shor, Peter. 1994. Polynomial-time algorithms for prime factorization and discrete logarithms on a quantum computer. *Proceedings of the 35th Annual Symposium on Foundations of Computer Science*. ACM Press. Reprinted in *SIAM J. Computing* 1997:1484–1509.

Simon, Herbert. 1996. *The Sciences of the Artificial*, 3rd ed. MIT Press.

Spector, Alfred. 1982. Performing remote operations efficiently in a local computer network. *Communications of the ACM* 25 (April):246–260.

Standage, Tom. 2003. *The Turk: The Life and Times of the Famous Eighteenth-Century Chess-Playing Machine*. Berkeley Trade.

Stewart, William J. 2009. *Probability, Markov Chains, and Simulation*. Princeton University Press.

Strassen, Volker. 1969. Gaussian elimination is not optimal. *Numerische Mathematik* 13:354–356.

Sutherland, Ivan. 2012. The tyranny of the clock. *Communications of the ACM* 55 (1) (October): 35–36.

Sutherland, I., and J. Ebergen. 2002. Computers without clocks. *Scientific American* (August), 62–69.

Tanenbaum, Andrew. 1980. *Computer Networks* (5th ed. with David Wetherall published 2010). Prentice-Hall.

Tanenbaum, Andrew, and Sape Mullender. 1981. An overview of the Amoeba distributed operating system. *ACM SIGOPS Operating Systems Review* 15 (3):51–64.

Tedre, Matti. 2014. *In Search of the Science of Computing*. Taylor & Francis.

Turing, Alan. 1937. On computable numbers with an application to the Entscheidungs problem. *Proceedings of the London Mathematical Society* 2:230–265.

Turing, Alan. 1950. Computing machinery and intelligence. *Mind* 59 (236): 433–460.

von Ahn, L., and L. Dabbish. 2004. Labeling images with a computer game. In *Proceedings of the ACM Conference on Human Factors in Computing Systems*, pp. 319–326. ACM Press.

von Neumann, John. 1945. *First Draft of a Report on the EDVAC*. In *IEEE Annals of the History of Computing* 15 (4):27–43. (Original work published as a technical report from the US Army project at the University of Pennsylvania, 1945)

Wikipedia. 2014. List of programming languages. Available http://en.wikipedia.org/wiki/List_of_programming_languages

Wilkes, Maurice. 1968a. *Time Sharing Computer Systems*. Elsevier North-Holland.

Wilkes, Maurice. 1968b. "Computers then and now." 1967 Turing Lecture. *Journal of the ACM* 15 (1):1–7.

Wilkes, Maurice. 1985. *Memoirs of a Computer Pioneer*. MIT Press.

Wilkes, Maurice. 1995. *Computing Perspectives*. Morgan Kaufman.

Wilkes, Maurice, and Roger Needham. 1979. *The Cambridge CAP Computer and Its Operating System*. Elsevier North-Holland.

Willinger, Walter, David Alderson, and John Doyle. 2009. Mathematics and the Internet: A source of enormous confusion and great potential. *Notices of the AMS* 56 (5):586–599.

Winograd, Terry. 1996. *Bringing Design to Software*. ACM Press Addison-Wesley.

Winograd, Terry, and Fernando Flores. 1987. *Understanding Computers and Cognition: A New Foundation for Design*. Addison-Wesley.

Wirth, Niklaus. 1989. *Programming in Modula 2*. Springer-Verlag.

Wolfram, Stephen. 2002. *A New Kind of Science*. Wolfram Media.

Wulf, William, W. Corwin, Anita Jones, Roy Levin, C. Pierson, and F. Pollack. 1974. HYDRA: The kernel of a multiprocessor operating system. *Communications of the ACM* 17 (6):337–345.

Xiang, Xiaoya, Chen Ding, Hao Luo, and Bin Bao. 2013. HOTL: A higher order theory of locality. *ACM Proceedings of the 18th International Conference on Architectural Support for Programming Languages and Operating Systems* (ASPLOS'13), pp. 343–356.

Zimmerman, Hubert. 1980. OSI reference model—The ISO model of architecture for open systems interconnection. *IEEE Transactions on Communications COM-28* (4):425–432.

Index